Routledge Revivals

Young Germany

First published in 1962, this book examines Germany's Free Youth Movement, a revolt of the younger generation in Germany from 1896 to 1933. This movement was one of the most significant factors in shaping modern Germany. Laqueur, who grew up in Germany, retraces the history of the movement, its central ideas, and its cultural background. He begins with its origins in 19th century, and goes on to examine the Jewish question, before moving on to the movement's roots in Germany around the time of the rise of National Socialism in the late 1920's and early 1930's. This book inspires all the ideas which continue to preoccupy proponents and students of generational conflict today.

Young Germany
A History of the German Youth Movement

Walter Z. Laqueur

First published in 1962
by Routledge and Kegan Paul Ltd.

This edition first published in 2018 by Routledge
2 Park Square, Milton Park, Abingdon, Oxon, OX14 4RN
and by Routledge
711 Third Avenue, New York, NY 10017

Routledge is an imprint of the Taylor & Francis Group, an informa business

© 1962 Walter Z. Laqueur

All rights reserved. No part of this book may be reprinted or reproduced or utilised in any form or by any electronic, mechanical, or other means, now known or hereafter invented, including photocopying and recording, or in any information storage or retrieval system, without permission in writing from the publishers.

Publisher's Note
The publisher has gone to great lengths to ensure the quality of this reprint but points out that some imperfections in the original copies may be apparent.

Disclaimer
The publisher has made every effort to trace copyright holders and welcomes correspondence from those they have been unable to contact.

A Library of Congress record exists under LCCN: 62014623

ISBN 13: 978-1-138-56896-9 (hbk)
ISBN 13: 978-0-203-70450-9 (ebk)
ISBN 13: 978-1-138-56898-3 (pbk)

YOUNG GERMANY
A History of the German Youth Movement

by
WALTER Z. LAQUEUR

with an Introduction by
R. H. S. CROSSMAN, M.P.

LONDON
ROUTLEDGE & KEGAN PAUL

*First published in 1962
by Routledge and Kegan Paul Ltd.
Broadway House, 68–74 Carter Lane
London, E.C.4*

© *Walter Z. Laqueur 1962*

*No part of this book may be reproduced
in any form without permission from
the publisher, except for the quotation
of brief passages in criticism*

For Naomi,
S.R.L., S.L.

CONTENTS

PREFACE *page* xi
INTRODUCTION BY R. H. S. CROSSMAN, M.P. xvii

PART ONE

1. ROMANTIC PRELUDE 3
2. THE BEGINNING 15
3. THE NEW STYLE 25
4. AT THE HOHE MEISSNER 32

PART TWO

5. METAPOLITICS 41
6. BLÜHER AND WYNEKEN 50
7. THE WAR OF THE SEXES 56
8. OTHER YOUTH MOVEMENTS 66
9. THE JEWISH QUESTION 74

PART THREE

10. THE FIRST WORLD WAR 87
11. 1919—LEFT V. RIGHT 99
12. YEARS OF DISILLUSION 111
13. THE END OF THE BEGINNING 121

CONTENTS

PART FOUR

14. THE 'WHITE KNIGHT'	page 133
15. ERNST BUSKE AND THE FREISCHAR	144
16. PANORAMA OF THE BÜNDE	155
17. TUSK OR THE TRIUMPH OF ECCENTRICITY	167
18. NATIONAL BOLSHEVISM	179

PART FIVE

19. IN HITLER'S SHADOW	191
20. THE ROAD TO RUIN	204
21. THE POST-WAR PERIOD	216
CONCLUSION	228
APPENDIX: THE FOREIGN POLICY OF THE BÜNDE	238
BIBLIOGRAPHY	244
INDEX	248

PLATES

1. *Wandervogel*—the earliest days (Easter 1898)   *facing page* 10
2. The Branco Stone in Berlin Dahlem which provided the name *Wandervogel*   11
3. *Wandervogel* girls' group (1909)   11
4. Competition in Camp (1913)   26
5. On Luneberg Heath (1909)   27
6. *Hohe Wacht*. The famous Fidus picture (ca. 1912)   42
7. Frontispiece of one of the *Wandervogel* periodicals before 1918   43
8. Ernst Buske in conversation with Luserke   58
9. Gustav Wyneken (1959)   59
10. The first and the last periodical of the German youth movement before 1933   194
11. Demonstration of Socialist youth group, Bielefeld (ca. 1924)   194
12. Eberhard Köbel (Tusk) (ca. 1930)   195
13. Hitler Youth (ca. 1934)   195
14. FDJ—East German Communist youth demonstration (Berlin, 1950)   195

PREFACE

THE story of the German youth movement begins about 1896. According to some historians it ended in 1914, according to others in 1933, and there are quite a few writers who believe it is still unfinished. It is a unique story, so much so that it is extremely difficult to describe in terms that are recognizable and familiar to British and American readers. But it is important for an understanding of Germany in the twentieth century, and for a number of other, more general reasons.

The course of German history during the past 150 years has been the subject of voluminous comment and discussion—not only in Germany and not only among historians. The writer believes that while further discussions in general terms can do little more to illuminate the problems involved, some fresh insights may perhaps be gained from an analysis of one particular aspect. For the youth movement in its way was a microcosm of modern Germany. Few are the political leaders, and even fewer the intellectual leaders among the generations born between 1890 and 1920, who were not at one time or another members of the youth movement, or influenced by it in their most impressionable years. And perhaps even more important than this personal element is the fact that all the great issues of the time are reflected in the history of the movement. At the outset it was non-political in character, or rather it wished to be so, yet it was gradually drawn into confrontation with the dominant issues of the age.

It was always the movement of a minority. Accurate figures do not exist, but it seems likely that the members of the youth movement proper, the autonomous groups, never exceeded 60,000. It was almost exclusively 'bourgeois' in its social composition. The vast majority of German boys and girls were enrolled in confessional organizations, not in the autonomous youth movement. And yet in some respects the impact of the youth movement on the mass organizations inside Germany, and even outside her borders, was decisive. The youth movement introduced new ingredients and a new style which, by the late nineteen-twenties, had spread widely among the younger generation in Germany and other European countries. Both the Hitler Youth and, later on, the Free German Youth of East Germany adopted many of its outward trappings.

Some of the difficulties that confront a historian of this movement should be mentioned in advance. It has been argued that the history of the youth movement can be written only by those who once belonged to it, shared its values, possessed the intimate experience supposed to be essential for a true insight into its past. Other movements, it has been said, may perhaps be understood retrospectively by analysis of their aims and programmes, but the youth movement had no such definite goals.

It is certainly true that most members of the movement went through an emotional experience *sui generis* which they believed, rightly or wrongly, to be incomprehensible to outsiders. And to have been oneself a loyal and committed member would doubtless be a valuable, perhaps a necessary qualification for writing a chronicle, a novel, or a poem descriptive of life in the youth movement. To write the history of any movement presupposes some understanding of the emotions of its members; but it also requires an appraisal of their long-range achievements and failures; and for this a measure of detachment and objectivity is necessary, difficult to achieve for those who were deeply involved in the movement's activities and aspirations. Nor is it altogether true to say that the youth movement had no aims and programmes.

Since in this connection the author's own approach and attitude could be relevant, a few personal remarks may be in order. My own origin is German-Jewish and I have recollections of the youth movement dating back to early boyhood. Some memories are vivid, others somewhat hazy; I was twelve when the *Bünde* were dissolved in 1933. I came to know, though at an early age and from the side lines something of the style of life developed by the movement and some of its leaders and members. It fascinated me for a time but I forgot about it for the most part, until, twenty-five years later, a general interest in the problems of nationalism and socialism (and their interaction) in the modern world induced me to undertake a study of recent German history—of which the present work is, in a way, a by-product.

One thing that makes it difficult to do justice to the movement is

PREFACE

that its politics, of the right, the left, and the centre, were singularly confused; it is hardly fair, however, to judge it exclusively on its political record. To its apologists, the youth movement had no responsibility whatever for the rise of the Third Reich, and any apparent resemblance to National Socialist ideology was fortuitous or limited to externals; whereas, according to some searching critics, the German youth movement from the first, knowingly or unknowingly, paved the way for National Socialism. The writer believes that, although the truth is not necessarily at the half-way point between these extreme positions, it happens to be vastly more complicated.

Questions of principle apart, the historian encounters obstacles of a technical character: notably a deficiency in the quality—not the quantity—of documentation. The *Wandervogel* and the *Bünde* were not, as a movement, literary; their books and periodicals are pale reflections of activities that were richly and vividly lived. Those most gifted in literary expression were not necessarily central figures in the movement or typical representatives of it. I have tried, whenever possible, to rely on the memories of people who participated in the events described, but I have also attempted to check these recollections by reference to contemporary publications.

A truly staggering mass of literature was produced by and around the movement during the past sixty years: perhaps as many as a thousand periodicals, including of course those published by religious and party youth organizations, as well as those put out by regional groups. Dozens of dissertations on its various aspects have been written in Germany since the First World War, and some have been written elsewhere. Yet some of the essential source material could no longer be traced even in the thirties, and much more was lost when the movement's central archives disappeared in the last stages of the Second World War. In view of the intrinsic interest of the subject, one would currently expect to find, at any rate in Germany, a good deal of literature concerning it. There are, it is true, literary essays, sociological reflections, and the personal recollections of individual leaders about particular periods and branches of the movement; but, strange to say, there is only one historical study covering the whole period up to 1933, and this, published in 1939, presented a National Socialist version.

The German youth movement was composed of many dozens of groups, large and small. In attempting to review the main lines of its development, I have had to neglect a good many minor events which might well reward further study. In some respects the present work covers a narrower field than its title indicates: I have not been able, for example, to deal with such subjects as the considerable

PREFACE

achievements of the youth movement in music, nor has it been possible to mention, still less to analyse, all the pedagogical problems involved. The main purpose of the present study is to retrace the history of the movement, its central ideas and its cultural background. Since it was impossible to present this subject in isolation from other contemporary developments, it was necessary to bring into the narrative some groups and personalities who did not, strictly speaking, belong to the movement but were influenced by it (such as the Socialist and Church youth groups), as well as others who for a variety of reasons had a powerful effect upon its political and cultural orientation.

The use of certain German expressions for which there are no equivalents in English proved unavoidable: *Völkisch* is not folkish, but indicates a specific trend in German right-wing thought and politics. It is not synonymous with nationalism, since it puts people (or, to be precise, the race) above state and nation as a supreme good. A *Bund* is neither a bond nor an association, but a nation-wide (youth) organization consisting of local groups with a fairly strict discipline. In these groups the emphasis was on collective life, on leadership and service. The *Wandervogel* represents the first phase of the youth movement (1896–1919); the *Bund* emerged as the main form of organization in its second phase (1919–33).

Other difficulties of presentation go deeper. Some of the theories, speeches, and manifestoes of which an account is given here may appear vague and ambiguous, occasionally quite incomprehensible to the British or American reader. The author could have enhanced the readability of his book by clarifying issues that were not clear, and by reading a meaning into statements that had none, but to eliminate the absurdities and inconsistencies would have been to attribute to the youth movement ideas and attitudes it never had.

It has unfortunately not been possible to make the references to quotations uniform in style. Youth movement periodicals were neither professional newspapers nor scientific journals. They appeared infrequently, sometimes without pagination, often without bearing a date.

It is my pleasant duty to record my gratitude to the staff of the Wiener Library, London, to Herr Hans Wolf, director of the youth movement archives on Burg Ludwigstein, and the director and staff of the American Document Center in Berlin-Dahlem. The unpublished dissertations of Drs Michael Jovy, Felix Raabe, Harry Pross and Franz Strebin were put at my disposal, and I received information concerning certain specialized problems from H. W. Belmore, Dr Heinz Dähnhardt, Colonel Hans Dehmel, Rolf Gardiner,

PREFACE

Ferdinand Göbel, Franz Ludwig Habbel, Walter Hammer, Werner Kindt, Heinz Lippmann, Franz Luft, Prof. Hans Raupach, Bernhard Reichenbach, Prof. Carlo Schmid, Heinz Westphal, Prof. Karl August Wittfogel, Dr Gustav Wyneken, and Walter Zadek. To Mrs Jane Degras and Mr Philip Mairet I owe thanks for reading the manuscript and suggesting improvements in style.

INTRODUCTION

by R. H. S. Crossman, M.P.

BEFORE I read Mr Laqueur's remarkable book I had not realized what a large and curious gap in our knowledge of Germany had remained unfilled. *Young Germany* is, I am assured, the first full-length history of the German Youth Movement to be published in English—the first, indeed, to be published in any language, except for a Nazi compilation issued in 1939. This, as Mr Laqueur rightly observes, is a very remarkable omission. For, whatever one's judgment of its merits and achievements, no one can deny the importance of the Free Youth Movement in shaping the outlook of the German middle class. It is reckoned that membership never exceeded 60,000, but its influence in Germany was at least as great as that of Eton and Harrow in this country. Indeed, the names—infamous as well as famous—of those Germans who passed through the Youth Movement make one realize that it was indeed, in its strange way, the German analogue to the public school system.

While staking this claim, it would perhaps be wise to make it clear to the British and American reader what exactly it is that we are studying. When Mr Laqueur talks about the German Youth Movement, he does not mean the confessional youth movements, run by the Catholic and Protestant Churches. Nor is he referring to the youth organizations attached to the political parties—the Young Socialists and the Young Communists, for instance. Nor, again, does he mean the Boy Scouts. Certainly all these organizations existed in Germany before 1933 and most of them have grown up again since 1945. But they are paralleled by similar organizations in other countries. The story Mr Laqueur tells is of a special and quite unique German phenomenon, the Free Youth Movement, which was self-assertively unattached to any confession or political party—which

INTRODUCTION

was, in fact, an end in itself—a movement *of* youth, *by* youth and *for* youth.

This Free Youth Movement started, and remained, as an exclusively bourgeois phenomenon and, despite many efforts, failed to strike any roots in the German working class. The function it served was to provide a peculiarly German framework for that rebellion against parent and home which, in any bourgeois society, so many adolescents experience at some stage in the course of their higher education. In the British upper class it usually takes place within the complex and rigid framework of public school and university conventions and has created, in the 'public school novel,' a special minor genre of literature. In pre-1914 Germany—where the bourgeoisie had neither grown into government nor developed its own educational system, separate from the State and the Army—it was the adolescent himself who fashioned his own institution of revolt. The *Wandervogel* perished in Flanders and at Verdun; and the Wilhelmian order, against which its young members had revolted, collapsed in 1918. Once again there was a vacuum to be filled. What roots would the new Weimar democracy strike in a disillusioned bourgeoisie, embittered by the effects of inflation? What stable social structure would its architects build to correspond to its political structure?

The answer, of course, is that they built nothing, and they cannot be blamed for that. For the social institutions that consolidate a democracy cannot be constructed from an intellectual blueprint. Given the right time and the right conditions, these institutions grow —and neither were available in the 1920s. So the German educational system failed to provide any social and ethical framework within which adolescent rebellion against home and authority could take place. Instead, the *Bünde* emerged, less individualistic, less easy to caricature and a great deal less harmless than those long-haired, untidy bacchants and super-bacchants of the *Wandervogel*, who used to wander through the fields and woods, strumming on their guitars their collective revolt against bourgeois respectability.

They were still formally unattached to political parties or churches; but most of them were *völkisch*, i.e. racist, and all of them were *nationalgesinnt*, passionately nostalgic for the lost territories in the East and contemptuous of the 'liberalism' they associated with Weimar. When the 1930s began, the American slump had already spread to Germany. The Weimar Republic was being defended by recourse to emergency decrees, which destroyed its liberties, and democracy was becoming a battlefield, on which the Nazis and the Communists could fight it out with totalitarian weapons. It was the year which, my degree taken and my Oxford Fellowship safe, I

INTRODUCTION

decided to spend studying Aristotle's doctrine of the soul, first at Frankfurt and then in Berlin. In these two cities I got to know a number of Germans of my own age associated with some of the organizations Mr Laqueur mentions. It is with special sympathy, therefore, that I read his chapters on the final agonies of the *Bünde*, their attempt to avoid the choice between Nazis and Communists in achieving a national bolshevism that synthesized both.

Mr Laqueur's perceptive description of this phase in the history of Weimar Germany is based on personal experience—and something else. Brought up a German Jew, he is just old enough to remember, though not actively to have participated in, the activities of the German Youth Movement, in which, as he points out, the Jews, including the Zionists, played an active and independent role. He has been a witness in Israel, in the 'thirties and 'forties, of the astonishing success of this young nation in integrating a homeless and uprooted youth into its ranks. No nation's educators have been set a more difficult task than those of Israel, when confronted with the problem not merely of thousands of orphans and child survivors of the gas chambers but also with a potential clash between immigrants with totally different standards of culture and civilization. In Israel today—largely thanks to the work of the Army—one can see the triumphant solution of an educational problem far more difficult than that presented to the German nation either before or after World War I.

It is, I think, because he both experienced the German problem from inside and later obtained an objective, exterior standard by which to measure it that Mr Laqueur has so largely succeeded in his difficult task of producing a readable history of the Free Youth Movement. Without doubt it was the most Germanic of all German institutions, inclined to prate in those abstract German concepts (*Bund, Gemeinschaft* and *völkisch* are three outstanding examples) for which there is no English equivalent. A movement that indulged in such metapolitical claptrap must test the patience of the British or American student, determined to get at the hard historical facts. For what exactly are the facts about it? What exactly did it do to its members? What exactly was its social and political significance? Mr Laqueur has wisely avoided the temptation to indulge in too much moralizing or generalization, preferring to tell what is inevitably a shapeless, ragged story as tidily as possible. As an ex-German youth, he feels in his bones that what happened on October 11th, 1913, at the top of the Hohe Meissner was of cosmic significance. And if we never quite understand the Nordic inflatus those German youths took back with them into their solid middle-class homes, the fault, I think, rests not

INTRODUCTION

with Mr Laqueur's powers of explanation but with the *Wandervogel* themselves.

Nothing is more illuminating in this book than the chapters devoted to the literature of the Movement. We learn that *Helmut Harringa*, which was published in 1910, sold 320,000 copies in a few weeks. This novel describes a shining example of German youth, who devotes his whole life to the struggle against three devils, alcoholism, premarital sexual intercourse and the contamination of the German race. The book culminates with the German peoples, united under the black, white and red flag, storming the enemy in his fortress of death, and its last sentence runs: 'The world owes the idea of freedom to the Nordic peoples, the Germans.' Another example of Youth Movement literature was the famous war story, published in 1918, about a student of theology 'whose God was girded with a sword, and his Jesus too had a bright sword when he went with him into battle.' Mr Laqueur quotes the scene after the hero's death, when his friend pays a Christmas visit to his mother.

> 'Did Ernst take part in an attack before his death?' He nodded. 'Yes, at Warthi.' Then she shut her eyes and sat back. 'That was his greatest desire,' she said slowly, as though it was a painful joy to know that what she had feared so long had come to pass. A mother should know what was the deepest desire of her child. And it must be a deep desire indeed if she is anxious about its realization after his death. O mothers, you German mothers.

The literary influences on the post-war *Bünde* were even odder. Few of his countrymen, I suspect, still remember, even if they had ever heard of, Kibbo Kift, the Woodcraft Kindred, and its founder, John Hargrave, of Kings Langley, Hertfordshire. Hargrave had been a Scoutmaster but seceded in 1920 to form the Kibbo movement, a curious mixture of Scoutery, Red Indians and Social Credit. In England the movement never prospered, but its ideas and methods were adopted by a large part of the German Youth Movement, including the 'White Knight' circle of Martin Voelkel, a youth leader whose mental outlook can be savoured in the following quotation from *Der Weisse Ritter*:

> The next thousand years belong to the Slav soul. But when this is past, the Third Reich will come. It will be neither culture nor civilization, it will be both of them and more than both. . . . Nobody but the German knows in which direction he is moving; between death and perdition the German Reich, devoted to the eternal in man, is emerging.

'Nobody but the German knows in which direction he is moving.' When I first read those words, my memory was taken back to something that had happened to me in 1934. I was visiting one of the

INTRODUCTION

brand new German labour camps at Rendsburg in Schleswig-Holstein, in an attempt to understand the Hitler Youth. That evening, in the youth hostel, we got into a fierce argument and I accused the Nazis of leading Europe to destruction. At this point my opponent, a handsome, uniformed blond, drew himself up and shouted, 'At least Germany is leading, and you are dragging along behind.'

The tragedy of the Youth Movement was precisely its 'freedom.' Refusing to tie itself to any practical adult education, it floated, directionless, on the waves of public emotion. Despising liberalism and suspicious of intellectual analysis, its leaders were inevitably swept up in the gigantic mass movement of National Socialism. But what kind of men were these leaders? Mr Laqueur has tried hard to bring these ghostly figures to life. But a youth leader is either someone who grows up normally and looks back on his adolescence as a passing phase, or else an adolescent who never grows up. Most of the men who shaped the Free Youth Movement seem to have belonged to the latter category, and the real-life Peter Pan appears even more unattractive when he is born in Germany.

The only leader the movement threw up with any real gifts was Gustav Wyneken. I remember meeting this Platonic athlete and educator at Wickersdorf, high up in the Thuringian mountains, an experimental co-educational school, where the girls were all treated as boys. It is perhaps because Wyneken was a teacher with a real touch of genius that he only irrupted personally on two occasions into the Youth Movement. When I saw him in the early 1930s he had become a prophet of that Hegelian communism which I was later to rediscover in that tragic and genuinely heroic product of the Youth Movement, Adam von Trott.

Mr Laqueur is surely right in dismissing the charge that the *Bünde* were the precursors of National Socialism. True enough, Goebbels, Hess and Rosenberg, who all had academic pretensions, felt an affinity for the Free Youth Movement. But Hitler himself despised it. Indeed, in his mouth *'Wandervogel'* was an insult, which he used on one famous occasion in order to write off Otto Strasser. Moreover, the National Socialists, up to the seizure of power, showed no particular aptitude for organizing youth. The Hitler Youth, in the form one can still see by visiting East Germany, was only created after 1933. Nevertheless, it remains true that the existence of the Free Youth Movement greatly assisted the Nazis in their seizure of power. From Hitler's point of view, its vitally important function was to prevent the development of any concrete belief in freedom among the sons and daughters of what should have been the Weimar Establishment. Everyone knows the devastating effect on German democracy of the aggressive nationalism current among professors, schoolteachers and leaders of public opinion. What is less well known and what was far less evident at the time was the political vacuum created by the *Bünde*. Middle-class boys and girls, in their period of adolescent rebellion, might have been expected to react against the older generation by espousing the cause of democracy. That they failed to do so was largely due to the fact that their emotions and enthusiasms were captured by a movement which smothered any intelligent doubts in a welter of vague racist metaphysics.

And what of post-war Germany? In the Russian zone, as we have seen, the rigid structure of the Hitler Youth has been carried on almost intact in the Communist Youth Movement. In Western Germany, despite some feeble efforts, the Free Youth Movement has shown little power of revival. In view of its history, I am inclined to regard this as a healthy symptom. There are many complaints that youth in the Federal Republic is materialistic, egotistical and unwilling to assume any civic or political responsibilities. In themselves, these characteristics are unattractive. But, in the case of Germany, they may well be a stage on the road to normality. A healthy democracy is impossible without a healthy scepticism, constantly corroding that adulation of leaders and uncritical acceptance of ideology on which totalitarian rule depends. If the Federal Republic is to become a reliable member of the Western community, what it needs above all is a solid middle class, whose belief in democracy is rooted in sceptical self-interest.

The other day I was talking to a distinguished German General with an impeccable Resistance record, who had spent some years teaching at Salem when Kurt Hahn's old boarding school in Bavaria was started again. 'You know, these boys are lacking in something,' he said to me rather sadly. 'After all, you'd have thought they would have been interested in what I did in Russia and Italy. But not one of them has ever asked me a single question about it. For them, it is all a dead past.' Reading Mr Laqueur's account of the *Wandervogel* and the *Bünde*, with their Wagnerian nostalgia for death, I can't help feeling that, in the case of German youth, crass materialism is a good deal less dangerous than the nostalgic longings for a hero's death which, in two generations, brought the Free Youth Movement to disaster.

PART ONE

PART ONE

One

ROMANTIC PRELUDE

I

OFFICIALLY, the German youth movement was born in the late hours of the evening of 4 November 1901 in a back room of the *Ratskeller* in Steglitz, a suburb of Berlin. Its roots can, however, be traced back for at least one hundred years, to the period of 'Storm and Stress,' the *Burschenschaft*, and above all to German romanticism. One was a literary revolt against the repression of individual emotions and the canons of classicism, the other a movement of patriotic students who disliked both Prussian autocracy and the French Revolution. Heir to so old a tradition, the youth movement of 1901 cannot be understood without reference both to its historical roots and to the spirit of the age that engendered it.

Europe had made unprecedented economic and technical progress between 1860 and 1900. While standards of living rose faster than ever before, not all classes benefited equally and strong social tensions were generated. But in most European countries the working class could view with satisfaction and confidence the constant growth of its political influence, as well as its economic and social achievements. There had been no major war in Europe for several decades, and there was every reason to expect another long period of peace, progress, and general well-being.

But serious symptoms of cultural decline were not lacking in that world of growing plenty and rapid technical advance. It would be interesting to speculate about the psychological sources of the discontent, the sense of emptiness and general dissatisfaction that found its expression in a *fin de siècle* mood even in a country like Russia, which faced more urgent political and social problems than the West. Why did so many people throughout Europe welcome the outbreak of the First World War as a 'liberation'? Such an investigation might show that man has often found it difficult to suffer serenely a prolonged period of tranquillity and well-being. When no major problems exist, minor problems tend to take their place.

We tend to look back on the world that ended in 1914 with a nostalgia mixed with a certain amusement. It is true that the great crisis of 1900 seems somewhat unreal, if not artificial, in comparison with the problems of the twenties and thirties. But for those who lived then, the cultural crisis was real enough; it turned some towards socialism, others towards an attitude of aristocratic disdain of the masses and hostility to bourgeois society and its culture or lack of culture. Politically, this rejection of society and its values could lead to either left- or right-wing extremist solutions. The German youth movement was an unpolitical form of opposition to a civilization that had little to offer the young generation, a protest against its lack of vitality, warmth, emotion, and ideals.

The angry young men of 1900 were found among the more articulate sections of the younger generation throughout Europe. Some developed a new cult of youth in an attempt to bring fresh air into the stale and musty atmosphere surrounding their elders. The writings of 'Agathon' in France, and of the early Italian Futurists, are evidence of this trend. The *Wandervogel* was one of the specific German forms of protest. It was and remained unique in many respects, since Germany's situation in Europe was different from that of other countries. The triumph of liberalism in France, Britain, and the United States had never extended to Germany; the 'bourgeois revolution' had never been completed; the middle classes were not fully emancipated. Capitalism had indeed prevailed in Germany and industrialization had made rapid strides, but in many sections of the population a medieval, anti-liberal, and anti-capitalist mentality survived because the people themselves had not taken a prominent and active part in these developments, which had frequently been initiated from above or from outside. The conspicuous part played by the Jews both in banking and in the German Liberal party during the second half of the nineteenth century was a natural consequence of this situation.

The official ideology of this society and its declared values were not those of individual freedom and the pursuit of happiness, but consisted of aristocratic Prussian ideas about loyalty and service to Kaiser and Reich. If the middle classes had been the leading force in German society, dissatisfaction would have taken very different forms from those it eventually did; it would have been a protest from inside or a post-liberal critique of society. In Germany, because of the weakness of the liberal movement itself, the movement was pre-liberal, romantic, in some respects medieval. These characteristics can be more clearly discerned in the second period of the German youth movement, its *bündische* phase after 1920. In its first period, between 1900 and 1914, the movement was to a certain extent individualistic; young people wanted to lead their own lives and demanded a partial release from the tutelage of the parental home and the *Oberlehrer*. But even in that early period the beginnings of a retrograde development can easily be traced. The official ideals in which the young generation was educated had a powerful attraction, even though they were curiously unreal, unrelated to the daily experience of middle-class youth. Only comparatively few could expect ultimately to enter professions in which they would be of direct service to Kaiser and Reich; they had to put up with the fact that the leading positions were barred to them, and not only those in the army. Hence the wide prevalence of *völkische* ideas as a form of middle- and lower-middle-class protest against the official upper-class nationalist ideology of the Germany of Wilhelm II.

The pioneers of the youth movement were young men without great cultural pretensions. Their literary taste was strictly middlebrow; they read not the classics of German literature but Grimmelshausen's *Simplizissimus* and Jörg Wickram's *Rollwagenbüchlein*, which when taken in massive doses had a deplorable effect on their style. They were succeeded by a more refined and articulate generation who had read Hölderlin and Novalis, and who were to echo time and again Hyperion's lament upon Diotima's death after he had parted again from Alabanda:

> It is a hard saying, and yet I say it because it is the truth: I can conceive of no people more dismembered than the Germans. You see workmen but no human beings, thinkers but no human beings, priests but no human beings, masters and servants, youths and staid people, but no human beings. . . .

The youth movement wanted above all to be integrated human beings, as one would put it today, and they were critical of a society that was not conducive to the development of such men and women. They felt very strongly what an earlier—and a later—generation of philosophers called 'alienation.' They were vague in their diagnosis and even less clear in their proposals for remedying the situation. But they felt strongly and sincerely about it. Broadly speaking, two ways of revolt were open to them: they could have pursued their radical critique of society, which in due course would have brought them into the camp of social revolution. But Social Democracy had little attraction for sons and daughters of middle-class German homes. They wanted a change in human relations, and there was no certainty that these could be changed by a new political and social system, however radically different from that under which they lived. The *Wandervogel* chose the other form of protest against society —romanticism. Their return to nature was romantic, as were their attempts to get away from a materialistic civilization, their stress on the simple life, their rediscovery of old folk songs and folklore, their adoption of medieval names and customs. Romanticism probably has a closer hold on Germany than on any other country. There have been classical schools in every culture, but nowhere has romanticism been so deeply rooted as in German literature, music, art, and the general *Zeitgeist*.

But there is more to the story of the German romantic school than the search for the blue flower, Schubert *Lieder* and Schumann concertos, the verse and stories of Arnim, Brentano, Tieck and Eichendorff. The political philosophy of the romantic school had a fatal impact on German thinking throughout the nineteenth century and beyond. Not every Romantic was a reactionary, but reactionary the mainstream of romantic opinion certainly was; having rediscovered the Fatherland and national history, they proceeded to reject alien influences and to hate the foreigner. A religious revival degenerated into religious intolerance and obscurantism. The Middle Ages became the great ideal: the manly virtues and poetic love, true faith and loyalty had disappeared with the age of chivalry. The only way to re-establish a harmonious society was to model it as closely as possible on the medieval pattern with its knights and vassals, its guilds and estates. The romantics glorified the peasantry in its bondage and were opposed to the growth of industry and trade. The whole development of the German youth movement was shaped by the impact of romantic philosophy, by a glorification of the past fraught with misgivings for the future. It was a repetition, on a smaller scale, of the general German misfortune: The German national consciousness was first awakened under reactionary auspices, in a war of liberation that put an end not only to Napoleon's rule but to the achievements of the French Revolution.

It could be argued with some semblance of justice that political views have been read into the *Wandervogel*'s intentions which did not really exist at the time. It did not discuss politics, nor did it in any way encourage its members to participate in what were believed to be the shabby affairs of parties and vested interests. The youth movement was anti-political, hostile to the hurrah patriotism of the beer halls, the nationalist swagger and pomposities of official Germany. All this is only too true, but it hardly goes to the root of the matter. The *Wandervogel* was certainly opposed to party strife and many of its members believed themselves to be profoundly uninterested in politics. But underneath they had accepted as articles of faith, not open to discussion and re-examination, many of the basic tenets of the official ideology propagated in the school, the parental home and elsewhere. The German youth movement talked politics, as M. Jourdain talked prose, without being aware of it.

II

The youth movement emerged spontaneously, not as the result of intellectual reflection, nor with the intention of copying the past. There were no ulterior motives; it was strictly rambling for rambling's sake. In later years its medieval mannerisms (Teutschtümelei) were occasionally criticized, as were its attempts to imitate the style of the wandering scholars of the Middle Ages. But this was not an act of political identification; the itinerant scholars were, if anything, practical anarchists, not political thinkers. Their latter-day admirers simply liked the style with all its crudities because it was rough, friendly, and free of many of the conventions of the first decade of the twentieth century. It was precisely those who had criticized Karl Fischer, the first *Wandervogel* leader, for his primitive and boorish style, his 'lack of ideology,' who were later to introduce the openly political element. To walk twenty-five miles a day in the dust of the roads was boring and stupid, they argued. Rambling was an art, they said; it had to be purposeful, those who engaged in it had to learn to be observant, to become more familiar with the Fatherland and its people.[1] This education by rambling was to produce a new German who had a better, more rounded picture of his country, and whose identification with and love of that country was deeply rooted in his personal experience.

The gradual introduction of the ideological element can be traced in the introductions to the *Zupfgeigenhansl*, the famous song-book of the *Wandervogel*. In the Introduction to the first edition in 1909 Hans Breuer, the editor, merely wished his readers happy rambling. In the Introduction to the fourth edition in 1911 the patriotic element first appeared: our search and striving is the sincere German way of life deeply rooted in our native soil. In the Introduction to the war edition of the song-book—which by then had passed the half-million mark—Breuer writes: 'We should become ever more German. Rambling is the most German of all innate instincts, it is our basic existence, the mirror of our national character.' Shortly before his death on the Western front he wrote to his father: 'I consciously cultivated the German, the national element (in the *Wandervogel*) long before the war came, and the war has shown that this was the right way.'[2]

[1] Frank Fischer, *Wandern und Schauen* (Hartenstein, 1921), p. 30.
[2] Quoted in Werner Helwig, *Die blaue Blume des Wandervogels* (Gütersloh, 1960), pp. 63–4.

It was probably inevitable that the youth movement should become 'ideological' as the first generation of its leaders grew up and came into closer contact with public affairs. In the universities they first heard in detail about a movement that seemed to have been a precursor of their own, Father Jahn's gymnasts and the *Burschenschaft* of the early nineteenth century. Father Jahn introduced a mixture of organized physical culture and patriotism in Germany, and he has not fared badly in recent German historiography. He was adopted as a fervent nationalist, Jew-hater, and Francophobe in the Hitler era, and he is now considered a progressive figure in East Germany because of his opposition to the reactionary forces of his time. Jahn, and the members of the *Burschenschaft*, whom he greatly influenced, were indeed democrats of sorts and were deeply aggrieved by the setback to their hopes of reform and greater freedom that followed the victory over Napoleon in 1815. But apart from such harmless antics as living in a cave (Jahn) or walking about in bear-skins (Karl Sand), there were disturbing elements in their general attitude. They hated everything foreign and firmly believed in the superiority of the German race. Some of the members of the *Burschenschaft* subsequently adopted a more consistent democratic line, but most of them were attracted by the purely nationalistic elements of the movement. It was perhaps symbolical that at the great meeting on the Wartburg in 1817 not merely the symbols of Prussian autocracy were burned but also books that were disliked for very different reasons. If the youth movement of the twentieth century traced some of its origins to the *Burschenschaft* it is only fair to add that it usually ignored the less savoury aspects.[1]

However, neither Jahn nor the *Burschenschaft* could be regarded as a living influence, since the problems they had faced almost a century earlier were very different from those facing young men in Germany around the turn of the century. More modern teachers and prophets were needed. It was said that the German students went into the First World War with Nietzsche's *Zarathustra* in their knapsacks, but in the youth movement Nietzsche became known comparatively late; his impact was of short duration and in some cases not very deep. The early *Wandervogel* was not interested in philosophy, and the *Oberlehrer* who were influential then were right not to consider Nietzsche one of their own kind. There was much in Nietzsche's writing that endeared him to the nationalists, but there were other, dangerous and heretical ideas as well, and on the whole he was not considered a beneficial influence on the younger generation. Nietzsche entered the youth movement only around 1912

[1] Cf. *Die Urburschenschaft als Jugendbewegung*, ed. Max Hodann and Walther Koch (Jena, 1917).

through the *Freideutsche* youth. His impact was felt during the early part of the First World War,[1] but the ecstatic rhymes did not stand up too well to the great test. Those who had been through the holocaust of Flanders and the mud and ice of the Eastern front knew all they needed to know about the spirit of tragedy. After the end of the war another, more human Zarathustra[2] had, for a while, a deeper impact than Nietzsche's.

Two other writers, more consistent and infinitely more pedestrian, had a greater effect on the pre-war generation: Paul Lagarde, a biblical scholar whose real name was Boetticher, and Langbehn, who wrote *Rembrandt as Educator*. Both were extremely critical of modern democracy, and favoured an aristocratic order in which the Germans would rightfully rule the world. Langbehn was mainly concerned with *Kulturpolitik*, Lagarde with the younger generation's lack of ideals, for which he blamed the leaders who withheld those ideals. If they would only give marching orders, if they would only permit German youth to come to the assistance of their persecuted brethren outside the Reich, if only there were a war, if the banners were flying, if the trumpets were to sound—what idealism would be released!... Langbehn also had magic powers, or so he thought; before visiting Nietzsche in his asylum he proclaimed that he would exorcise the demons that possessed Nietzsche's soul. Nietzsche, mad as he was, had enough sense to ask that Langbehn be thrown out.

Other countries have had their Lagardes and Langbehns, but they never acquired such a mass following. In Germany their books were sold by the hundred thousand, and the Kaiser himself was proud to be a pupil of Houston Stewart Chamberlain. All this could perhaps be more easily understood if the Germany of 1900 had indeed been a cultural desert. Actually, at that very time, Germany produced a crop of philosophers, sociologists, and historians hardly to be equalled anywhere in the world. But they were academicians, not leaders; they were engrossed in their specialized studies and left public affairs to the charlatans with their half-baked ideas. This lack of contact between the younger generation and those who should have been its leaders is perhaps one of the most tragic aspects of the German situation at that period. It was a failure of the older generation, as Lagarde had claimed, but not in the way he meant. There was so much enthusiasm in German youth that could have been channelled into the struggle for freedom in Wilhelmian Germany; it could have become a

---

[1] 'At the beginning of the war the comrades carried *Faust*, Dante's *Divine Comedy*, or *Zarathustra* ... in their knapsacks. Now it is quite different; these people also ask for entertaining literature, for novels.' Quoted in Inge Ehrenhaus, *Die Lektüre unserer Frontsoldaten im Weltkrieg* (Berlin, 1941), p. 80.

[2] Hermann Hesse's *Zarathustra's Wiederkehr*.

national struggle in which a liberal nationalism might have prevailed over the aggressively chauvinistic trend.

A number of adverse circumstances combined to frustrate any such possibility, among which it is easiest to identify the delay in German unification, the defeat of the 1848 revolution, and the weakness of democratic and liberal traditions.

III

The *Wandervogel* was born in Steglitz, then a semi-rural middle class suburb in the western part of Berlin, the capital of the Second Reich. There was no industry in Steglitz, and the real aristocrats had their stately homes elsewhere. Some of the local families belonged to what Blüher, himself a native of Steglitz, somewhat contemptuously calls the 'half aristocracy.' Some were merchants or professionals, but many were employed in the middle or higher ranks of the civil service. There was a closely knit Steglitz establishment with a distinct code of behaviour. It was strictly Protestant, intensely patriotic, and monarchist. It voted Conservative, though a few may have given their allegiance either to the National Liberals or to the more radical right-wing groups. Liberalism was definitely undesirable, and the Social Democrats were beyond the pale. The few artists who lived in the area were tolerated, but hardly recognized as equals. All in all, it was a middle-class bulwark of Wilhelmian Germany, as convinced of the essential rightness and justice of the political and religious order as the British middle classes were in late Victorian England, and perhaps believing even more in progress and its own security and in its country's mission in the world.

This society did not have much excitement to offer its young people. In general youth was considered a rather annoying age and state of mind. The community was adult-centred, and education was expected to produce a new generation of teachers, government officials, and reserve lieutenants that would be a more or less exact replica of its elders. Discipline was strict in the schools, the study of Greek and Latin being considered the only true education. Relations between the sexes were like those in late Victorian England, with, needless to say, the same double standards of morality. It was an efficient and successful society, but it must have been fairly boring to more enterprising spirits, perhaps even stifling, and there certainly was not much romance in it.

It was in these surroundings that the youth movement first emerged, and it retained its Protestant and middle-class character when it spread throughout Germany. Some *Wandervogel* groups developed independently at about the same time or slightly later, without knowing of the Steglitz movement—the Hamburg group for instance. But most of the early branches came into being in little university towns, founded by ex-Steglitz leaders after their graduation from school. These were the groups in Heidelberg, Jena, Göttingen, and other places. Between 1904 and 1906 the movement spread to most of the other big cities in the Reich, such as Stettin, Hanover, and Breslau. In 1907 the first groups in the German parts of the Sudeten were founded, and soon afterwards it took root in Vienna and Prague. The composition of the Austrian *Wandervogel* was somewhat different. The predominantly Catholic composition of the Hapsburg monarchy was reflected in the youth movement, but even there the Protestant element was more widely represented than in the population at large. In addition, the Austrian *Wandervogel* was much more consciously political from the very beginning. It was part of the general movement that fought for the preservation of the German character of the monarchy, against Slavs and, of course, Jews.

In Germany proper the youth movement never really struck deep roots in such Catholic areas as the Rhineland, Hesse, Alsace-Lorraine, or Upper Silesia.[1] When young people were organized there they joined religious youth groups. The youth movement did not make much headway in such exclusively Protestant provinces as East Prussia or Schleswig-Holstein either, but for different reasons. There were few, if any, big cities in these outlying North and East German regions, and the youth movement was mainly a big city movement.

The heartland of the *Wandervogel* was the region where Lower Saxony, Thuringia, and Hesse meet. Most of the geographical landmarks in the history of the youth movement are located within a radius of seventy miles or so of Eisenach in Thuringia: the Hohe Meissner, Burg Ludwigstein, Kronach, Hofgeismar, Jena, Göttingen, and so forth. This, it may be argued, used to be the geographical centre of Germany, and it was only natural that the youth movement should choose meeting points convenient for most of its members. But there may be more to it than that. It certainly was no coincidence that one of the most fascinating though not quite typical offshoots of the *Wandervogel*, the *Neue Schar*, appeared shortly after the First World War just in that area. This was a small group that had left one of the bigger youth organizations, practised primitive communism, travelled from town to town and preached

[1] According to a regional breakdown of *Wandervogel* membership in 1914, the strongest districts were Berlin-Brandenburg, Lower Saxony, Thuringia, and Westphalia. Each of these regions had as many members as the whole of Southern Germany. *Wandervogel*, January 1916, p. 27.

the salvation of mankind in semi-religious, semi-sexual ecstatic surrender to folk dancing ('swinging') and singing. It had a phenomenal though short-lived success, and attracted tens of thousands of people in a manner than can only be compared to the Pied Piper and certain medieval sects.[1] The very largest of the 'Orden' that emerged after the First World War, the 'Jungdo,' was founded in Cassel. There are many more examples of this kind. Only in the middle and late twenties did a certain geographical shift set in. Many of the leading figures of the *Freischar* came from Eastern Germany, while the leaders of the *Jungenschaft*, the last significant group to emerge before 1933, hailed from south-west Germany.[2]

The youth movement never really overcame the denominational division, and it was even less able to break down the class barrier. It came into being as, and remained, an exclusively middle-class phenomenon. There was Wolf Meyen among the early *Wandervogel* who had to work for his living. But he played a leading role only in the very early days and soon faded out. The schoolboys had their own interests, which were different from those of the young workers and apprentices, who still had to win an eight-hour working day. It was natural that the schoolboys and students should keep to themselves, but in the long run the narrow class character of the youth movement was probably its greatest weakness. All the fine slogans about deepening the community of the people (*Volksgemeinschaft*) and the 'break-through to the nation' were bound in these circumstances to remain futile. Under the impact of the great economic crisis of the late twenties some groups made a considerable effort to attract members from social classes other than their own. They succeeded to some extent, especially in the work camps of the *Deutsche Freischar*. But by then the days of the youth movement were already numbered.

Nor was the aristocracy widely represented. Social mixing with other classes was still thought to be slightly disreputable. The interests of the young aristocrats were different, as was the milieu in which they grew up, and they often went to separate schools as well. The *Wandervogel* has frequently been called by left-wing critics a petty-bourgeois movement, but while this label may have served certain polemical political purposes, it was not, strictly

[1] The itinerary of the *Neue Schar* was Kronach–Koburg–Sonneberg–Rudolstadt–Jena–Weimar–Gotha–Eisenach. See Adam Ritzhaupt, *Die Neue Schar in Thüringen* (Jena, 1921).

[2] Certain 'Catholic' elements infiltrated into the youth movement after 1918 and particularly affected the rites and symbolism of the *Bünde*. But on the whole it remained Protestant (Lutheran), and the part played in its leadership by sons of parsons and students of theology was quite considerable.

speaking, accurate.[1] In so far as lower middle-class youth was organized at all, it found its way far more frequently to the para-military mass organizations, the gymnasts or the denominational associations, than to the autonomous youth movement. The young people of the *Wandervogel* and the groups that succeeded it were for the most part sons and daughters of professional people, middle or higher government officials, or people of similar status in the world of industry and commerce, i.e., the middle classes proper.

Analysing the biographies of one hundred leading personalities of the youth movement, Walther Jantzen reaches the conclusion that they hailed, almost without exception, from middle-class families: 'The aristocracy, the officer corps, the rich entrepreneurs and the proletariat are never, or only very seldom, represented. From a geographical point of view Middle and East Germany prevail over Western Germany by a wide margin. Catholic origin was at first almost as infrequent as Jewish.'[2]

The demand to include boys and girls from elementary schools in youth movement activities was first made in 1907. Some groups thought it a rather hopeless enterprise, while other leaders such as Hans Breuer asked that the *Wandervogel* be opened to all German youth, not just to a happy few. His call found a certain echo, and a number of boys from primary schools joined the movement; but there were never very many, and with a few exceptions they remained in separate groups and did not mix with their social superiors. Even Wyneken, who certainly wanted to inculcate an anti-capitalist mentality in his Wickersdorf pupils, noted regretfully after several years' experience that his pupils were mostly children of rich or very well-to-do parents—'there was not one of real working-class origin among them'.

Class differences were too great (and too rigid) in Wilhelmian Germany to be overcome by mere good will. Nor is there much evidence that there was a widespread and intense desire to make the *Wandervogel* a popular movement with roots in all classes. The majority of its members wished to be in a congenial and more or less homogeneous group in which outsiders were not really wanted. Their social conscience was not highly developed and the 'going among the people' that had so appealed to a whole generation of Russian students would have struck them as somewhat comic and quite unrealistic. Missionary activity among the lower orders remained the monopoly of religious and political organizations.

[1] See for instance Alfred Meusel in *Jahrbücher für Soziologie*, vol. II (1926), p. 243; Ernst Bloch in *Freiheit und Ordnung* (Berlin, 1947), p. 163.
[2] 'Die soziologische Herkunft der Führungsschicht der deutschen Jugendbewegung 1900–33', in *Führungsschicht und Eliteproblem* (Frankfurt, 1957), p. 130.

It would be pointless to condemn a non-political youth movement for not bringing about the social revolution that even the biggest political party in Germany was unable to effect. But there was more than one occasion on which it might have tried to overcome class barriers during the First World War, in the immediate post-war period, and again during the depression. Under the impact of the world economic crisis of the late nineteen-twenties the *Freischar* and a few other *Bünde* took a step in this direction with their work camps, which became a meeting-place for young people of various classes.

The youth movement could never really have become a mass organization, for its élitist views were incompatible with such a movement. The mass youth organizations in Germany and other countries borrowed and successfully popularized many of the outward activities first developed by the autonomous youth movement. But its main substance could not be transplanted since it was wholly nurtured, for better or worse, in the shelter of a middle-class world.

Two

THE BEGINNING

I

HERMANN HOFFMANN, a student at Berlin University, founded in 1896 a shorthand study circle at Steglitz Grammar School which also from time to time arranged group excursions. Hoffmann was then 21, impecunious and idealistic; tuition was free in his class, and many were attracted by his initiative and joined in the walks to the Grunewald and other targets in the neighbourhood of the German capital. The following year the group went on a more ambitious trip, traversing the Harz mountains for two weeks, and in 1898 they went to the Rhine. In 1899, to crown it all, they wandered for four weeks through the Böhmerwald, the chain of mountains dividing Bavaria from Bohemia. Out of this group there grew what subsequently became known as the *Wandervogel*, and is commonly called the German youth movement.[1]

It may not be readily obvious why a circle of shorthand-writers who liked rambling on Sundays and holidays should have provoked a near revolution in the habits of large numbers of young Germans, and ultimately made their influence felt on many young people throughout Europe. Rambling in itself was not exactly a discovery made by Hoffmann and his friends. There were picnics and family excursions in those days as there are now; pupils went with their teachers, soldiers with their officers, on various excursions, while amateur naturalists scoured Germany's forests and streams. But the

[1] Documents pertaining to its early history have now been collected and sifted by Walther Gerber: *Zur Entstehungsgeschichte der deutschen Wandervogelbewegung* (Bielefeld, 1957). Hoffman dropped out even before the *Wandervogel* was officially established (1901) and became German consul, eventually Consul-General, in Turkey. At the time of the Armenian massacres he was stationed in Alexandretta and played a very creditable part, doing more for the Armenians than he was entitled to do (as Franz Werfel put it in the *Forty Days of Musa Dagh*). He retired from service in the late thirties and died in Kiel in 1955.

early *Wandervogel* put itself into deliberate opposition to a society whose interest in nature was by and large limited to yearly visits to mountain or seaside resorts, with all their modern comforts. There was more to it, too. It was, or at any rate became, a somewhat inchoate revolt against authority. The youngsters knew that a trip with parents, teachers, or supervisors would not be the real thing, but they were ready to bow to the authority of the group leader, only a few years their senior.

Whether Hoffmann envisaged a great popular movement that was to spread throughout all Germany is more than doubtful. He left Berlin in autumn 1899 on the completion of his studies, and did not come back except for a short stay in the following year. On the eve of his departure for Constantinople in late January 1900, he had a long conversation with Karl Fischer, who had been his chief aide on the trip to the Bohemian mountains the year before. He walked with Fischer to the Fichteberg in Steglitz, and on the way, according to his own testimony, tried to win his companion over to his idea of youth-rambling beyond the borders of Steglitz itself.[1]

Karl Fischer was not in need of much persuasion; he knew that he was cut out to be a leader of German youth. Hoffmann was a pleasant and able man, an enthusiastic rambler, but he had neither vision nor charisma, and the brooding, over-bearing Karl Fischer, with all his intellectual limitations, had precisely these qualities; he was the born leader. He was also a very unhappy man, and there is an element of tragedy in his later life. But nineteen-year-old Karl Fischer, when he took over from Hoffmann, was perhaps the only one who could have made that small and informal group of ramblers and amateur stenographers into the much more ambitious movement that was to spread throughout Germany and beyond its frontiers.

Fischer introduced a new style and a new content. The trips became more frequent and more extensive, and the friends from the Steglitz school met not only on Sundays and holidays, but also during the week. They now had a form of greeting of their own ('Heil'), a whistle of recognition; gradually they developed a specific garb, in order not to be mistaken for vagrants or pedlars; they developed their own taste in folk and marching songs. Fischer became the 'Oberbachant,' the medieval itinerant scholar ('Bachant') being the ideal. Newcomers to the group started with the rank of 'scholar,' and gradually became 'Bursche' and later 'Bachant.' Promotion depended upon participation in trips and on the way in

---

[1] See his letter to Ahrens in 1952, quoted in Gerber, p. 38. But Copalle (*Chronik der Freien Deutschen Jugendbewegung*, Bad Godesberg, 1954, p. 11) adds, also on the basis of a letter from Hoffmann, that it is unlikely that the concrete form of a movement (*Bund*) was envisaged at that time.

which the individual established himself on these occasions; frequently Fischer demanded some written homework also.

The activities of the group continued throughout the years 1900 and 1901 on a very informal basis; it is doubtful whether more than a dozen people outside Steglitz, let alone outside Berlin, knew of its existence. It had no name, no newspaper of its own, not even a written sheet. It was just a group of friends. And it is doubtful whether any of its members, with the exception of Karl Fischer, thought of their circle in any other terms. They liked it tremendously, they were enthusiastic about it, but it would be misleading to describe them as pioneers conscious of a mission.

Karl Fischer was not a great thinker, and he was an indifferent speaker. Blüher once noted that it was sometimes painful to listen to his long, rambling discourses, and that to see this man wrestling with his unformulated ideal moved onlookers to pity. But with all that, Fischer sensed quite correctly what were the first steps that must be taken to get his group recognized by their parents and by their school. He understood that in the Wilhelmian Germany of his day recognition as an 'official association' was an absolute prerequisite to getting his group accepted, to winning over new members, founding new groups, and ultimately making it a great movement. No professional diplomat could have tackled this delicate task more efficiently.

And so, on the evening of 4 November 1901, in the back room of the Steglitz Town Hall cellar, five 'old boys' (four free-lance writers and one physician) and five youth leaders, including Karl Fischer, came together and decided to establish an association, 'Wandervogel, Ausschuss für Schülerfahrten' (*Wandervogel*, committee for schoolboys' rambles).[1] The writer Heinrich Sohnrey (1859–1948) was elected president; together with Karl Fischer he drew up a constitution to give the committee the proper legal façade.

Two days after the Steglitz meeting the first printed leaflet was published in an attempt to raise support among parents and enlist new members. A new movement was on the march to conquer German youth.

[1] The name 'Wandervogel' was proposed at that meeting by Wolf Meyen, the youngest of the group, by trade a mechanic. The word 'Wandervogel' apparently first appeared in an Eichendorff poem published in 1837, and was first used with a wider meaning (referring to human beings), in a poem by Otto Roquette in the eighteen-fifties. Wolf Meyen, on a walk to Dahlem, the Berlin suburb, came across a tombstone (the 'Branco stone') with an inscription that began as follows:

> *Wer hat euch Wandervögeln*
> *Die Wissenschaft geschenkt*
> *dass ihr auf Land und Meeren*
> *die Flügel sicher lenkt . . .*

II

The story of the youth movement in the first decade after the meeting in the Steglitz Ratskeller is one of steady and inconspicuous growth, not of great deeds and memorable events. New groups spread throughout Germany—the first branch outside Steglitz was founded in Berlin-Lichterfelde in 1902, the first group outside Greater Berlin, in Lüneburg. It is a story of more frequent, longer, and better-planned trips; on one occasion in 1903 eighty boys took part, a mammoth outing by the standards of those days. A certain style developed in *Wandervogel* activities. Karl Fischer was the advocate of a simple life, and it became the rule to cook meals on a stove set up in the fields, while barns served as quarters for the night; later on there were tents too. The authority of the group leader was, indeed had to be, unquestioned. All this was very different from the trips organized by schools, or the holidays that the boys of that time spent with their parents. Soon the *Wandervogel* developed the rudiments of its own culture. There were amateur theatricals (with Hans Sachs a favourite instructor), as well as puppet shows. The members were encouraged to put on paper their impressions and experiences. Some wrote poems, while drawing and especially the preparation of silhouettes was expected from those who had any inclination in that direction, and the first *Wandervogel* photographers appeared on the scene.

By and large, the artistic harvest was disappointing. Youth movement literature was curiously flat and formless; its early magazines are almost unreadable. Deep feeling there undoubtedly was, but the capacity for artistic expression was notably absent. The humour was heavy and the style fairly routine. In literature the *Wandervogel* was neither an innovator, nor did it keep up the best traditions of German writing. The decade before World War I was not, it is true, a particularly fruitful one in the annals of German literature, but there were better preceptors for the *Wandervogel* to choose. Dozens of German writers were at one time or another members of the youth movement, among them some novelists of real distinction. But curiously enough scarcely one of them later wrote about the youth movement, and it is difficult to trace in any of their work the influence of themes and attitudes peculiar to the movement.

Artistic taste was, if possible, worse, for that generation of German youth modelled themselves on some of the most inferior trends then prevalent in German painting. The great impressionist masterpieces were practically unknown, but Fidus' beautified young heroes and heroines were greatly appreciated. It is only fair to add that a notable improvement set in after the First World War; some of the youth movement magazines of the late twenties were indeed pioneering in the quality of their photographs, their lay-out, the revolutionary use of lettering.

But there was one field in which great work was done. The youth movement did probably more than any other movement at the time to develop musical culture on a very broad basis. It brought about a renaissance of German folksong, which had been neglected for a long time. It collected and published old songs, and here, in contrast to literature and painting, it revealed a sure touch and applied high standards. Choirs and orchestras were encouraged; group singing became an integral part of meetings. *Wandervogel* songs are known and sung today wherever the German tongue is spoken; they in their turn have become real folksongs. The lute and the guitar were rediscovered by the youth movement, and folk dancing too was cultivated, though not with equal success.

All these were by-products, so to speak. The authentic and deepest experience of the youth movement is difficult to describe and perhaps impossible to analyse: the experience of walking at night and at sunrise, the atmosphere of the camp fire, the friendships that sprang up. There was much romantic exaltation, and it is easier to ridicule the extravagances of this state of mind than to do them justice. Very deep emotional chords were struck; the genuineness of this experience cannot be doubted. For many of the best of the younger generation in Germany it was a cherished experience remembered all through their life. Whether, and to what extent, it shaped their subsequent life, is a question that cannot be easily answered.

III

The early history of the youth movement is one of idealistic endeavour and high aspirations. It was also beset by splits, personal quarrels, and conflicts between various leaders and groups. Karl Fischer had been extremely prudent in enlisting the assistance of an *Eufrat* (Parents and Friends Advisory Council), which undoubtedly helped to remove many obstacles. Above all, it made it much easier for the *Wandervogel* to be recognized by the school authorities.

Fischer was less happy in his relations with his contemporaries, the *Wandervogel* leaders. The regulations drawn up in the Steglitz Ratskeller were calculated to give constitutional sanction to Fischer's undisputed and absolute leadership. This worked well for a while, but when the youth movement spread there was an influx of people who were not willing to accept Fischer's dictatorship, as some of them called it. There were complaints about the coarseness of the *Wandervogel*, the lack of elementary good manners, about the neglect of intellectual interests; one member drew attention to the fact that the groups at that time were composed chiefly of pupils with a bad scholastic record; others contended that Fischer had over-exerted his group during the trips.

The leaders of the opposition were Siegfried Copalle, Bruno Thiede, and Richard Weber, who were just one rank below Fischer in the *Wandervogel* hierarchy. There was less of the itinerant scholars' spirit in their activities, and there was also a greater willingness to compromise with society and its established rules. Blüher, a not altogether reliable witness, relates that on trips conducted by Fischer everybody got the same food, whereas on an excursion led by Copalle those who had the money ordered *Wiener Schnitzel* in a restaurant while their less fortunate comrades could only watch them.

Karl Fischer, never an easy character, became more difficult to handle as the years went by. Whether the accusation of 'Caesarism' was justified or not, Fischer overruled his assistant leaders on various occasions, and Copalle, Thiede, and Weber retired in midsummer 1903 from active participation in the *Wandervogel*, while retaining their membership. Not one of them was a born leader of men as Fischer was, but they had qualities which the 'Oberbachant' sadly lacked, and they were genuinely concerned about the wrong and 'anti-cultural' course the movement had taken. They had their friends and sympathizers in Steglitz and continued their private meetings with the younger members. During the 1904 Easter holidays they arranged a trip with their followers without first asking Fischer's permission. This was an act of open defiance and rebellion, since according to usage every major activity had to be authorized by Fischer. The conflict soon became the talk of the town in Steglitz, or at any rate of that part of the town that cared. It was discussed by both teachers and schoolboys and an open clash became inevitable. The decisive meeting took place on 29 June 1904, in the same Ratskeller in which only three years before the *Wandervogel* had been officially established. Fischer found himself in a minority on that evening; he left the meeting and a split ensued, the first of many secessions and reunions in the history of the German youth movement.

Copalle and his friends, who were supported by an influential member of the 'Parents Council,' Professor L. Gurlitt, an internationally famous educationist, set to work at once and founded a new group, '*Wandervogel*, registered association in Steglitz'. The 'registered association' was a pure technicality, but it symbolized the greater readiness of the group to conform with society, to accept the leadership of the parental home and the school. The term 'Registered Association' in Germany raises unfortunate memories of rabbit-breeders and skittle-players, but Copalle and his friends apparently did not mind this. They founded a movement that was certainly to place much more stress on cultural activities, but was also somehow more domesticated than the early *Wandervogel*. Fischer's verve was sadly lacking. Their periodical had a much higher standard than the bulletins published by Fischer, they were more democratic, they established an excellent orchestra and published a first collection of songs. But the excitement and the spirit of rebellion were absent, and the *Wandervogel* (Steglitz) did indeed remain confined to the German capital in subsequent years, when the other groups spread throughout Germany.

Fischer had declared at the fateful meeting that he intended to retire altogether. But at a meeting with a group of those who had remained faithful, held at night in a forest near Berlin (and dramatically described by Blüher), he reconsidered his decision and thus became the first leader of a new organization, the *Altwandervogel*. It had less money at its disposal than its rival, and fewer classical philologists to give it respectability; but it continued to some extent the old itinerant scholars' romanticism, and was both less 'reasonable' and more successful. Soon, however, it too was torn by internal dissension; Fischer moved to Halle University after having promoted himself to the rank of 'Gross Bachant,' and wished to continue to direct the affairs of the movement from his new domicile. But Friese, his deputy in Berlin, had different ideas, and Fischer lost control.

The situation was further complicated by the Jansen affair. Wilhelm Jansen, a man in his forties, owner of a large estate in Hesse, had met by chance some *Altwandervogel* groups, made friends with them, and came to be regarded by them as both leader and father confessor. A rich man who was genuinely interested in young people and their problems, he had great charm and his personality in a very short time captivated many of the younger members of the movement. The leaders and some of the older friends of the movement were somewhat distrustful of Jansen's intentions, his championship of nudism, and other strange ideas. But the younger element prevailed, and when Karl Fischer resigned Jansen was appointed in his place.

We are nearing the end of another chapter in the history of the youth movement, and the remainder of the story can be briefly told. After more internal crises, Fischer decided to make his exit; in October 1906 he left for Tsingtao, China, to do his national service with a German battalion stationed there. But Jansen, too, soon found himself in difficulties. This was a time when people in Berlin reacted very violently to the sight or sound of the word 'homosexual'; there had recently been a number of scandals affecting high, even the highest circles in the country. The inclusion of certain homosexuals among Jansen's friends gave rise to various insinuations, and his position in the *Altwandervogel* became untenable. He and his followers seceded, and founded the *Jungwandervogel*, which was to be the longest-lived, though not the most important, of all the groups we have so far mentioned.

IV

Hoffmann-Voelkersamb dropped out of the *Wandervogel* before it was even officially born, and his role as one of the pioneers was soon forgotten. Hoffmann was a pleasant man whom everybody seems to have liked. Nobody would have called Karl Fischer pleasant or inoffensive, but in his prime he was a great leader, and as such he is remembered to this day. Blüher, admittedly an easily impressionable witness, recalling his first meeting with the 'crazy Fischer' (as a pillar of Steglitz society allegedly called him), says that everyone who had any dealings with him invariably realized that he was a man of highly unusual capacities. One day Blüher saw a fresh wound on Fischer's arm: 'I burned the flesh a bit; I wanted to find out the state of my nerves. It's still all right.' With all his antics, however, and despite an indifferent scholastic record, Fischer retained the confidence of the director of his school. And even Copalle, his main rival, wrote after many years that when in the early days their group returned to Steglitz on a Sunday evening, dirty and tired after a strenuous trip, Fischer marched in front of his group, completely indifferent to the sneering comments of passers-by, while he (Copalle) was very happy with his less conspicuous place in the second or third row.

Fischer was anything but articulate, yet he knew how to impart his own enthusiasm to others. His autocratic regime in the early days was presumably justified, but it became a great problem and ultimately caused his downfall. A friend wrote later: 'I have not yet found any single person who has really seen through Fischer. To me he was always sinister, like a thundercloud coming over. Presumably he had much wider plans than he ever publicized.' And even Blüher says that Fischer was undoubtedly sincere when he talked about the German mission of the movement, but what he really wanted in his innermost self nobody could say.

There was a streak of melancholia and depression in Fischer which as time went by became progressively stronger. Like Achilles he retired brooding and sulking to his tent, and in the end there were no friends to comfort and encourage him. He did not complete his university studies, and his stay in China lasted much longer than had been expected—fifteen years, of which several were spent in a prisoner-of-war camp. When he returned to Germany in 1921 a new generation of youth leaders had come into existence with whom he could find no common language. He was made editor of a youth magazine that soon ceased publication, and after that he did not look for or find any permanent employment. Blüher reports that at one time he sold newspapers near a swimming pool in Berlin, and that at a different period he was scrubbing floors in the villa of a *nouveau riche*. He rejected attempts made by friends to help him, but apparently did not refuse a monthly honorarium (*Ehrensold*) from the Hitler Youth after 1933. He had never married, and in 1941, a few weeks after the death of his mother, whom he had loved very much, he died in Berlin at the age of sixty-one, an embittered and forgotten man. He was remembered again on the fiftieth anniversary of the youth movement, which was celebrated in the early fifties, and there is now a Karl Fischer Society in Berlin.

What became of those who provoked the first big split in the *Wandervogel*, the men who had wished to follow more decorous and intellectual paths? Both Bruno Thiede and Richard Weber died while still young; Copalle became a teacher in Schweidnitz, Silesia, where he founded a youth orchestra, but otherwise lost contact with the youth movement. When Silesia became part of Poland in 1945, he worked for a while at an East German university, but then settled in West Germany, where he died in 1957. Jansen, too, dropped out of the picture; he lived to see Hitler's advent to power and died, an old man, in the late thirties or early forties.

After these pioneers had disappeared the leadership of the movement passed first to Hans Breuer and Hans Lissner, and eventually to Edmund Neuendorff. Breuer was one of the very earliest ramblers, a member of Karl Fischer's group; he and Lissner became close friends when students at Heidelberg. He is now remembered chiefly as the editor of the *Zupfgeigenhansol*, the song-book of the youth movement which had such a tremendous success. Breuer became a physician and was killed, like so many others, during the First World War. Lissner, a teacher, was for years editor of the *Wandervogel* magazine and member of its executive. He survived two world wars, was arrested in East Germany and kept in prison for several years, but released around 1957—perhaps in view of his advanced age. Neuendorff had an interesting and unusual career. Shortly before the First World War, while headmaster of a high school in Western Germany, he became head of the united *Wandervogel*. In the twenties he served as head of the Prussian Academy of Gymnastics. In the Third Reich he studied theology, and in 1945 (at the age of seventy) became a parson in a small West German village. There were other leaders (including a whole host of Fischers—such as Walter Fischer, Frank Fischer, *et al.*—unrelated to Karl Fischer) whose names will come up in our narrative. Many of them did not return from the First World War, and those who did no longer found it possible to make contact with the new generation that had meanwhile grown up in the youth movement. Common to them all was a youthful enthusiasm and the desire to make the movement a great and positive force in the German fatherland. These things apart, it would be difficult to bring under one common denominator men who differed widely in character and outlook. It is of interest that many of that generation chose teaching as their profession, and Eduard Spranger has rightly observed that if the youth movement did indeed have a lasting impact, it was precisely in that field. They liked teaching because it gave them the opportunity to continue in a different setting the educational work they had done in the youth movement; they thought of teaching as a vocation.

Three

THE NEW STYLE

I

EVERY youthful experience is strong and lasting; but each is also different. Members of the youth movement have come to believe that only those who belonged to it know what it was all about. This is not altogether surprising; some Germans have always maintained that neither West nor East can understand their deepest motives and feelings.

It is doubtless true that the facts and figures of the historians, sociologists, and educationists do little to communicate an understanding of the central experience of the movement. It is the business of poets and novelists, perhaps of painters and composers, to depict the quality of life in the *Wandervogel* for the wider, uninitiated public. Unfortunately they have not yet produced works of art that do this; we have hardly more than a few transitory glimpses and pale reflections of these so-long-cherished experiences. It is no insurmountable psychic barrier, however, that has hitherto impeded such communication, but the simple fact that the members of the movement were not remarkably articulate; there was no creative writer or artist of genius among them who chose life in the movement for his subject.

One who belongs to a different generation and a different people cannot hope to succeed where members of the *Wandervogel* itself have so far been silent or ineffectual. The following notes and observations will deal, therefore, mainly with the more formal aspects of youth movement life. For the spirit of the youth movement we shall have to rely on the testimony of its members and on our evaluation of their evidence.

II

Members of the youth movement were as a rule between twelve and nineteen years of age. Those under twelve were in most cases physically unequal to the rigours of long expeditions, nor were they presumably much interested in the other activities. Those over nineteen had normally left school; they had gone to do their service in the army, were undergoing professional training, or had become students at a university. There were few students apart from group leaders; most of those who had passed through from the *Wandervogel* joined the Academic *Freischar*, or, later, the *Freideutsche* youth, whose activities differed greatly from those of the younger boys and girls in the *Wandervogel*.

The group leader was in most cases three to six years older than his followers, but there were exceptions in both directions, and no hard and fast rule. A difference of more than six or seven years was often considered unduly great; the disparity in the interests and general attitudes of leader and group might be a handicap. On the other hand, it was not considered desirable that the leader should be of the same age as his followers, for leading demanded greater maturity and experience, more knowledge, and if possible more physical strength; it also presupposed a certain respect that youngsters are usually more ready to grant to those slightly older than themselves.

The group (*Gruppe* or *Horde*) had seldom less than seven or eight members; the exceptions were those that had just been founded or those in small cities. Those with more than twenty members were regarded as too large; it was thought that there could be no real friendship and cohesion in them. Where there was more than one group in a given city, they were united in a local branch (*Ortsgruppe*), and all the local branches in a given province had a central organization of their own, called the *Gau*. There was collaboration but also competition between the various groups in a local branch. The leaders of the groups would meet once every few weeks, and from time to time there were joint activities between two groups of the same branch, or between all of them. The *Gau* often had its own internal bulletin, hectographed or printed, and the various branches of the *Gau* met at a camp or on some other occasion once or twice a year. The leader of the *Gau* was responsible to the head of the whole *Bund* for the groups under his control.

It was comparatively easy to convene a meeting of all the members of the *Gau*, for in the entire history of the German youth movement there were few that counted more than a thousand members, and most of them had only about a couple of hundred, not all of whom appeared at the meetings. A camp of the whole *Bund* was a different proposition, and in view of the great technical difficulties involved such camps were but seldom convened. Even so, the number of participants at the very biggest meetings of the youth movement before the First World War (such as the Hohe Meissner or the *Bundestag* at Frankfurt-am-der-Oder in 1914) did not exceed 2,000 to 3,500.

Karl Fischer had, in the circumstances of the time, to appoint himself leader. But in later years a regular procedure for choosing group leaders was adopted, although hard and fast rules never existed. Those who were believed to have the qualities thought necessary to lead a group were asked to do so by their superior leader, or else they volunteered to take over an existing group, or to form a new one. The technique of attracting new members varied: a youngster would be approached in school or in a sports club, or, more frequently, simply in the street. He was invited to come along to a group meeting or a ramble. If he liked it—and was liked by the others—he would be invited again, until he became a full member.

All the youth groups were selective, but standards and criteria varied greatly from group to group, and at different places and times. In some of the small, highly exclusive *Bünde* of the late twenties good looks were an important, though admittedly not the only, criterion, whereas the *Wandervogel* and the bigger organizations were less particular in this respect. A serious physical defect would frequently preclude membership, but so would asocial behaviour, or the group's unwillingness to accept a candidate, whatever the reason. Nobody became a full member at once; everyone had to go through a trial period during which he was submitted to various tests. The scouts, in the early days, merely demanded a knowledge of the basic commandments, familiarity with knots, and the ability to find one's way in a strange place; elsewhere the tests were far more elaborate and included anything from participation in a certain number of marches (endurance tests) to weird and complex tests of courage in groups with higher pretensions to the formation of an *élite*. Some organizations consisted of leaders, full members, and candidates, but others had several grades and degrees in between. At first, selection was made on an entirely *ad hoc* basis, and in some groups it never became very complicated. But in the bigger organizations, the hierarchy dividing the novice who had just taken part in his first trip from the *Bundesleiter* was not much less complex than the distance separating an aspiring Freemason from the position of Grand Master, or a raw recruit from that of a field-marshal. It should be added, however, that the *Wandervogel* was, by and large, and for reasons to be discussed later, more democratic than many of the *Bünde* formed in the period after the First World War.

III

Initially (and for many years after) the big expedition was at the centre of youth-movement activities. For obvious reasons (school holidays) a big expedition had to take place in the summer months. In addition, there were rambles or camps of shorter duration during the Christmas vacation, around Easter and in autumn. There were also half-day excursions on Sunday, or sometimes week-end trips into the immediate neighbourhood of one's native city.

In the pioneering days the preparation and planning of these activities was a bit haphazard: necessarily so, because there was as yet no ubiquitous network of youth hostels to facilitate the planning of the successive stages of an itinerary. And it was an unwritten law, almost from the beginning, that the group must make do with the very minimum of money; if the railway had to be used, the *Wandervogel* went in the very cheapest compartment, and they made it a rule to sleep in barns rather than hotels and to cook their own food. In the early days everybody turned up in different garb and often wearing flamboyant hats, with or without feathers. The different groups had their own little badges or pins, marks of distinction that were invariably worn; and in the twenties the wearing of uniform clothes became obligatory—short trousers, blue, white, brown, green or grey shirts, according to the *Bund* that one belonged to, and scout neckties, red or blue cords, distinctive headgear, and so forth.

The group-travelling itself developed, both in technique and in geographical range. In the earliest days, a *Wandervogel* group explored only the immediate vicinity of its native city; journeys to other parts of Germany were exceptional. Gradually the desire to visit remoter regions prevailed, until after a few years there was a reaction against the tendency to measure the value of an expedition by the remoteness of the objective or the number of miles walked. But after the First World War every self-respecting group went abroad at least once a year, and the more adventurous, professional *Wandervogel* (such as the *Nerother*) toured the African deserts and the Himalayas, while Lapland became a favourite target for others.

These travels had to be elaborately prepared; the boys—and still more their group leaders—had to consult works of reference and, if they were going abroad, acquire a smattering of a foreign language. After their return, reports had to be prepared, for which drawings, paintings, and photographs had been collected; and if the quality of the material warranted it, these were published in book form.

THE NEW STYLE

Valuable as these activities could be, it was soon found that expeditions and preparations for them could never fulfil all the aims or employ all the energies of the movement. The members of a group met informally in school or in the home of a member, and it was decided to give these meetings a more organized and systematic form. From this arose the idea of the *Nest* or *Heim*, which consisted of one or more rooms, or frequently of a shed, on the outskirts of the city, decorated with the emblems of the movement and containing perhaps a small library and other group property, including the banner and sports gear. Members of the group met here once or twice a week, in the afternoon or evening. Such meetings were likely to be opened and concluded with a couple of songs accompanied by lute or guitar; they would include a reading, by the leader, of a few pages from a favourite writer of the youth movement, or the leader might tell a story of his own; there might also be a discussion on the aims of the movement or on school problems, or perhaps of the personal problems of individual group members.

There were other activities, too, such as the sports competitions of the local branch, 'war games,' amateur theatricals, and competitions in group singing. In some *Bünde* the summer or winter solstice was a central event, when some youth movement groups held religious services in the open, conducted by clergy from among their own associates. Group leaders and aspirant leaders were called together once or twice a year for special training courses.

Songs played a vital part in all youth movement activities, but there were considerable changes in taste and fashion. The romantic folksong was typical for the movement, but in the twenties, with the advance of the so-called 'liturgical movement,' there was an anti-romantic trend towards stricter discipline and back-to-Bach. In the later twenties group declamation (*Sprechchor*) came into fashion, and seemed for a while to have supplanted the folksong.

The rediscovery of the folksong had been the great achievement of the *Wandervogel*, but love songs and innocent ditties did not seem to suit the mood of the twenties. Military songs became generally popular, including a revival of *Landsknecht* songs, both authentic and faked. Songs from many countries were imported, celebrating such different heroes as the men of Harlech, William of Orange, Hetman Platoff, Field-Marshal Radetzky and Admiral Kolchak. In some groups there was a nihilistic, Brechtian or quasi-Brechtian vogue in the late twenties and early thirties: drums and trumpets were more and more often used to accompany the singers on their march. The soldier was supplanting the strolling scholar as the ideal type.

IV

Shared experiences and adventures welded a more or less accidental group into a disciplined community. There might be a more intimate friendship between two or more members, but the feeling of comradeship and solidarity extended to every member of the group. A group usually disintegrated when its members reached the age of seventeen or eighteen; a few would stay on as leaders, but most would leave when they left school, made new friends, and acquired new interests. But the feeling of comradeship would linger on; in many cases it would persist for decades, and this was not merely a sentimental interest in what-became-of-so-and-so. If some grew indifferent, others preserved something more than the old school tie feeling.

There were decisive differences between the *Wandervogel* and the *Bünde* of the twenties; the former was more individualistic in character, whereas the latter laid more emphasis upon the collective, and it is difficult therefore to generalize about the youth movement as a whole. But there were certain ideals and qualities which the whole movement tried to instil into its members. Above all, it acted as an important corrective to selfishness; neither the school nor the parental home could provide boys and girls of that age with the inner discipline and the comradeship that the youth movement demanded from every member. This was a practical introduction to ethical and aesthetic values that would otherwise have been denied to many of the young generation. Church youth groups and the Socialist movement could provide these too, because they had the guidance of an accepted set of values; but a "bourgeois youth" which was neither religious nor socialist and had no specific values of its own was in danger of growing up destitute of ideals, preoccupied with its careers, lacking any sense of social obligation, and with no desire but to enjoy itself. But even if the youth movement had not performed this or any other function, it would require no justification, for it arose as the natural and necessary revolt against a society that denied the young generation a right to its own ways of life. Those who speak for the movement claim something more. The youth movement, they say, inculcated a certain spirit or attitude (*Haltung*) that made its members different from most other boys and girls of their generation. Even if they afterwards joined the S.S. or became Communists, they had human qualities that distinguished them from their colleagues. One of them has said that 'It is impossible to imagine anybody who ever felt anything of the ethos of the youth movement as a commandant of Auschwitz or as a GPU man-hunter.'[1]

This is not a very happy example,[2] but it should be added that the sterling qualities of character which the youth movement encouraged in its members were frequently corrupted in the twenties by the politics of moral nihilism: it was neither a Hitlerite nor a Communist who declared that 'even the most heinous means is consecrated if used in the struggle for national liberation,' and that 'we must say "no" to humanism, we must use even the most barbaric means, if it is necessary to further the national resurrection'[3]—it was Ernst Niekisch, who enjoyed great authority in the youth movement and who spent many years in the prisons of the Third Reich.

But these were problems of the *bündische* youth; the world of 1913, and the *Wandervogel* in it, had less critical issues to face. Their aspirations were best defined in that famous formula of 1913 of the *Freideutsche* youth who wanted, standing on their own feet, to shape their own lives—'at their own initiative, on their own responsibility, and with deep sincerity'. This in its vagueness left room for various interpretations. Socialists and Pan-Germans, Jews and anti-semites, girls and masculine anti-feminists—all were undoubtedly sincere, and wanted to be responsible for their actions. The Meissner formula was not exactly a call to action, but as a moral maxim it probably did make sense in the world that came to an end in August 1914.

[1] Karl O. Paetel, *Das Bild vom Menschen in der deutschen Jugendführung* (Bad Godesberg 1954), p. 53.

[2] The commandant of Auschwitz, Rudolf Höss, was a member of the *Artamanen*, a group that was commonly regarded as a part of the youth movement.

[3] Ernst Niekisch, *Was will die Widerstandsbewegung*, p. 21; idem, *Politik deutschen Widerstandes*, p. 25.

Four

AT THE HOHE MEISSNER

I

THE Hohe Meissner is a mountain to the south of Cassel: Lady Holle, a prominent figure in German mythology, is said to reside there. On the evening of 11 October, 1913, a great number of groups of boys and girls, including a good many students from Göttingen, Jena, Marburg and other universities, converged upon the Hohe Meissner. So did a certain number of men and women of more advanced age, friends and well-wishers of the youth movement. It was a miserable evening, cold and rainy, and several hours' marching had done nothing to improve the general mood when the ramblers, wet and exhausted, arrived at their destination: the failure of the meeting seemed a foregone conclusion. But the rain stopped next morning, the sun came out, it grew warmer, and the spirits of the assembly rose with the barometer. In fact, the stage was set for what they all wanted to make the most important convention in the annals of the youth movement.

The date of this event was the centenary of the war against Napoleon. The *Wandervogel* did not greatly relish the usual patriotic festivals, but the idea of a youth mass meeting had found much response. And there were other, more cogent reasons for holding a rally. Between 1910 and 1913 the youth movement had spread throughout Germany and taken root in Austria and Switzerland. Various new organizations had come into being, and it was generally felt that some larger measure of unity among them would do no harm—even if a merger was impossible. In addition, there was the problem of the older members of the *Wandervogel*, those above the age of twenty, who had clearly outgrown the youth groups. Many of them had joined student groups which carried on the tradition, and it was from these circles that the suggestion came to found an organization which should unite all the older members of the

Wandervogel without distinction of *Bund* or group. The name *Freideutsche Jugend* was proposed, and the first meeting was convoked for October 1913. The organizers of this convention met in Jena in July, and at once faced a number of ticklish problems. The main *Bünde*, with one notable exception, refused to commit themselves, and merely permitted their older members to take part in the meeting. As organizations they did not want to become too closely involved. The 'Jungwandervogel' was ready to appear on the Hohe Meissner, but complained in its manifesto that by now too many groups were led by teachers acting on behalf of the authorities. Was it for this purpose that the *Wandervogel* had come into being? The Austrian comrades protested that it must insist on racial purity in its ranks; Jews and persons of Slavonic or Franco-Italian blood were excluded. So far this was intelligible enough, but after it came this remarkable *non sequitur*—'We regard with contempt all who call us "political". '

There were representatives of two or three organizations present preaching abstinence, advocates of 'Free School Communities' (including Wyneken's), and a group with strong *völkische* views (the *Volkserzieher*). 'We regard Germany, not Palestine, as the promised land,' they declared; for further information the enquirer was referred to the *Germanic Bible* and *Under the Swastika*, the household books of the movement.[1] The Academic *Freischar* announced that it did not want to make its members visionary utopians; on the contrary, it intended to educate them in practical idealism in the spirit of Carlyle, Fries, Fichte, and Paul de Lagarde. Most original of all was the declaration of aims by the *Sera* circle in Jena (founded by the publisher Eugen Diederichs) which was made in hexameters; and the most tolerant was the *Wandervogel's* description of itself as '. . . a chequered community of very different people. Within its walls even the queerest fellows get along famously, if they do not quarrel. This, happily, occurs only on secondary issues. On the main thing—rambling—we are in complete agreement.'

There was an obvious conflict from the very beginning between the *Wandervogel*, which saw its main purpose in rambling, and the other organizations which only wanted the youth movement's co-operation in their campaigns for various kinds of *Lebensreform*.

[1] The leader of this group, Wilm Schwaner, is now mainly remembered because he figured prominently and for many years in Walther Rathenau's letters. There were more intelligent correspondents then available in Germany for such exchanges, and the relationship between the two can only be explained, as it is by Rathenau's biographer, Harry Graf Kessler, by the deep-seated inferiority feeling of the intellectual Jew *vis-à-vis* the nordic *Lichtmensch*. It is only fair to add in this context that the Swastika, which, incidentally, was frequently used as a sign in the *Wandervogel*, became the symbol of extreme anti-semitism only after 1918.

Many leading figures of the day declared their support for the *Freideutsche* youth, among them Gerhard Hauptmann and Gertrud Bäumer, Ferdinand Avenarius and Friedrich Naumann. Others were invited, or felt themselves obliged, to send greetings. Alfred Weber, for instance, sent a few sentences to the effect that the older generation should not offer too much advice to the youth movement; the greatest danger facing youth was that it would not stand on its own feet. Others were more prolix, like Ludwig Klages, who filled eighteen pages with savage condemnation of the ideas of progress and reason as guiding principles in life.[1] Among those who sent their greetings were some of the leading pedagogues of the day, such as Gurlitt, Kerschensteiner, and Paul Natorp, who contributed what were perhaps the most thoughtful estimates of the tasks and the dangers confronting the youth movement. Politically, they were more or less equally divided between the right wing and the liberal centre. One attacked clericalism; another suggested that German *Geselligkeit* should form the vanguard in an imperial march to the triumph of German culture; a third uttered warnings against the State's encroachment upon the rights of the individual. There were some first-rate minds among them, and some obvious cranks, but most of the advice offered had nothing at all to do with the youth movement and its specific tasks and pursuits. It must have been somewhat disconcerting to find that, with very few exceptions, these friends and sympathizers of the youth movement were at a loss even to find a common language with the younger generation.

II

The Meissner convention started with a meeting of the steering committee on the Hanstein, a neighbouring mountain height. Bruno Lemke, a student of Marburg,[2] opened the proceedings by summarizing the views of the *Wandervogel* and of the other organizations present, and a general debate ensued. Some of the speeches were forceful and enthusiastic, and Hans Paasche's peroration, 'The German house is on fire, and we are the fire brigade!' was received with acclamation. There was some common ground

[1] Klages had a considerable and pernicious influence on the youth movement for many years. His strictures against moral conscience and his attacks on the spirit, the 'adversary of the soul', paved the way for fascist philosophy in many important respects. The National Socialists ultimately refused to accept Klages because of his 'softness' and pacifism, but this does not diminish his responsibility as an intellectual pacemaker for the Third Reich.

[2] A young mathematician and philosopher, he remained a leading member of the youth movement for about a decade. He was editor of the *Freideutsche Jugend* in 1921–22.

between the *Wandervogel* and the puritan reformers: the Meissner formula was to include a passage urging that alcohol and nicotine should be banned from all meetings of the *Freideutsche* youth. It was also realized, however, that the life-reformers had their own special interests and rather narrow purposes, which were by no means identical with the aims of the *Freideutsche* youth. Wyneken and his friend Luserke thought that youth was the age for getting to know oneself (*Sammlung*), and that before entering upon the stress and struggle of adult life, young people needed to withdraw into the wilderness, as Christ withdrew into the desert, to acquire inner knowledge. They were not yet ready to decide what leader or what party to follow. There was a distinct danger of their being captivated by a modern pied piper, lured to perdition by some spellbinder appealing to vague emotions.

At the end of the evening no agreement was in sight; and after the long speeches and heated exchanges not much good will or brotherliness remained. But next day the scene shifted to the Hohe Meissner, where there was communal singing, folk dancing, and a general relaxation of tension. Gottfried Traub, a pastor, made a speech recalling the patriotic spirit of 1813, but also appealing to youth not to sell itself to any political party, however commendable its aims and activities. Later in the evening, when they were all assembled around a great camp fire, Knud Ahlborn, the spokesman for the *Freideutsche*, repeated Paasche's words about the house—built by Bismarck—being now on fire: yes, something ought to be done, but the time was not yet ripe for youth to take its stand in this struggle. Their highest patriotic duty was to grow up, and not to become committed prematurely. Obscurantists had tried to bring confusion and fanaticism into the ranks of the *Freideutsche*, but youth ought to be tolerant and to respect everyone's opinion so long as it was arrived at in search of the truth and was sincerely held. The supreme good for these young men was serenity of mind untouched by party strife.[1]

Then, on the following morning, a Sunday, came the central event of the meeting, Wyneken's address, in which the results of the convention were to be summarized. Wyneken said that he approached this assignment with great reluctance after having heard what kinds of voices and ideas had been received by many with acclamation. He deplored narrow nationalist impulses, and for love of country itself he wished that there might never be a war. He recalled the patriotism of the great heroes of 1813—but had they not

[1] The full text of the Hohe Meissner speeches has not been preserved. *Freideutscher Jugendtag*, 1913 (second edition, Hamburg, 1919) gives the gist of them; and *Freideutsche Jugend* (Jena, 1913) contains the messages of greeting.

been citizens of the world at the same time? Had not Gneisenau written that principles were more important than countries, and that, if Prussia and its rulers were not capable of defeating Napoleon and restoring freedom, England had better take over Germany and give it a free constitution! We are ready to display our patriotism at the slightest provocation, said Wyneken, because we have acquired it so cheaply; there was something less than genuine about it. Germany was now no longer a geographical notion, it had achieved a political unity. But the German people was far from being united, a deep cleavage went right through it. The Austrians had talked of the danger of Panslavism and of the distress of German minorities outside the Reich; but inside the Reich, too, a great many Germans were in distress, and sabre-rattling should not be allowed to drown the voice of conscience calling for their succour. Before going to war, young men should be perfectly clear in their mind whether this really was the holy war of the spirit[1] that would lead all mankind from darkness to light. Everybody, and youth especially, was living in a time of transition, and nobody here would live to see a good and happy life. But if a happy life was not given to this generation, they could lead a heroic life; world history had only just begun, and the younger generation had a much greater assignment to fulfil than the extinguishing of a fire somewhere: they had to help in changing the world permanently.

It was an impressive speech, and the witticisms of Ferdinand Avenarius, a well-known editor, who spoke after Wyneken, about his own embonpoint were somewhat out of place. 'See you again next year,' Avenarius concluded. But there was to be no repetition, and for many of these young men this was the last autumn of their life.

The chronicler reports that the skies were overcast on the last day of the convention, when Goethe's *Iphigenie* was performed as the final event of the meeting. And meanwhile, all over Europe, the political clouds were massing for the war that so few foresaw, and for which no one, least of all the youth movement, was ready.

III

Many of those who returned from the Hohe Meissner were under the impression that the great alliance of German youth was at last in sight: a union of the various *Wandervogel* groups within the *Freideutsche* youth seemed to be just round the corner, and some

---

[1] The idea of an (abstract) Hegelian *Weltgeist* played a great part in all Wyneken's speeches and writings, and did much to impede the reception and understanding of his ideas in the youth movement.

AT THE HOHE MEISSNER

even thought that the nationalist and Socialist youth organizations would ultimately join too. These high hopes were not to be fulfilled; the *Wandervogel* did not unite after all, the main groups merely recommended their older members to join the *Freideutsche* youth, and refused to contemplate an organizational merger. It was the old, sorry story of petty vested and separatist group interests, and this prevented a union that might have become a real force in German life. The whole history of the German youth movement is one of splits and temporary reunions; frequently most of its energies went into these sterile activities. One would not, perhaps, judge these unending squabbles so harshly if the desire for a great united youth movement had not been proclaimed by all as the central article of faith. Everybody talked about the realization of this great dream, and so few did anything about it. Nor did unity even in the ranks of the *Freideutsche* last long. In January 1914 the storm broke against *Der Anfang*, a monthly magazine which had criticized school, and occasionally even the parental home, much more radically than the *Wandervogel*. Among those directly concerned was Wyneken, who was thought, not altogether wrongly, to be the guiding spirit behind *Der Anfang*, and soon the whole youth movement was under attack. Wyneken at once leaped to its defence; so did Alfred Weber and a few other friends of the youth movement. But many of the *Wandervogel* leaders and some of its advisers, such as Paul Natorp, thought that Wyneken and his circle had become a liability, and they decided to get rid of him. Some of their reasons were legitimate. The youth movement had not been founded, they argued, to follow a leader, however gifted, who wanted to spread ideas about a 'youth culture' that he himself was to provide. Other considerations were less creditable: Wyneken and his circle were too extremist and revolutionary for the Ahlborns and Lemkes, who had assumed the leadership of the *Freideutsche* youth and probably feared his intellectual superiority; nor did they like his left-wing liberalism.

As the result of a long and heated discussion at a meeting in Marburg in March 1914, Wyneken and his circle, as well as all the other fellow-travelling organizations of adults (such as the 'Vortrupp') were asked to leave;[1] and this they did, though not all of them with a good grace. The split had two important consequences: it emasculated the youth movement, for, with all his weaknesses, Wyneken was probably the only man who could have brought clearer ideas into the movement, and he would certainly have guided their cultural endeavours into more productive channels. In addition, Wyneken's expulsion was followed by the formation of left

[1] *Die Marburger Tagung der Freideutschen Jugend* (Hamburg, 1914), passim.

and right wings in the movement. Wyneken's sympathizers, the leftists, continued to fight for their ideas, whereas the right wing, who had carried the day in 1914, had to retreat in 1917 and accept Wyneken's reinstatement. These developments were probably inevitable: the left- and right-wing trends were inherent in the movement, and if the Wyneken crisis had not brought them into the open, the split would have occurred upon some other issue.

Little, after all, came out of that historic Hohe Meissner meeting, apart from a promise that was never fulfilled and a formula that meant different things to different people, and in any case was not specifically a youth formula. To the boys and girls of the *Wandervogel* this may not have mattered much: at the Hohe Meissner they had watched with some amusement the attempts of left and right to mobilize them for their purposes. Less than a year later the First World War broke out.

PART TWO

Five

METAPOLITICS

I

THE youth movement was not intended to be a political organization; 'Our lack of purpose is our strength' was its most frequently repeated tenet. It did not encourage its members to take part in politics and as a body tried hard to avoid political commitment. Those of its leaders who gave public issues more than passing thought were convinced that the changes they wanted to effect in society could not be brought about by political means, but only by the improvement of the individual. Yet for all this dislike of party strife, the movement could not remain entirely immune to it. Political parties and organizations tried to draw the promising youth movement into their orbit. And, apart from such external influences, both leaders and members of the movement were children of their time and accepted, thinkingly or unthinkingly, much of the official German ideology of the day.

A determined effort was made by the right-wing extremist Pan-German association (*Alldeutscher Verband*) to win over the *Wandervogel*. In June 1902, and again in the following year, they took part as guests in the *Alldeutsche* solstice festival near Berlin. Professor Förster, one of the leading anti-semites of the day, who had a son in the *Wandervogel*, talked at great length and with much eloquence about the detrimental influence of the Jews. Whether he made a great impact on his audience is not known; there is reason to believe that some of Förster's theses were accepted while the more extreme statements were disregarded. We know that Jahn, Lagarde, and Langbehn were Karl Fischer's favourite political authors, and Copalle says that he and his friends knew all the nationalist and völkische writers[1] such as Lagarde, Langbehn, Chamberlain, Gobineau, Bartels, Ammon, Sohnrey, Lienhard, and many others.

[1] Quoted in Gerber, *Zur Entstehungsgeschichte, etc.*, p. 83.

This list is fairly representative of the reading matter circulated in right-wing nationalist and racialist circles at the time.

But it would be neither fair nor correct to regard the early *Wandervogel* as part and parcel of the right-wing racialist camp. The reading of such books was more or less obligatory in the middle-class circles in which the movement found most of its followers. They never revolted against this heritage nor did they draw any militant conclusions. They simply did not think it was their business to extract political lessons from the nationalist writings: they left that to parents and teachers. On occasion they were criticized by the more militant right-wingers for retreating from the holy struggle, for showing detachment and individualism.

They were convinced that something ought to be done to strengthen the German minorities outside the Reich, notably in Austria-Hungary. An attempt was made to establish a unified German-Austrian youth movement, but the authorities vetoed this proposal. The strident nationalist approach of the Austrian *Wandervogel* was not universally accepted in Germany, although it was conceded that for the Austrian comrades there were extenuating circumstances. After all, they had to fight a defensive struggle against Slavs, Italians, Jews and what not. The Austrian *Wandervogel*, and some German anti-semites such as Theodor Fritsch, pressed for the exclusion of Jews from the movement and so brought on the crisis of 1913, of which we shall have more to say.

In international affairs the youth movement was altogether innocent; members of the *Altwandervogel* went for their first trip to England in July 1909 and visited some Boy Scout camps, but in contrast to the trips of the twenties there was no political intention or significance behind this. Shortly before the outbreak of the war, the Academic *Freischar* sent a cable from its annual conference to the Kaiser asking him to do everything in his power to prevent a world war. But at the same time it assured him of the full support of the young generation if there were to be a war of self-defence. . . .

There had been a first clash between right-wingers and liberals on the Hohe Meissner. The meeting had been convened in deliberate contrast to the official beer-hall commemorations of the anniversary of 1813. Nevertheless, among the messages of greeting from well-wishers there were quite a few in the conventional chauvinistic style. 'Forward the German culture commando!' were the final words of one speaker, and another ended with the peroration: 'German units are taking over the guardianship of culture, Germany is awakening, and no other people in the world will be able to retain its place. They flourish while Germany slumbers and they will perish when Germany awakes.' A third, in somewhat more moderate vein, predicted that Germany would become the cultural centre of the world, not because it wanted to dictate its laws and customs to others, but because 'the spirit of human culture is crystallized in the German people in its purest, clearest, and most manifold form . . .'[1]

But there was also Gustav Wyneken—who in sheer force of personality eclipsed all others present—sternly rebuking the aggressive speech of an Austrian representative: 'I beseech you, do not easily give in to your enthusiasm . . . it is impossible for me to exult when one speaker calls "To arms" and then, after a few minutes, to sing "Seid umschlungen Millionen, diesen Kuss der ganzen Welt".'

Wyneken ended in a very unorthodox vein: 'We must dare to keep a certain distance from the Fatherland and from the unthinking patriotism in which we have been educated.'[2] But he was, for the time being, a voice crying in the wilderness. The *Wandervogel* did not want to be bothered by what appeared to them extraneous problems and assignments; among the *Freideutsche* youth there was a vague awareness that political and social questions did matter and ought somehow to be tackled. But this was all very nebulous, for the intellectuals of the youth movements preferred a pre-occupation with the ultimate questions of philosophy and religion to a confrontation with political realities. They were critical of society but not of the pillars of society; they thought that a reform of society was quite feasible within the given political framework of Wilhelmian Germany and that it could be combined with loyalty to Kaiser and Reich.

II

Few if any members of the youth movement studied political theory, but almost all read novels with a political message. Some of these books had a huge success in the years immediately before the outbreak of the First World War; they affected the thinking of tens of thousands of young people, but also reflected the spirit of the times. Hermann Burte's *Wiltfeber* is probably one of the gloomiest novels in the German language; the mood is pure Wagner (of the Götterdämmerung), but without Wagner's genius. Martin Wiltfeber, a young German, returns to his native country after having spent some nine years abroad, during which time he had been consumed by homesickness. But his return brings a chain of disappointments. Everything is rotten and decayed, the people are sharply divided into

[1] *Freideutsche Jugend* (Jena, 1913). A. Luntowski, p. 119; Ulrich Rauscher, p. 139; F. Jodl, p. 87.
[2] *Freideutscher Jugendtag, 1913* (Jena, 1919), pp. 34, 36.

classes, the middle class is lazy, foreign cultural influences abound, and the old traditional, popular culture is in a state of decomposition. Wiltfeber goes to church—the action takes place on Midsummer Day—but does not find the preaching about the 'Jewish desert god' congenial. He meets both the pious of the land and the public figures, and everywhere encounters resignation or disappointment. The peasant he meets has lost his farm and is now deluded by the false doctrines of socialism.

There is a double climax to this novel. Wiltfeber takes part in a gymnastic competition and is by far the best, but the judges are persuaded to believe that nobody can be as good as that and refuse him the victor's laurel. (Apparently this is meant to signify that standards have declined in Germany, and that those who excel and stand out from the multitude will face only hostility and ingratitude.) Having suffered this rebuff, Martin takes a walk in the fields with Ursula, the woman he has chosen as wife. It is now near midnight; a thunderstorm breaks; Martin Wiltfeber and Ursula are struck by lightning and killed.

Wiltfeber, published in 1912, became the Bible of the right-wing *Wandervogel*. The author, Burte, remained very much a 'man of one book'; in later years he published several more works, none of which attracted much public interest. *Wiltfeber* was not intended as a party manifesto, but expressed the unformulated discontents of a young German patriot. Hence its great appeal to Burte's contemporaries in the youth movement.

III

The story of *Helmut Harringa*, the man who abstained (published in 1910) had an enormous success in the youth movement and among a wide circle outside it; 320,000 copies were sold in a few years; even the Berlin liberal papers were enthusiastic despite the fact that they had been roundly abused beforehand by the author, Hermann Popert. It is impossible to sketch the narrative of the book, for there is hardly any connection between its various episodes. The hero, Helmut Harringa, is a young Hamburg judge of Frisian origin, the most shining example of young manhood imaginable. He has three main enemies, and he devotes his whole life to the struggle against them, notwithstanding the fact that it diminishes the chances for promotion in his career. These great foes are alcoholism, premarital sexual intercourse, and the contamination of the German race. Alcohol is really the root of all evil because it always leads to drunken excess and ultimately to the brothel and syphilis. One of the main characters in the book, a reserve lieutenant, infects and ruins his wife and many other innocent girls, although he knows about his disease. Harringa's own brother, a young man with sterling qualities of character, is seduced one night into taking part in a students' drunken bout which ends up in a whore-house, and Friedrich Harringa commits suicide when he discovers that he too has contracted the terrible disease.

Alcohol and lust are at the root of most crimes, Harringa concludes—theft, murder, prostitution. In one scene is described a ghostly street fight of the drunkards and debauchees of the Hamburg underworld against the forces of light (the police). Unlike Burte, Popert is not hostile to the Socialists in principle, at any rate not to those who are abstinent. The class-conscious worker joins the police in the struggle against the underworld. Helmut Harringa has decided at an early age to be one of the warriors in the army of light. His favourite reading consists of the songs of Beowulf and of Gudrun, and the tales of the Nordic gods. He adores everything Nordic and Germanic, which in his eyes is the incarnation of true heroism, loyalty, and every other high ideal. Enemies are somewhat vaguely characterized: they include the vested interests opposing Harringa, the brandy distillers, the scribblers of the yellow press, the French (who drink too much) and so on.

Like *Wiltfeber*, *Helmut Harringa* ends with an apotheosis, though in a more optimistic vein. Harringa's first son is born, for all we know following an act of immaculate conception. And then the great struggle, the 'last, decisive' fight starts. Under the great banner of freedom, the 'Black-White-Red' flag of the Reich, all the Germanic peoples unite to storm the enemy in his fortress of death. Victory is achieved, and the novel ends as follows: 'The world owes the idea of freedom to the Nordic peoples, the Germans.'

What appealed to the youth movement above all in *Helmut Harringa* was the savage attack on the way of life that was practised in the students' corporations with their drinking bouts, duels, and other not-so-innocent antics. Popert was an excellent and enthusiastic speaker who travelled from town to town to gain supporters for his ideas. Even so it is somewhat difficult to explain the overwhelming impact this book had on a whole generation of German youth. The reaction, however, did not fail to appear: Helmut Harringa, the idol of one generation, became the laughing-stock of the next.

Popert's group, the *Vortrupp*, was closely associated with the youth movement for several years; it was among the sponsors of the Hohe Meissner meeting, and under its influence the anti-alcoholic clause was included in the Hohe Meissner declaration of 1913. Popert's closest collaborator at the time was Hans Paasche, a former lieutenant-commander in the German navy. Following his experience in a small colonial war in Africa he had become a convinced pacifist, and while he shared the *Vortrupp's* views, pacifism became his overriding preoccupation. During the First World War he was charged with high treason but never brought to trial.

Paasche wrote *Lukanga Mukara*, the imaginary letters of an African visitor on his impressions of Germany. This book too was sold in tens of thousands of copies, and in its effect upon youth it has outlasted *Helmut Harringa*. *Lukanga Mukara* is a very funny book, very much in contrast to *Helmut Harringa* whose only humour is involuntary. Much of its criticism of society and its customs is splenetic, but it never exhibits the fear-ridden fanaticism of *Helmut Harringa*. Paasche was killed on his farm in May 1920 'while trying to escape'—a formula that was to become very famous in later years—when a search was being made, by some Black *Reichswehr* unit, for a store of arms alleged by an informer to have been hidden there. His murderers were not brought to trial and the whole affair was dismissed by the authorities as an unfortunate incident.[1]

The Popert-Paasche tradition of abstinence lived on in the youth movement, and endowed some of its sections with the particular anti-alcoholic militancy that survived in groups such as that formed by the Göttingen philosopher Leonard Nelson, and in the widely-read monthly *Junge Menschen*, which combined pacifism with a general appeal to 'life reform' (vegetarianism etc.). They veered towards socialism; some of their members became prominent leaders of German Social Democracy after the Second World War, and through others this group has even had a certain impact on individual leaders of the British Labour movement.

IV

'A war experience,' as the story of Ernst Wurche is called, was published in 1917, shortly before the author's death on the field of battle. It introduced the *Wandervogel* into German literature. Ernst Wurche was a twenty-year-old lieutenant and student of theology from Silesia, who served in the same regiment as Walter Flex, the author. 'Defiance and humility, the grace of youth, gave an air of splendour to the tense body, the slender and forceful limbs, the proud neck and the self-willed beauty of mouth and chin. His walk was elastic, an easy-going strength, the kind of walk that is called

[1] The Paasche affair is the subject of the play *Kolonne Hund* by Friedrich Wolf (1927). Friedrich Wolf, himself an early member of the youth movement who probably met Paasche on the Hohe Meissner, subsequently became a Communist, and served East Germany as its ambassador to Poland and China.

striding—a calm proud stride that is arrogant in the hour of danger. The gait of this man could conjure up a game or a battle or a divine service according to the hour. It was devotion and joy. When this slim, beautiful man in his shabby grey coat walked down the mountain, the bright grey eyes full of splendour and of a longing that was sure of its aim, he was like Zarathustra coming from the heights, or Goethe's Wanderer.'

In this little book dedicated to the memory of a dead friend there is no place for subtle psychological explanation or for half tones: Ernst Wurche was a good comrade, a pure youth, a hero, an ideal and model to his men. He was a student of theology, but 'his God was girded with a sword, and his Jesus too had a bright sword when he went with him into battle.' The cause of the youth movement, and a Germany revived by it, was perhaps his deepest concern: 'To remain pure and to grow mature, this is the most beautiful and most difficult art of life,' he said one night at the end of a conversation. From his lieutenant's pay he sent home money to his comrades at school and university. 'We must fill up the war chest of youth,' he said smilingly. And then came the replies written in awkward letters, and the yellow numbers of the *Wandervogel* magazine with its black silhouettes and its reports of the latest expeditions, and there was no greater joy for Wurche than to read all this. Politically, Ernst Wurche was rather naïve; when he read about Italy's joining the Allies he compared it to the action of Judas Iscariot, and on another occasion he talked to Flex about personally avenging his many fallen friends.

Perhaps the most revealing scene is that after Wurche's death, when Flex came at Christmas to visit the mother of his fallen friend. After a silence she asked: ' "Did Ernst take part in an attack before his death?" He nodded: "Yes," at Warthi. Then she shut her eyes and sat back. "That was his greatest desire," she said slowly, as though it was a painful joy to know that what she had feared so long had come to pass. A mother should know what was the deepest desire of her child. And it must be a deep desire indeed if she is anxious about its realization after his death. O mothers, you German mothers.'[1]

The moving story of Ernst Wurche cannot blind one to its implications. Had Wurche lived, he would probably have continued to believe in the just cause of his country, in the 'stab in the back' that caused the downfall in November 1918. He would probably have joined one of the right-wing extremist groups. For how could so much heroism and suffering have been in vain?

[1] *Der Wanderer zwischen beiden Welten* (Munich, 1918), p. 53. Flex's novel too was a tremendous success; several hundred thousand copies were sold in the two or three years after its publication.

Wiltfeber, Helmut Harringa and Ernst Wurche were the heroes of the youth movement. But they were not its only heroes: during the war years there was a pronounced move away from the conventional in literary taste. The *Wandervogel* had no great literary ambitions, but under the influence of the students of the *Freideutsche* youth, the leading writers and poets of the younger generation gradually became known among the youth movement: Stefan George and Hugo von Hofmannsthal, Rilke and Hermann Hesse, Spitteler and Trakl.[1] Hermann Hesse had for a while his own little youth magazine (*Vivos voco*) and there was a veritable craze for the newly discovered wisdom of the East—Russia, India, and China. There was undoubtedly much intellectual snobbery about this, and it was sometimes difficult to differentiate between the publications of the youth movement and the *avant-garde* literary magazines of the day. But it affected not only the left-wing, where the expressionists had a field day; the right-wing nationalist groups, too, where cerebral exercises and 'cold intellectualism' were not highly appreciated, improved very considerably between 1913 and 1920. It sometimes appeared that seventy, not seven, years divided the world of 1920 from the world before the war.

V

If lack of interest in politics could provide an alibi from history the *Wandervogel* would leave the court without a stain on its character. However, it has been realized for a considerable time that lack of interest in public affairs is no civic virtue, and that an inability to think in political categories does not prevent people from getting involved in political disaster. The youth movement, moreover, was wider in its appeal and more ambitious in its scope than a sports club. It was concerned with the whole human being, it stood for revival and reform, not merely in one particular section of life, but in life whole and entire. It is not difficult to think of extenuating circumstances: the boy, or the young man, is not yet called upon to take part in public affairs, for which he has neither the knowledge nor the experience. But he ought to be educated towards that aim, and it was in this respect that the *Wandervogel* and even the *Freideutsche* completely failed. They did not prepare their members for active citizenship. The Ernst Wurches had many admirable qualities: they were honest, pure in word and deed, loyal to their comrades, and

[1] To give but a few illustrations: the January 1918 number of the monthly *Freideutsche Jugend* opened with a couple of Werfel poems, the March 1918 issue with Rilke; in June there were excerpts from Walter Hasenclever's 'Antigone,' the August 1918 number opened with excerpts from Chuang-tse's sayings (in the Martin Buber edition), the October issue with parts of the *Bhagavad Gita*, the November/December issue with poems by Hofmannsthal.

brave. But their humanist education was largely restricted to the study of Greek and Latin; their teachers and leaders usually forgot to tell them that humanism also meant a belief in the rights of the individual, in the human dignity, not of the member of one's own group alone, but of every human being. Nor was very much done to develop their social conscience. What a former member of the youth movement said in retrospect about the late twenties is to some extent true of the pre-war period too: 'We had no real principles. We thought everything possible. The ideas of natural law, of the inalienable rights of man were strange to us. . . . As far as our ideas were concerned we were in mid-air, without a real basis for our artificial constructions.'[1]

Both the Socialist youth and the Catholics had firmer ground under their feet; each had a set of values to which they adhered. But in the education of the free youth movement there was a dangerous vacuum all too ready to be filled by moral relativism and nihilism. These trends became much more pronounced in the nineteen-twenties, but they all go back to the pre-war period. Of the members of the youth movement who returned from the war a small but vocal and influential minority joined the Communists. A considerably larger group joined right-wing extremist groups, and eventually National Socialism.[2] The largest section remained neutral and uninterested after the immediate post-war crisis had passed. This was no accidental development; nor was it very auspicious for the future of the young Weimar Republic.

[1] E. W. Eschmann (Leopold Dingräve) in a conversation with Kurt Sontheimer. *Vierteljahreshefte für Zeitgeschichte*, 3, 1959, p. 260.
[2] The comment of an observer on the situation in 1919 is of interest: 'A great part of the youth voted nationalist (*Deutschnational*) while others voted USPD (the left-wing of the Social Democratic party). Youth was not much attracted by the centre parties.' Else Frobenius, *Mit uns zieht die neue Zeit* (Berlin, 1927), pp. 204–5.

Six
BLÜHER AND WYNEKEN

I

MEMBERSHIP book No. 33 of the *Wandervogel* was issued to Hans Blüher when he was a 14-year-old student at Steglitz *gymnasium*. His nickname was 'Gestalt,' and we know that in the following year Copalle excluded him from a trip to Westphalia, for lack of discipline and other unspecified reasons. But Fischer defended young Blüher, and a quarrel ensued which eventually led to the first great schism in the movement.

Blüher was the most articulate *Wandervogel*—and the movement suffered from the consequences. The first part of his *Wandervogel: the History of a Movement* is a beautiful description of Steglitz about the turn of the century; Fontane would not have been ashamed of its broad sweep, of the richness and clarity of the language, the poignancy of the characterization. But Blüher was a man of extremes. He combined a deep shyness in his personality with an extreme aggressiveness in his writings; an unprepossessing appearance with a belief in beauty and racial superiority. In his writings occasional profound insight alternates with frequent downright nonsense; and a megalomania that set in at a very early age seems always to have been coupled with painful doubts about his own creative gifts. His radical antisemitism did not exclude personal friendships with individual Jews, just as his staunchly right-wing political views did not prevent him from realizing that nobody on the right, but many people on the left, were interested in him. Many of his extremist *obiter dicta* were undoubtedly theatrical, or intended to shock, and sometimes betrayed an element of snobbery, such as appeared in his friendship with Wilhelm II—after that potentate had been exiled.[1]

---

[1] The list of Blüher's writings is extremely long. Of general interest are *Die Rolle der Erotik in der männlichen Gesellschaft*; *Die Aristie des Jesus von Nazareth*; *Secessio Judaica*; *Die Achse der Natur*. Of specific interest for the youth movement are *Wandervogel* (first edition, 1910); *Die deutsche Wandervogelbewegung als erotisches Phaenomen*; and his autobiography *Werke und Tage* (1953).

Blüher wrote the history of the *Wandervogel* at the age of twenty-two, as an act of revenge against those who had slandered Karl Fischer, and to a lesser degree Wilhelm Jansen. The net result was a distorted picture of the early *Wandervogel* days which it took almost fifty years to correct, for Blüher's work had gone through many editions and, being very well written, had become the standard work on the subject. *Wandervogel* scandalized many, but his later book on the youth movement as an erotic phenomenon raised an even greater storm, and brought him into disrepute and virtual isolation: a man of the right was not supposed to dig up such 'dirt.'

Friendships between boys that were not entirely asexual or purely platonic were not rare among the students of Steglitz gymnasium around the turn of the century, or among the pupils of other institutions of learning in Germany—or, indeed, in some other countries. The fact as such was well known, but had hardly ever been investigated or commented upon in that age of prudery. Blüher, however, was not so easily shocked. Far from denouncing erotic attraction between boys and young men as reprehensible or calling for suppression, he upheld the view that only an association of men (*Männerbund*) could be positive and creative, and that the family was destructive. Blüher was a fervid anti-feminist, and wrote with great frankness about his own erotic inclinations as a youth (later, he married and had a family). Such ideas were not altogether new; they had been propagated in the German capital during the same period by another brave *paterfamilias*, Benedict Friedländer, an anthropologist, who founded the 'Association for Male Culture' which was expressly directed against 'female domination.' Blüher was one of the first German laymen to realize the importance of Freud's work. He exchanged letters with Freud, and the latter commissioned from him an article for *Imago*.[1] But Blüher did not agree with the psychoanalytic assumption that inversion ought to be regarded as a disturbance if persisting after a certain age: he developed his own theory according to which most homosexuality was congenital. Later on he wrote that while Freud's discoveries had been basically correct, they had, like all Jewish revolutionary insights, a corrupting effect. 'Only after passing through a German brain did these ideas become productive' (*Secessio Judaica*, p. 23). By this Blüher undoubtedly meant his own brain, for he subsequently published a treatise on medicine and another on the theory of neuroses.

Blüher's writings were a source of much annoyance to the youth movement, for two different reasons. In the wake of the Harden-

[1] On, characteristically enough, *Niels Lyhne* and the problem of bi-sexuality. *Niels Lyhne* is the famous novel by Jens Peter Jacobsen, so much loved by two generations of German youth.

Eulenburg affair, everybody in Germany had become very sensitive about homosexuality: allegations and rumours about its prevalence aroused suspicion and antagonism towards the youth movement on the part of the authorities—schools and parents in particular. Worse still, according to some witnesses, it tended to poison relationships inside the movement. Most youth leaders thought that Blüher made many young men conscious—and self-conscious—about the erotic nature of their friendships with others. And since most of them could not tolerate Blüher's opinion that such relations were desirable, but shared the public detestation of them as unnatural and despicable, they found themselves in an unexpected moral dilemma.

Homosexuality thus became and remained a problem for the German youth movement, though hardly anybody dared openly broach the subject after Blüher's scandalous initiative, for it was always feared that malevolent outsiders would use any 'revelations' for attacks upon the movement.

Blüher lived to the middle fifties, but his subsequent career is of no particular interest in the present context. To those who went to see him in his later years he said he had lost interest in the youth movement thirty years before. His interests and publications ranged over a wide field: anti-feminism, theology, political science, a new theory of medicine and in particular of neuroses, and, above all, a peculiar type of anti-semitism.[1] Blüher welcomed the swastika as a sign of redemption and proposed the re-creation of the ghetto as the ideal solution for the Jewish problem, but he did not join Hitler's movement, and in the Third Reich he was regarded as a cranky outsider.

In our day, Blüher is remembered chiefly as the one *Wandervogel* historian and amateur sociologist who wrote clear, occasionally brilliant German. These qualities are notably absent in other German writers who were in the youth movement or wrote about it, and Blüher's achievement is therefore not to be belittled. Some of his theories contained more than a grain of truth; others are too silly for serious discussion. He was partly sincere, partly a poseur and charlatan, and the clarity of his style is not, unfortunately, the reflection of a basic clarity of thought. In England, which is more tolerant of gifted cranks and eccentrics, such a man might have been a modest success. But in Germany such characters were completely out of place.

[1] 'The world pogrom is approaching beyond any doubt. Germany will be the only country that will be deterred from mass murder. It is ignoble to torment the disarmed enemy. The German is no Frenchman' (*Secessio Judaica*, 1922). It is of some interest that this little book was put out by one of the publishing houses of the youth movement, the *Weisse Ritter Verlag*.

II

Whatever impact Blüher had on the *Wandervogel* was through his books. Wyneken, too, wrote books, and especially pamphlets, in great number, but his main impact on the youth movement was through his personality as a leader and educator. In contrast to Blüher he had never been a member of the movement, but while Blüher dropped out of it after a few years Wyneken remained in touch with it—except for long enforced intervals—for a much longer period.

He started his career as a teacher in the year 1900 in one of the very first German progressive schools, which had been founded a few years previously by Dr Hermann Lietz. Soon Wyneken quarrelled with Lietz, and in 1906 he decided to found, together with Paul Geheeb, the 'Free School Association' of Wickersdorf in the Thuringian Forest. After a little while he fell out with Geheeb also, and before long there were difficulties with Martin Luserke, Geheeb's successor.[1] Meanwhile Wyneken had come into conflict with the local authorities, an episode that is of no interest here, but which led to his removal from the school for some considerable time. There was another major dispute in 1913–14 with right-wing and Catholic circles when a magazine whose editors were close to Wyneken came under fire for the unorthodox views it preached. Wyneken returned to Wickersdorf in 1919, but after less than two years there was a fresh crisis and in consequence of this he was again compelled to leave the school.

Wyneken thrived on polemics, was intransigent to the verge of foolishness and, to put it mildly, did not get on well with other educators. But for all his conspicuous weaknesses he was also an educator of genius, who could perhaps in different circumstances have effected a revolution in German education.[2] His influence on the youth movement was enormous during the short period he co-operated with it (1913–14 and 1916–20). It can be said without exaggeration that his appearance at the historic Hohe Meissner gathering was by

---

[1] Lietz had been strongly influenced by the educational system practised at the Abbotsholme School in England. In later life he was influenced by National Socialist ideas. See G. L. Mosse, 'The Mystical Origins of National Socialism,' in *Journal of the History of Ideas*, January 1961, pp. 94–5. Geheeb subsequently became known as the head of progressive schools in South-west Germany and Switzerland. Luserke continued to teach in Wickersdorf, despite his quarrels with Wyneken, for some twenty years, and then decided to devote all his time to writing plays and novels. He is better known now as a writer than as an educator.

[2] He had an important post in the Ministry of Education for a short while after the 1918 revolution, but his ideas were not accepted and he soon resigned.

far the most impressive, and largely shaped the thinking of the whole youth movement for years to come. Wyneken, who did not suffer from undue modesty, once said of himself that he was a born leader who would be a leader even if there was no one to follow him. This may be quite true, but does not make it any easier to explain in what exactly his charisma as leader and educator consisted. He had his own ideas and system, which in cold print do not appear to be particularly revolutionary, for, as with so many other educators of genius, it is the personality of the man behind the ideas which makes the methods work. Wyneken's central idea is 'youth culture' (*Jugendkultur*). He claims that, until his own appearance on the scene, young people had never had the right to, or the opportunity for, self-expression. Youth was regarded as a transitional stage between childhood and maturity, without specific, positive characteristics, or a style of its own. He had much affinity with the *Wandervogel*—with its opposition to the mode of life of youth in the big cities, to the progressive mechanization of life, and to the arid intellectualism that made for a degeneration of body and soul. He thought his own school superior to the *Wandervogel*, however, for, as he said, the youth movement had a style but as yet no culture of its own. It merely 'organized' the leisure hours of boys and girls, whereas the Free School Association was comprehensive, embracing school life also, combining it with agricultural work, a modified school syllabus, physical education, and life in community, in an attempt to train a new type of man and woman.[1]

Teaching in Wickersdorf was in groups rather than in classes, and it was one of the very first schools in Germany to practise co-education. Wyneken had very definite ideas of his own with regard to the curriculum of the German school; he wanted, for instance, to abolish the study of Greek and Latin as obligatory subjects. (This should be interpreted in the specific German context of the times: those who were clamouring most insistently for a revival of the educational ideals of Hellas[2] were by no means convinced humanists. They stood for an aristocratic order, despised the plebs and its democratic ideas.) In the teaching of German literature Wyneken,

[1] While Wyneken's educational ideas found few imitators in Germany, the Soviet government during the first years of its existence was interested in his experiment. A special commission was appointed to study and report on Wickersdorf, and Wyneken's ideas had a certain impact on Soviet education in the twenties during its early experimental phase.

[2] Eine kleine schar zieht stille bahnen
Stolz entfernt vom wirkenden getriebe
Und als losung steht auf ihren fahnen
Hellas ewig unsere liebe.   (Stefan George)

whose political orientation was left-of-centre, opposed the glorification of the second-rate writers and poets whose reputation rested on their ultra-patriotism rather than on their intrinsic literary achievement. He wanted to replace the teaching of religion by instruction aiming at a certain spiritual attitude (*geistige Haltung*), arguing that traditional religion was no longer generally believed, was no longer popular religion, and ought not therefore to be taught.

It was intended that Wickersdorf should not be ruled by the head of the school, but managed by an executive of teachers and pupils. In practice, however, this frequently amounted to enlightened dictatorship.

Wyneken's connections with the *Anfang* group are described elsewhere, and so is his part at the Hohe Meissner meeting. In the nineteen-twenties his relations with the youth movement became much less close; by this time the *Bünde* had not only a style but a culture of their own, and Wyneken did not greatly like what he saw. The emphasis on nationalist and militarist forms and motives appeared exaggerated to a man who was essentially an old-fashioned liberal; and the exclusion of girls from many of the *Bünde* was not in accordance with his educational system and ideas.

'The hour of Wickersdorf is long over,' an official commentator wrote in 1933, and the Free School Association was indeed dissolved by the authorities in that same year.[1] Wyneken survived the Hitler era, and even continued to publish; he was one of the very few German writers who, shortly after the Second World War, could afford to reissue, without change, a book that he had brought out under the Third Reich. This points to the integrity of the man, but it also shows that his work was not considered offensive by the authorities, which was very unlike the Wyneken of earlier days. But in 1946, when in his seventies, he added his efforts to an attempt to revive *Freideutsche* groups and study circles, and the old quarrels of 1914 soon reappeared, since Wyneken's views were still very much to the left of those of his colleagues. There were fresh polemics, pamphlets about *Freideutsche* politics, rival meetings and negotiations. But these disputes between men in their sixties and seventies had little to do with youth and the youth movement. After a while Wyneken decided to retire from these activities, and returned one evening in March 1955 to Burg Ludwigstein, the old and new centre of the youth movement in Germany, to celebrate his eightieth birthday. Here he pronounced a discourse on the future, on the responsibility for distant generations, and 'the courage to wish to be happy' —a fitting valediction to a life lived to the full. Whether it was a happy life, one would hardly dare to ask.

[1] In Wickersdorf (now East Germany) a school continues to exist. Wyneken was invited to be present at its fiftieth anniversary in 1956.

Seven

THE WAR OF THE SEXES

I

IT was in the spring or summer of 1907 that girls took part in a *Wandervogel* outing for the first time. This was a truly revolutionary event, as for the first decade of its existence the youth movement had been exclusively a boys' society. Karl Fischer in particular took a dim view of the presence of girls in these groups; he thought they would be a distracting and disruptive element. Personal relations in the groups were apt to be somewhat rough and uncivilized: the style of the medieval vagrant scholars, which they frequently imitated, made no allowance for the presence of the gentler sex. Moreover, this was a time when German women were not fully emancipated in other respects either. Co-education was almost unheard of, and there was no outside pressure upon the *Wandervogel* to revise its original opinion of what was to become known, later on, as 'the problem of girls' rambling.'

As the youth movement developed and spread, it became more conformist and civilized. Hans Breuer relates an incident that illustrates this point. When he and Wolf Meyen were returning from a particularly rough and adventurous trip in Hesse,[1] they had to enter a railway compartment full of young peasant girls, neatly dressed in their local costume. For the first time Hans Breuer felt ashamed of his own attire. 'This must stop,' he said to Wolf Meyen. 'You know we have been looking for dirt and wallowing in it.'

The first application for the admission of girls, made by the mother of an early member in 1905, was rejected out of hand. But two years later the leader of a Jena students' group again proposed the establishment of mixed groups, and when his ideas were rejected his group seceded and founded the *Wandervogel, Deutscher Bund* which soon spread throughout Gemany; girls took part in all

[1] Blüher, *Wandervogel*, vol. I, pp. 116–17.

this group's activities without any known untoward consequences. The other groups, however, remained sceptical for some years. The *Altwandervogel* and the Steglitz *Wandervogel* tolerated girls at some of their meetings and festivals—though not on their trips—if they were accompanied by their mothers; the *Jungwandervogel* remained opposed on principle. By 1911, however, most leading members of the youth movement agreed in principle to have girls as full and equal members in their movement, though many of them favoured the existence of separate girls' groups. In mixed groups, it was argued, the boys would become effeminate and the girls would tend to become wild; anyway, it was much better for the girls to have their own holiday camps and not to participate in the big, rough-and-tough outings.

Girl students took part in the *Freideutsche* youth from the beginning, though in the early days they constituted a small minority. This changed only during the First World War, when so many members were mobilized and much of the organizational work at all levels had to be taken over by young women.

II

In January 1914, during a debate in the Bavarian Landtag, a speaker of the Catholic Centre Party denounced the *Wandervogel* as a 'club of homosexuals' and a den of free love. An official campaign ensued, and for a time even the songbook of the movement, the *Zupfgeigenhansel*, was banned. It was a stupid accusation: far from favouring any sweeping sexual reforms, the youth movement of those days might perhaps have been best characterized as an organization for sublimating the juvenile libido.

At that time, when it was the fashion to discuss everything about the youth movement in terms of a 'problem'—the alcohol problem, the social problem, the Jewish problem, the school problem and many others—there was, of course, a problem of the relationship between the sexes: this was a highly constrained one, in accordance with the strict moral code of the day. Society as a whole was regulated with a view to 'extended puberty' among middle-class youth; marriages before 25 were rare in these circles. Few psychologists have studied the youth movement—perhaps because they thought it atypical—and those who have written on the subject argued that the *Wandervogel* were refugees from both the threats and the temptations of the parental home. In this view, the youth movement became the rallying ground for more or less unconscious homosexuals (homosexuality being a way of escape from incest); it was supposed to have strengthened the basically neurotic attitude of these youngsters by tending to produce a fixation on the youth movement experience, and a reluctance to face life and reality.[1]

Such views are contested, and not only by those who deny categorically that 'sex' was of importance in the youth movement, and affirm that the *Wandervogel* experience can never be understood by applying analytical principles. The problem of 'facing reality' at the age of sixteen is rather complicated, and so is the question of repression during adolescence. The Soviet Komsomol discourages outward manifestations of sexuality during puberty as firmly as any bourgeois youth movement, and it is misleading to single out the taboos and repressions of bourgeois society as the factors mainly responsible for the development of neuroses; these phenomena seem to be common to all modern societies.

Questions of sexual morality preoccupied the youth movement for many years. The 'struggles against prostitution and masturbation' were occasional subjects of discussion. In taking up this position the movement was for a while much influenced by the impassioned advocacy of sexual abstinence before marriage in Popert's *Helmut Harringa*, whose hero embodied all the manly virtues.

It would be tempting to trace the differences between right and left wing opinion from the political into the sexual domain. But, like so many generalizations, this would soon prove misleading. The right wing was frequently anti-feminist. But the *Jungwandervogel*, the group that was most strongly opposed to admitting girls to youth movement activities, was certainly not the farthest to the right in its political temperament. The 'd.j.l.ll.' came into being as an exclusive boys' group, but politically it veered towards the extreme left. Wyneken was one of the pioneers of co-education and politically a man of the left; but his championship of the 'Eros that has two wings' is well known.

In its earliest days the *Wandervogel* had on the whole evaded discussion of sexual questions. There was an unspoken assumption that the relationship between the sexes was so pure, so devoid of any sexual character, that any discussion of these topics could only do harm by destroying the implicit innocence of the existing relationship. At the same time, close friendships between individual boys and girls were discouraged. Some observers were aware that this asexual relationship—if indeed it could be maintained—had its disadvantages. The average male *Wandervogel* was shyer, less confident, less mature than other young men of his age. 'Behind the pretended comradeship between the sexes... was hidden a mothering

---

[1] Fritz Jungmann, 'Autorität und Sexualmoral in der freien bürgerlichen Jugendbewegung,' in *Studien über Autorität und Familie* (ed. Max Horkheimer), *Schriften des Instituts für Sozialforschung*, vol. 5 (Paris, 1936), pp. 680 ff.

of the young men by the girls.'¹ The insights of psychoanalysis—and, indeed, of modern psychology in general—were rejected, so far as anything was known about them in these circles. Open discussion of sexual problems did not start in the youth movement proper, but in certain circles of the *Freideutsche* youth, notably the student groups and Wyneken's group *Der Anfang* around 1912–13. Their common ground was a belief in the equality of the sexes, and in the value of the girls' participation in youth movements. (Some of them went rather far in this: in Wyneken's school, the girls had to compete with the boys in the two-mile race, and any improvements in their score were proudly announced in the school prospectus.) They were all in favour of comradeship, but as to the exact nature of comradeship there was for a long time little clarity and no unanimity. Wyneken was on the whole in favour of 'heroic asceticism' and frequently stressed his belief that in the existing social order the sexual question was insoluble. (He did not make it clear whether it was soluble in any social order that could be envisaged in the twentieth century.) Heimann and the few others who went on record before the outbreak of the First World War favoured abstinence before marriage, out of an 'erotic-mystical orientation'² which, they insisted, was not at all identical with the spirit of abstinence preached by the professional philistine abstentionists. But already, during the last year before the outbreak of war, some voices were heard demanding a much freer relationship between the sexes, to the scandal of Wilhelmian society. Among them were some of the contributors to *Der Anfang*, a periodical edited by Siegfried Bernfeld of Vienna and George Barbizon, which came into being independently of Wickersdorf, but soon became the mouthpiece of Wyneken's circle.³ One of them, the student 'Friedrich Mono,' argued that since 'Jugendkultur,' at any rate in its sexual aspects, was impractical in present society, it was nonsense to demand an 'heroic style of life.' The unfortunate reality of bars, dance halls, and shop girls would continue to exist as far as the male sex was concerned (*Anfang*, November 1913). Another, Herbert Blumenthal, noted that young people in the big cities had discovered that they had a strong sexual urge, the existence of which had been concealed by the philistines. They had found the courage to protest and were not prepared to be

[1] Eduard Heimann in *Freideutsche Jugend* (Hamburg, 1920); E. Busse-Wilson, *Die Frau und die Jugendbewegung* (Hamburg, 1920).
[2] Heimann, *op. cit.*, p. 12.
[3] The first number was published in May 1913; most of its contributors were students in secondary schools. Many articles were not signed, because the authors feared expulsion from their schools. Walter Benjamin, to name but one, signed himself 'Ardor.' Among other early contributors were Wieland Herzfelde and Prof. Carlo Schmid.

suppressed any longer. Blumenthal asked the youth movement to recognize and accept this rather than engage in solemn and futile accusations against the 'ugly eroticism of the big city' (*Anfang*, October 1913). Measured by the approach and style of 1919, these student articles were harmless enough, but in the general climate of 1914 they provoked violent attacks from without[1] and led eventually to a split in the *Freideutsche* youth.

The war brought revolution in more than one domain, with results that became obvious even before it ended. There was a general loosening of sexual morals; nevertheless it is somewhat strange that the discussion of sexual reform should so often have been given first place on the agenda of meetings held during the war years. The general tenor of the debates was now very different from the attacks on 'dirty masturbation' and the call to 'heroic abstention.' Towards the end of the war the left wing of the youth movement accepted in full the principle of premarital sexual freedom. This position was reached gradually, by various stages, and some of the theories developed *en route* revealed both a sincere groping for 'solutions' and, to put it mildly, great muddleheadedness and strange flights of fantasy. According to Fritz Klatt, some form of coitus interruptus was recommended, since the sperma had (in his view) a tremendous importance as a kind of spiritual force which was to be expended only for procreation, not in the act of passion. Alfred Kurella elaborated a more widely accepted notion on the parallelism of body and soul: Sexual intercourse was justified only when two souls met, but a meeting of souls also demanded physical expression. More down to earth were the early writings of Max Hodann, subsequently a well-known physician-sexologist in Weimar Germany, which were destined to spread enlightenment and fight ignorance on sexual matters in the youth movement.[2]

These discussions on sexual topics lasted until about 1921; they took place among a comparatively small circle of university students, not all of whom continued to be leading figures in the movement. But their ideas had a certain impact on the movement, especially on the left-wing groups. A similar trend towards greater freedom between the sexes could be traced during the war and immediate post-war

---

[1] See the anonymous pamphlet *Jugendkultur* (Munich, 1914), and Wyneken's answer, *Die neue Jugend* (1914).

[2] Hodann subsequently moved to the far left; Kurella became a leading Communist, spent many years in the Soviet Union, and is at present responsible to the East German Politburo for cultural activities in the German Democratic Republic. Fritz Klatt set up an educational institution of his own and developed various ideas, frequently with a somewhat mystical strain ('Die schöpferische Pause,' etc.). His school in Prerow existed until 1939, and he died shortly after the end of World War II.

period in many other countries, with and without ideological justification; there was nothing specifically German in it. The impact of the Kurellas and Hodanns did not, however, extend to the new phase of the German youth movement that opened about 1923, when the new *Bünde* began to develop on lines quite different from both the *Wandervogel* and the *Freideutsche* youth.

The youth movement and modern psychology never met.[1] Psychoanalysts were studying primitive cultural types in search of a theory of human nature and its basic motivations; whereas the young men and women in the youth movement would certainly have resisted any attempt to 'reduce' their own way of life to what must have appeared to them psychological mumbo-jumbo. This may, in retrospect, be a matter of some regret to psychoanalysis; social psychology too, might have enriched its knowledge of such phenomena as group mentality, or the emergence of group leadership, not to speak of the more specifically sexual factors, by an intimate study of the youth movement. But from their own point of view the young people were probably justified; for what would have been left of comradeship and the leader-follower relationship, if all the motives, hidden or manifest, that entered into them had been analysed? Would this not have opened the door to a profanation of all that was held most sacred? There was a basic incompatibility between the rational psychiatric approach and this essentially romantic and non-reflective movement—or so it may well have appeared at the time.

It was not in Germany but elsewhere that the attempt was made—after 1913 and in particular after the First World War—to combine the idea of the youth movement (especially of Wyneken's *Jugendkultur*) with some of the insights of modern psychology. Certain early supporters of *Der Anfang* in Vienna tried to inject these insights into the activities of the Austrian Socialist youth movement, not without success; and some young left-wing Zionists who had studied in Vienna during that period, afterwards applied their experience to the establishment of schools and youth movements in Palestine. There, albeit with many modifications, something of this psychological approach survives in the education of the younger generation in the collective settlements.

[1] It has been said, but quite inaccurately, that the early history of the *Wandervogel* has been 'interpreted in psychoanalytic terms by the notorious Hans Blüher' (Howard Becker, *German Youth, Bond or Free?* (London, 1946), p. 64). Blüher never accepted (probably never understood) psychoanalysis, but substituted for it concepts and a terminology of his own. Harald Schultz-Hencke, formerly a leading member of the *Freideutsche* youth and afterwards a leading psychiatrist, did accept some of Freud's basic conceptions and established a school of thought related to psychoanalysis; but this was long after Schultz-Hencke had left the youth movement.

Pedagogical ideas, no less than books, have their unpredictable fate.
Was the youth movement homosexual? The question is not a particularly easy one to deal with, but it cannot be shirked, since it is so important. It is impossible to give a clear-cut answer, for the simple reason that homosexuality is not a clear-cut condition. It is not a distinct psychological or clinical state, but includes a great variety of symptoms of varying intensity, and affecting various types of people. Nor is there unanimity among psychological schools about the origin and essence of homosexuality.

One of the most likely hypotheses holds that man is bisexual in origin. Part of the libido is channelled in a homosexual direction, but this is later sublimated—or may turn into overt homosexuality, thus possibly becoming a source of neurotic difficulties. The transition from bisexuality to heterosexuality usually occurs during adolescence, while pre-adolescent homosexual play seems to be the rule rather than the exception.

In Germany as elsewhere, the whole subject was embedded in a morass of repression and taboo. Only a small minority had the courage to deal with the subject, and even they usually preferred to call a spade an agricultural implement, using recondite or coined Greek terms in their discussions. Homosexuality, after all, was both a criminal offence and considered to be morally reprehensible. Paradoxically enough, at the same time German society (except for the working class) did much to promote homosexuality. The whole educational system tended to postpone the meeting of the sexes as long as possible. The heterosexual taboo was even stronger than the homosexual one, for in the world of adolescent boys there was no room for girls, and vice versa. Restrictions of this kind have been and still are to be found in various parts of the world, with similar consequences. In Germany they frequently led to the idealization of *Männerbünde* (exclusively male societies).

What we know about the youth movement is based more upon impressions than statistics, for the *Bünde* were no more willing than the British public schools to supply information to inquisitive outsiders. In some groups erotic relationships were openly recognized and sometimes glorified, while in others they were less conspicuous, or there was no overt homosexuality at all. There were 'cases' in each *Bund*, and probably in each group, but they hardly ever became public. According to one of the few investigations into adolescent delinquency, made in Munich,[1] the incidence of homosexuality in

---

[1] K. Seibert: 'Die Jugendkriminalität Münchens in den Jahren 1932–33,' table IV, quoted in Herbert Schierer, *Das Zeitschriftenwesen der Jugendbewegung* (Berlin, 1939). The validity of such statistics is problematical, since it is obvious that among youth that is not organized at all, in the towns and still more in the countryside, homosexuality comes to public knowledge far less often.

the youth movement was more than three times as high as the average in German society at large. But these figures were published in the Third Reich when the general tendency was to discredit the *bündische* youth.[1] It was a very common National Socialist practice to charge political enemies—Catholics, for example—with homosexual deviations.

Those who joined the youth movement went through an emotional experience which was also an act of sublimated sexual gratification. The majority—and especially the younger members—felt more attracted to their own sex, more comfortable and less inhibited. Thus one could say that some sexual attraction was required in order to hold the group together, but that too much was disastrous, for an overt 'darling relationship' would soon subvert discipline in a group. This was an extremely difficult situation, and it was up to the leader to find the right balance.

Up to a certain age this phenomenon was natural. However, above that age there was a danger of the *Bünde* perpetuating inversion, or, in other words, preventing the young men from finding their way to girls. This is why all attempts to preserve the youth movement above a certain age were bound to fail. As the groups dissolved, most of their members established normal relationships with the other sex. Some did not, and among these a number have come to sad ends, in which homosexuality was perhaps combined with character disturbances.

The whole issue is worthy of detailed study, and it would be presumptuous to present conclusions of general validity without closer investigation. It is rather surprising, for instance, that overt homosexuality was more of a problem for the *Bünde* than for the *Wandervogel*, despite the fact that there was more sexual freedom in Weimar Germany than in the Wilhelmian Empire. This probably shows that homosexuality was not only a response to repression but that other factors must have been involved as well.

Such an investigation would be outside the scope of the present study, and would, of course, be speculative. Most members of the youth movement would probably regard such an enquiry as a profanation of some of their most cherished memories. In present-day society—both in Germany and elsewhere—frank discussions of sexual problems still encounter tremendous resistance.

Liberal and socialist well-wishers at one time wrongly considered the German youth movement an ally in the struggle for sexual

---

[1] See for instance, *Oberbannführer* Tetzlaff: 'Homosexualität und Jugend,' in *Der H. J. Richter*, February 1942. But some of the leaders of the pro-Hitlerite Sudeten German *Bünde* were also arrested on similar charges after October 1938; totalitarian states have an inclination to disparage manifestations of sexuality regardless of the direction of the libido.

emancipation. There were such stirrings among the members of the *Anfang* group (1913–14) and there was a demand to put an end to the 'sexual monopoly' of the adults. Wyneken observed in 1915 that the youth movement needed a new 'erotic orientation.' Its old programme of sexual abstinence and a comradely relationship between the sexes was not a solution but a subterfuge.[1] At this time too Blüher published his book on the *Wandervogel* as an erotic phenomenon; since Blüher used psychoanalytic terminology his study was at first welcomed in these circles.[2] But there were many who already had misgivings about Blüher's preoccupation with one of the new insights gained by psychoanalysis—the nature of sexual inversion. The most prominent of these well-wishers of the German youth movement was Siegfried Bernfeld of Vienna (1892–1953) who, as an editor of *Der Anfang* had belonged to the Wyneken circle and who at the same time used fairly orthodox psychoanalytical methods in his own pedagogical work.[3] Writing in 1917 he clearly exaggerated the probable impact of psychoanalysis on the youth movement. He was aware of the fact that the majority of the youth movement leaders preferred to ignore the Freudian school and that in view of its 'Jewish character' it was said to be inapplicable to German youth, with its different emotional and mental make-up.[4] (Even Blüher, ironically enough, was suspected of having Jewish antecedents.) Among the more serious arguments against psychoanalysis in the youth movement was the reference to the close relationship between sublimation and cultural achievement. Would not sexual freedom lead to cultural impoverishment? Bernfeld admitted that this was a real dilemma but expressed optimism, saying that it was a difficult pedagogical problem but could be solved. He expected to find the empirical justification of this optimism in a mass experiment: the exposure of a sizeable part of the youth movement to psychoanalysis. However, this mass experiment did not take place and Bernfeld's own pedagogical activities were not crowned by success. He founded a children's home, 'Baumgarten,' in 1919 as part of a plan to resettle and re-educate uprooted and orphaned Jewish children in Vienna. It had five disused military barracks at its disposal and was intended to become the nucleus of further such establishments. 'Co-education paired with administrative responsibilities and a more enlightened

[1] *Die freie Schulgemeinde*, October 1915.
[2] 'Die Psychoanalyse in der Jugendbewegung,' in *Imago* V, 3 (1917), p. 283 et seq.
[3] Among his more important early publications that are of relevance in the present context: *Die neue Jugend und die Frauen* (Vienna 1914); *Vom Gemeinschaftsleben der Jugend* (Vienna, 1922); *Sisyphos oder die Grenzen der Erziehung* (Vienna, 1928).
[4] S. Bernfeld, *Imago loc. cit.*

approach to sex problems based on Freud were to be realized there.'[1] But Bernfeld fought a losing battle against a rather narrow-minded charity organization and there were conflicts with his co-sponsors. The only lasting result was a book in German called *Kinderheim Baumgarten, a Report on a Serious Attempt at New Education*. . . . Bernfeld was both too early and too late in his pedagogical endeavours.[2]

[1] Obituary on Siegfried Bernfeld by Hedwig Hoffer in *The International Journal of Psycho-Analysis*, vol. 36 (1955) p. 66.

[2] For other psychoanalytical comment on the youth movement see Otto Fenichel: *Sexuelle Aufklaerung. Schriften zur Jugendbewegung*. Heft 3. (Berlin, 1916). The early writings of Wilhelm Reich and Max Hodann should also be mentioned in this context. Reich explained the 'secret meaning of the bourgeois youth movement as the quest for sexual freedom' (*Unter dem Banner des Marxismus*, III, 1929, p. 767). But the youth movement rejected these and similar attempts to explain the background, real or imaginary, of their movement as 'detrimental to the simplicity of the soul.'

Eight
OTHER YOUTH MOVEMENTS

I

IN June 1904 the body of a boy was found in Berlin Grunewald, and proved, on investigation, to be that of an apprentice who had committed suicide after being maltreated by his master. The case found its way into the Press and provoked a wave of indignation among the organized workers; it was this incident that gave birth to the first apprentices' and young workers' association in Germany. The idea of a Socialist youth movement had been in the air for some time; in Vienna there was a fairly sizeable group already in existence; and in Mannheim in South-west Germany, an association of young workers was founded in September 1904 without any such dramatic and tragic stimulus as that which prompted similar action in Berlin.

The history of the Socialist youth belongs only in part to our story of the youth movement. The leaders of the Socialist youth were grown-up men (as were some of the leaders of the *Wandervogel* and most of the officers of the Boy Scouts). They had founded the Socialist youth because, among other reasons, they felt concern about the progress made by religious youth groups in working class circles; they were not particularly worried by the 'bourgeois' youth movement, which was numerically much smaller and made no effort to appeal to proletarian youth. Not that the Socialist youth movement was altogether sponsored and led from above: there was a spontaneous urge from below as well, and a growing belief among young workers that they ought to take independent action in view of their own specific problems. They wanted independence, up to a point, from the political party—and this 'separatist' inclination on their part did not get much sympathy from the Social Democratic leaders.

In many important respects the Socialist youth movement differed from the *Wandervogel*: it represented common political and economic aspirations rather than a common emotional experience. The personal element, and the inner cohesion of the group, were much less developed, and there was no cult of an *élite*. But, in contrast to the bourgeois youth, the young Socialists had to face strong outside opposition, and to fight for their very existence. The authorities thought the *Wandervogel* slightly crazy, but they regarded the Socialist youth as highly subversive.

It was from two independent centres in the same year that the Socialist youth movement in Germany developed. The northern section spread to a few cities besides Berlin, but its main strength remained in the capital. In the earlier period it had no outstanding leader and, to a much greater extent than the movement in the south, it was trade unionist in character; that is, preoccupied with immediate economic aims, such as the reduction of working hours, higher wages, and better working conditions. It also faced much greater difficulties in view of the openly hostile attitude of the Prussian authorities; at every meeting, on every outing, the inevitable police lieutenant and sergeant were in attendance, ready at the first sign of 'disloyalty' to dissolve the meeting. The northern section could not afford to give itself an openly socialist character in those early years.

In the south, those who had established themselves in February 1906 as the 'Association of Young Workers in Germany' had a first-rate leader, a comparatively well-written magazine (*Junge Garde*), and were able to make open profession of their Socialism and anti-militarism, which would have been unthinkable in Prussia at that time. The trade union character of the movement was, however, less emphasized than its cultural activities, and its socialism was based more upon ethical obligations than upon historical materialism. Its leader was Ludwig Frank, a young lawyer from Mannheim and a Social Democratic deputy in the Reichstag, an extremely able speaker and organizer who, but for his early death in battle in 1914, might have become one of the ablest leaders of German Social Democracy.

The government of the day followed the whole development with considerable misgivings, and sought some legal means to nip the Socialist youth movement in the bud. This they contrived by the new Law of Association of 1908, which banned all political work among the younger generation. In practice, this law was invoked only against the Socialist youth, and never applied to *bien-pensant* youth associations. The southern Socialist section was harassed by it far more than the northern, which had never established itself openly as a political group, and could not therefore be compelled to dissolve.

There were ways and means of circumventing the restrictions, but to do so made great demands upon internal discipline. The Socialist youth claimed that they were not associations in the legal sense, and therefore needed no licence. But this meant that henceforth they could have no statutes, no executive, no membership books, and could not —officially at least—collect any dues. One could neither join them nor resign from them. The groups continued to meet, and the police to forbid them any large-scale activities—including amateur theatricals! There were occasional arrests, and some Socialist students at high school were debarred from study at universities. But all in all, it was a fairly mild form of despotism under which they suffered; the two bodies of Socialist youth flourished, eventually united, and by 1913 their periodical *Arbeiter Jugend* had a circulation of one hundred thousand. But trouble was brewing elsewhere. The Social Democratic party executive had been watching the growing independence of these youth organizations with some concern; it now issued a condemnation of semi-autonomous associations of young workers. Some of the leading Socialists also thought that the pronounced anti-militarism of the youth was out of place; they did not want to condone militarism, but thought that the Socialist youth endangered their very existence by trying to challenge a power so deeply entrenched in Germany. On the other hand, it was the very anti-militarism of the youth which made the left-wing Social Democrats support them; in *Die Neue Zeit* Pannekoek, Parvus, and the other orthodox Marxists defended their right to self-determination. The Socialist youth movement thus became to some extent a pawn in the contest between 'revisionist' and 'orthodox' Marxists; but in the end the party executive accepted a compromise which regulated the relationship between the party and the youth organizations. This remained in force until the general crisis of German Social Democracy in 1916 put an end to party unity.

The war of 1914 gravely affected the fortunes of the Socialist youth groups established during the previous decade; many of their leaders and active members were mobilized, those at home had to work longer hours, their political activities were narrowly circumscribed by the authorities, and their publications controlled by a strict censorship. The Socialist youth protested against the introduction of a compulsory saving scheme, and against compulsory military training for those under eighteen. But on the whole the leaders were by no means anti-war, and it was against this background that the split occurred which was to paralyse the whole Socialist youth movement for many years to come. A large part was attracted to the leftists and their struggle against the 'traitorous policy of the party executive.' The left had its representative in the Party commission responsible for youth work (Luise Zietz) and the most radical elements came from groups of young Socialist freethinkers in such cities as Frankfurt. At a secret meeting in Jena in April 1916 the oppositionist 'Free Youth' was founded, but it was at once attacked by extremists in Bremen as being still too moderate. The Socialist youth gradually lost the bulk of its members in so many key places, such as Berlin, Leipzig, Dresden, and Hanover, that it had to start afresh after the end of the war. True, it was not long before the left wing split again into a Communist (Spartacist) section and a left-wing Social Democrat group, but this was cold comfort for the majority Social Democrats. Among those who helped to rebuild the Socialist youth movement between 1918 and 1933 there were, however, some who were destined to become leading figures in German politics—including Erich Ollenhauer, the present leader of the West German Social Democrats.

The Socialist youth organization was always something of a problem child for the party leadership. It usually veered to the left, sometimes towards the right, but seldom toed the party line. Opposition is the privilege of youth, and the party executive should have been prepared for such deviations. Nor was the Socialist youth ever very numerous, not even during the period of its greatest influence. It has been argued that democratic socialism never attracts the young, since it has little to offer to their generation. This may be true; but strangely enough, the more extremist parties did not fare much better. In 1930–31, when National Socialism had more than six million voters and the Communists between four and five, the Hitler Youth counted only twenty thousand members, and the Communist youth at their most numerous probably never exceeded thirty thousand. One of the reasons was that no party, not even the most extreme, paid much attention to the under-eighteens simply because they had no votes. This was an age group that cared more for football and kindred pastimes than for a party programme, even at a time when political passions were running very high indeed. In Austria, on the other hand, the Socialists were much more successful among the younger generation. Here they developed an organization with a style of its own—combining the amenities of a sports club with those of the *Wandervogel* and a high level of political education —and this made a considerable appeal to a fair proportion of Austrian youth.

II

Surveying the German scene a few years before the First World War, a Socialist observer said that his party had far less to fear from the Protestant youth organizations than from the Catholic: 'The Protestants are more theoretical, more ignorant of the ways of the world than the Catholics, and they know much less about influencing and controlling the masses.'[1] Catholicism in Germany had more cohesion, was much more of a vital force than the quasi-official religion of the German Reich. Protestants were in a two-thirds majority in the country, but their youth organizations were never as numerous as those run by Catholics. Nor did the Protestant groups have anything like the same *élan*.

The history of the Protestant youth groups goes back to the early nineteenth century. Small Bible-reading circles were founded to provide spiritual comfort and moral support to the uprooted young workers who streamed into the cities from the countryside. In later years domestic servants became one of the main social reservoirs of Protestant youth groups. In the eighteen-eighties a new movement was formed, on the pattern of the American YMCA, which for a time was the most militant of all, and around the turn of the century a Protestant sect appeared in Germany calling itself 'Jugend für Entschiedenes Christentum.' All these groups engaged in youth welfare and had, strictly speaking, nothing to do with the autonomous youth movement. The Christian *Pfadfinderschaft*, founded in 1910, was more in touch with the spirit of the times, and less working-class in character, but it regarded the Boy Scout training merely as a means to the end of religious education. The *Bund* of the *Köngener*, which had originated in youth Bible-study circles, reacted differently when it had to choose in 1920 between the authority of the Church and the youth movement. It opted for the latter, and some of its leaders, including a number of students of theology, were subsequently to hold leading positions in the youth movement.

It would be difficult, however, to point to a specific Protestant contribution to the youth movement, apart from a certain pietist tradition that was sometimes discernible. To be a Protestant meant so much less in daily life than to be a Catholic; there were some important exceptions, such as the attempts of some Protestant sectarians in the youth movement to establish collective agricultural settlements on a Christian-Communist basis. Some leading Protestant theologians were members of the movement in their younger days (Paul Tillich, Gogarten) or were in close contact with it (Karl Barth). In so far as they had a certain influence on the movement, it was of a problematical character; their followers were not far wrong in concluding from their teachings in the early post-war period that a retreat from the world's realities into a communal life of dedicated labour on the land was the devotional duty of the day. Gogarten, in line with the Lutheran tradition, preached that the State was omnipotent (thus tending to confirm contemporary State-worship) and that the 'insane habit of reliance on *humanitas*' should be shaken off.

[1] Karl Korn, *Die bürgerliche Jugendbewegung* (Berlin, 1910), p. 44.

OTHER YOUTH MOVEMENTS

The leading Protestant thinkers of the day soon lost interest in the youth movement, and those who remained in contact with it—such as W. Stählin and Karl Bernhard Ritter—were not quite of the same calibre: some found the general confusion of the movement rather congenial to their own state of intellectual disarray, but had nothing of much consequence to contribute. No Protestant appeared to match the Catholic Romano Guardini—a leader with a first-rate mind who devoted many years of his life to the creation of a Catholic youth movement.

This Catholic movement had begun in the nineteenth century, not unlike the Protestant youth groups, with apprentices' and domestic servants' associations which had limited and clearly defined aims. There was a great variety of Catholic groups, but in contrast to the Protestant groups they did not often overlap or compete with one another; each had its own function and catered for some specific section of the younger generation. Nearest to the youth movement were *Quickborn* (led by Romano Guardini for many years and still going strong), and *Neu Deutschland* (also still in existence), established with the help of the Jesuits in 1919. Both were recruited mainly from middle-class high school students. *Neu Deutschland* was perhaps the more nationalistic in outlook, for in the *Quickborn*, in the twenties, there was a struggle for supremacy between a religious-Socialist and internationalist wing, led by Nicolaus Ehlen, and a nationalist right wing.

Both groups paid lip service to the Meissner formula, and adopted the educational methods and the forms of the youth movement. But the content of their work was very different; they recognized the Church, the family, and the school (in that order) as powers established by God. Their leaders, including Guardini, regarded the autonomy of youth as an extremely dubious achievement of modern times: the young human being was not divine, nor was he as yet a whole human being. 'He is assuming a burden which he cannot carry and which will lead to hopeless inner conflicts or to a wanton playing with words.'[1] In practice, these Catholic youth organizations had almost as much autonomy as the others; there was guidance and control, but it was exercised less obtrusively than in many non-confessional groups.

It seems somewhat strange, in retrospect, that the autonomous youth movement should have been, and have remained, predominantly Protestant. It was, after all, one of the descendants of the romantic movement, and romanticism had been in Germany a Catholic trend *par excellence*. But, as the late Waldemar Gurian

---

[1] From a booklet published in 1921, quoted in *Manifeste der Jugend* (Düsseldorf, 1956), p. 14.

complained in 1921, the youth movement simply did not want a confrontation with Catholicism. The Catholics on the other hand were from the very outset distrustful of a movement of somewhat pagan inspiration. The declaration of neutrality concerning religion might satisfy Protestants; it could never be a sufficient reassurance to Catholics.

III

Several other youth organizations were founded in the decade before the First World War, but only one of them, the German variant of the Boy Scouts, subsequently became part of the youth movement. The others were either sports clubs or semi-military patriotic groups of no specific interest to the present survey, and only to be mentioned in passing.

The gymnasts, who counted about a quarter of a million members in the pre-war period were, like the *Wandervogel*, officially neutral in politics. But the movement traced its origins back to *Turnvater* Jahn and the war against Napoleon, and the political element had never been quite absent from its history. Despite a paragraph in its statutes that forbade political activity, the gymnasts took part in patriotic demonstrations before the First World War and occasionally clashed with the Socialist youth. After the war, especially in the late twenties, the political trend became even more pronounced; the gymnasts took part, for instance, in the nationalist demonstrations against the performance of the Remarque film *All Quiet on the Western Front*; and E. Neuendorff, the leader of the gymnasts (who for many years had been head of the *Wandervogel*) declared in 1932 that there was no room for 'Marxists' (i.e. Social Democrats) in their ranks.

The *Jungdeutschlandbund*, founded in 1911, was a semi-official organization devoted mainly to military sports and led by adults. The *Wandervogel* groups were frequently invited to be corporate members of this new organization, but they did not regard military training as part of their activities. They much resented Field-Marshal von der Goltz's declaration that the youth movement was 'doing good work inasmuch as it provided soldiers who were particularly fit for marching.' Ultimately, however, most of the *Wandervogel* groups (with the exception of the *Jungwandervogel*) joined the *Jungdeutschlandbund* in order to benefit from the many important privileges that members of that organization enjoyed—such as a reduced rate on railway trips and permission to obtain lodging in army barracks. This step was not, however, of great political or organizational significance, and hardly affected the internal life of the *Wandervogel*. The *Jungdeutschlandbund* ceased to exist during

OTHER YOUTH MOVEMENTS

the First World War; later it became a kind of central clearing house for some of the right-wing groups in the youth movement.

In the same year 1911 a German Boy Scout movement was founded and soon counted some 80,000 members. Its first impulse had come, like Baden-Powell's initiative, from South Africa. Dr Alexander Lion, an army physician, wrote a book describing his experiences in what was then German South-west Africa, and made much of the importance of scouting. Soon after this Baden-Powell's book was translated, and the German scouts were modelled closely on the British pattern. Their Chief Scout was Captain Bayer (killed in the First World War), and all their leaders were adults. There was a world of difference between the rigidly organized activities of the Scouts, devoted almost exclusively to the physical betterment of the members, and life in the *Wandervogel*. There was no contact at all between the two movements prior to 1914. After the First World War, however, the Scout groups underwent a radical change, extended their activities, and ultimately became part of the *bündische* youth.

Nine

THE JEWISH QUESTION

IN 1916, in the middle of the First World War, at a convention of the *Freideutsche* youth, a certain Franz Rust declared that the Jewish question was the most important problem facing mankind.[1] He was by no means alone in that assumption; Blüher ('the Jewish question is at the very centre of all political questions') and many others shared his views. It may appear somewhat incongruous in retrospect that Franz Rust and his comrades should have been concerned about a minority of less than one per cent of the German population, at a time when the very existence of their country was at stake. But concerned they were, and they spent much time discussing what to do about German Jews in general and those in the youth movement in particular.

The youth movement had appeared on the scene a few years after the great antisemitic wave of the eighteen-eighties and nineties had subsided. Between 1895 and 1912 radical antisemitism persisted among certain groups on the extreme right, but on the whole the antisemitic movement was much less in evidence than in the previous two decades. Superficially, everything seemed to be quiet, or at any rate, relatively quiet as far as German-Jewish relations were concerned. But under the surface some ominous developments were taking place; the old-fashioned religious antisemitism *à la* Stöcker was being gradually superseded by racial antisemitism.

The younger generation, too, was affected by these new trends. Siegfried Copalle, one of the founders of the youth movement, has left an extremely revealing letter[2] in which he mentions the political

---

[1] *Freideutsche Jugend*, 10/11, 1916, p. 307.
[2] Walther Gerber, *Zur Entstehungsgeschichte* . . . , p. 83–4. Hans Friedrich Blunck, another early member of the youth movement (in Hamburg), mentions Houston Stewart Chamberlain as one of the main formative influences among his circle (*Licht auf den Zügeln*, vol. I, Mannheim, 1953, p. 98).

influences that made the greatest impact on the *Wandervogel* leadership: 'The attitudes towards political questions were more or less identical with those expressed in the *Deutsche Zeitung*. This paper had been founded in 1896 by Dr Friedrich Lange as an "Independent non-partisan newspaper." Its excellent weekly supplement, the *Deutsche Welt*, had a lasting impact.... The problems of the Jewish question were known through the handbook published by Fritsch. There was contact with the "Alldeutsche Verband" (Pan-German League) through one of our comrades whose father (Prof. Paul Förster) was a leading figure there.'

Lange was a right-wing extremist; his general outlook may be deduced from his recommended reading list of the best in German literature: Jews (including Heine) did not figure in the list, nor did a single Catholic writer, nor indeed Goethe and Schiller, the 'cosmopolitans.' Theodor Fritsch and, to a lesser degree, Paul Förster, belonged to the radical wing of the antisemitic movement; so extremist was Fritsch that the official, more moderate antisemites, embarrassed by his crude antics, frequently dissociated themselves from his writings.

The *Wandervogel*, consciously or unconsciously, was part of the general stream of right-wing nationalism, which in Germany is really a pleonasm; in contrast to other European countries, nationalism there has always been monopolized by the right wing. Antisemitism thus became one of the basic articles of faith of many members of the youth movement, but it was, at least at first, less pronounced there than in the other nationalist associations. For the youth movement did not claim to be a political organization, and rejected quite a number of the cherished beliefs of the older generation, of the parents and teachers. Rabid antisemitism was therefore suspect at least in some circles of the youth movement precisely because it was preached by the *Oberlehrer* as part of their official ideology.

Karl Fischer had social contacts with Jews and wanted them to establish an organization of their own, so that nation would stand beside nation and each would know its place. He believed that the Jews should profess a Semitic culture.[1]

There were no Jews among the early Steglitz *Wandervogel*, but around 1905 some of them joined or wanted to become members of the movement. While the Jews formed less than one per cent of the German population at the time, their representation in the middle-class intelligentsia in the big cities was much greater, and the percentage of Jewish pupils in the upper forms of the leading secondary schools (which were the mainstay of youth movement membership) sometimes reached 25 per cent or even more. German Jews were

[1] Hans Blüher, *Wandervogel*, p. 98.

prone to welcome every new and progressive movement and many of them followed with sympathy the beginnings of the *Wandervogel*. Many Jewish parents sent their children to Wyneken's school in Wickersdorf, because it was known as the most progressive of its kind. In 1914 about 20 per cent of the children there were Jewish, and the figure reached 40 per cent after the end of the First World War. Wyneken thought this undesirable: 'Jewish participation that is so much higher than their part among the German people, and even among the intelligentsia, gives rise to a certain intellectual one-sidedness, and, as experience has shown, lowers the level of physical fitness.'[1]

The Jewish question became one of the central topics of debate in the youth movement following the Zittau case in 1912. A Jewish girl in that Saxon city, who had successfully completed the tests of a 'candidate,' was refused admission on the ground that the *Wandervogel* was a German movement and had therefore no use for Jews.[2] This news reached the general Press (notably the *Berliner Tageblatt*) and was debated in the *Wandervogel Führerzeitung* (Guides paper); there were declarations and counter-declarations by the leaders in the various regions. Jewish boys and girls had been refused admission in previous years, but so had others, and even if the percentage of the rejected Jews was much higher, there was apparently no open and organized antisemitism involved.

All this now began to change rapidly; the radical antisemites such as Fritsch and P. Stauff established contact with leading members of the youth movement and published special leaflets to spread their views on the Jewish question (such as *Der Wandervogel deutsch*, by Paul Erlach); attempts were even made to establish a small *Wandervogel* movement on an antisemitic basis ('Wandervogel, Vaterländischer Bund für Jugendwandern'—Young Patriots Rambling Association). The Austrian *Wandervogel* had introduced the Aryan paragraph even earlier, at its annual convention in Krems in 1913, declaring that 'we do not want the Slavs, Jews, or Welsh in our ranks.'

The anti-Jewish campaign reached its climax with the publication of a special issue of the *Wandervogel Führerzeitung* which caused an uproar throughout the organization. This paper was edited at the time by Friedrich Wilhelm Fulda, the son of a teacher at the central institution for the training of officers at Lichterfelde. Fulda had to work as a mechanic after the death of his father, which left the family impoverished. But he returned to the university in 1911 and

[1] Gustav Wyneken, *Wickersdorf* (Lauenburg, 1922), p. 33.
[2] See Cora Berliner, 'Wandervogel,' in *Im Deutschen Reich*, December 1913, p. 547 *et seq.*

was studying philosophy and pedagogics at the time of the great discussion. Fulda's thesis was, in brief, that all Jews should be excluded from the *Wandervogel* because they were not of German (Aryan) origin, and because a Jew, in view of his blood, could never be a true German patriot.[1]

If Fulda had stated his views with moderation, they would probably have been accepted by a majority of the youth movement. Instead he and his friends resorted to violent vituperation, which not only shocked the few Jews in the *Wandervogel* but offended the good taste of many who were by no means philosemites. The famous 'Jewish number' of the *Führerzeitung* (October 1913) and some of its subsequent issues were efforts of which the late Julius Streicher would not have been ashamed. The Jews were charged with exploiting the German people, corrupting its culture, seducing German virgins, and organizing a sinister network of white slave traffic. The Jew was artful, never innocent; his lack of decency was innate. The Press, the Social Democratic party, the theatres, the big publishing houses, the banks, the department stores—all of them were Jewish. So were Caruso, the tenor, and Dr Crippen, the murderer, the poet Stefan George, and the Austrian Colonel Redl who had spied for the Russians.[2] All the youth groups who did not try to get rid of the Jews were committing suicide.[3]

The regional branches of the *Wandervogel* reacted in different ways. The Saxon region, Northern Thuringia, and several others excluded all Jews from membership; so did some sections in Berlin including the famous Steglitz branch. A few protested against the discrimination against the Jews and declared that they would have nothing to do with antisemitism—among them the Silesian region, Alsace-Lorraine, the Rhineland, and some Berlin branches as well as the *Jungwandervogel*. Leading members of the *Wandervogel* who opposed Fulda's views founded a rival 'Guides newspaper' (*Die Pachantei*) which existed for several months.

The whole atmosphere of the period is described in an account which is of great interest because it was written by one of the leaders of the anti-antisemitic faction:

[1] *Deutsch oder National: Ein Beitrag des Wandervogels zur Rassenfrage*, Leipzig, 1913.
[2] *Wandervogelführerzeitung*, 4/5, 1914, p. 74.
[3] *Ibid.* 11, 1913, p. 219. After completing his studies Fulda became headmaster of a secondary school in the Harz. He was killed in April 1945 on the Eastern front, a reserve officer, at the age of sixty. According to the *Wandervogel* hagiographers he is said to have dismissed his unit on the eve of a Russian attack but remained himself at his post. 'His last message to his wife was a quotation from the *Edda*—"To live in faith, to fight defying death, to die smilingly" ' (Copalle-Ahrens, *op. cit.*, p. 65).

The Jewish question ... had given us many headaches. The exclusion of all Jews would have been interpreted under the Kaiser as a lack of patriotism (*staatstreue Gesinnung*), as sabotaging national unity. It might have been the occasion for prosecution of the *Wandervogel*. Our experience with Jews in the local branches was chiefly negative. Their cool intellectualism remained largely alien to our inner feelings. There were exceptions: I remember Theo K., strong as a bear and a good friend, beloved by old and young and often the centre of gay fun. He looked strange enough as a soldier (I still keep his picture) with his swelling negroid lips and the expression of a faithful dog. He was a brave man and fell in France. But I also remember the Jewish student who importuned our boys in Jena and was excluded. I dissociated myself from the coarse attacks made by Fulda in the *Führerzeitung* against everything Jewish.[1]

Many youth movement groups, including the central leadership, did not want to get involved in a public discussion of the Jewish problem. But in view of the passions aroused, a showdown could not be much longer postponed. It came at the all-German meeting of the movement at Frankfurt-an-der-Oder at Easter 1914. Shortly before, at the Hohe Meissner, the movement had declared its 'political and religious neutrality.' Would it stick to that declaration—and how would 'neutrality' be interpreted?

The opening in Frankfurt was not very auspicious. Several groups of Jewish boys and girls were present, only to be attacked physically by the Bavarian group of Friedrich Weber.[2] This clash ended with what one eye-witness termed a compromise; the Jews had to leave the scene—though not the meeting. The convention ended with a similar compromise: the local branches were permitted to accept (or reject) whatever Jewish candidates there were. General resolutions by local branches not to accept Jews as members were not to be tolerated. At the same time the leadership of the *Wandervogel* refused to take any action against branches which had decided not to admit Jews. Finally, it reiterated its neutrality in all matters political and religious.

The resolution was extremely ambiguous; in practice it amounted to giving the local branches the right to select or reject whoever

[1] Georg Müller, 'Rings um den Hohen Meissner', in Will Vesper (ed.), *Deutsche Jugend* (Berlin, 1934), pp. 58–9.

[2] Weber, a veterinary surgeon, subsequently became one of Hitler's earliest associates, participated in the march on the Feldherrnhalle, and was Hitler's cell-mate in Landsberg prison. In the late twenties, as head of the para-military 'Bund Oberland', he broke with Hitler because he did not want to serve as 'praetorian guard of German capitalism.' On Weber's collaboration with the 'national Bolsheviks' see Ernst Niekisch, *Gewagtes Leben*, Cologne, 1958. Later he made his peace with Hitler, was appointed 'Reichstierärzteführer' (Führer of the Reich Veterinary Surgeons), and died in Munich in 1955.

they chose. Some regions refused to accept Jewish members altogether. (The leader of the Nordmark district wrote subsequently: 'Why all this fuss about the Jewish question? *We* have no Jews anyway.') Other branches apparently had no restrictions whatsoever, while the majority used some form of *numerus clausus*. A contemporary witness already quoted mentions what seems to be a fairly typical letter of a leader in Kassel: 'Almost everybody will admit in a moment of truth that the Jews are disagreeable. The argument that many Aryans are also disagreeable does not hold water, because of the Jews 95 per cent are disagreeable—98 per cent to be precise—and in a way in which Aryans could never be. If the *Wandervogel* decides not to exclude Jews in principle, in view of the two per cent who may be suitable and agreeable, this shows a large measure of moderation and decency. He who does not appreciate the magnitude of this decency shows that he is not worthy of it, and he demonstrates that the Jews in general have no sense of decency.'[1] Walter Fischer, the editor of *Wandervogel*, reacted in a similar way: If the Jews continued their obstinate complaints the movement would have to reply by taking more radical measures, namely by excluding them altogether.[2]

The compromise came in for some criticism, especially because of its attempt to explain that certain pronounced racial characteristics made Jews, by and large, unsuitable for membership of the *Wandervogel*. As Neuendorff, the leader of the movement, put it: Most of our boys may never have heard the word 'antisemitic.' But somehow, it seemed, they felt in their innermost being that the Jewish manner was absolutely alien to their own.[3] Neuendorff had originally denounced antisemitism in a declaration to the Press; he was the headmaster of a State school, and public antisemitic statements were frowned upon in Wilhelmian Germany, particularly if they came from State officials. Subsequently, however, he used much more outspoken language when writing on this subject for publications within the youth movement, where presumably he felt less constrained.

The Jewish reaction, too, was not uniform. The Zionist youth regarded the antisemitic debate as additional justification for their view that Jewish boys and girls should have organizations of their own. Their own association, *Blau Weiss*, had been founded several years before. The assimilationists, the great majority at the time, advised their sympathizers to stay in those local branches where they were wanted.

Occasionally, the Jewish attitude revealed what can only be described as a certain lack of dignity. There were quite a few who

[1] Georg Müller in Will Vesper, *op. cit.*
[2] *Führerzeitung*, 6, 1914, p. 109.   [3] *Ibid.* 6, 1914, p. 106.

tried to demonstrate that they were as good Germans as their Aryan compatriots, if not better. Popert, the author of *Helmut Harringa*, was of part Jewish origin. So were Wilhelm Jordan, Ernst Wachler, Max Bewer, and other pillars of the *völkische* movement, who were all widely read among the antisemitic wing of the *Wandervogel*. And there were not a few Jewish members of the youth movement who justified the *numerus clausus*. Max Bondy[1] said in the 1916 discussion that most Jews did not fit the German youth movement, not even the majority of those whose sincere aspirations were unquestioned. 'There are certain imponderabilia that remain strange to the average Jew, who lacks a certain freshness and simplicity. . . . I would not be surprised if the majority of Jews asking to be admitted were rejected.' This attitude completely disregarded the fact that the racial theories propagated by the antisemites were total, and a matter of principle. As one of them put it during the war: 'Please spare us the sentimental phrases about the friend, the noble Jew, who is not to blame that he was born a Jew. As if it was a question of one single Jew; the danger for the Germanic race is so great that the question of the individual does not come into it at all. . . . It is contemptible if a Jew leaves his own people and wants to work in our ranks. He will never become a German, he will always remain a Jew—at best a bastard.'[2]

Most of the antisemites strongly advised the Jews to join the national Jewish (Zionist) groups; some were ready to envisage the existence of separate Zionist groups in the wider framework of the movement. But the Zionists viewed these suggestions with considerable reserve. 'We shall have to wait and ask ourselves whether we can indeed be fruitful members of that community,' wrote Moses Calvary,[3] a noted Jewish educator.

The 1913–14 Jewish crisis in the youth movement has to be viewed against the wider background of developments in Germany at that time. It was noted that there were no Jews in the movement in its very early days, but that probably several hundred joined later on. It is conceivable that some of the 'Aryan' members were concerned by this influx of Jews and the consequent gradual 'judaization' of the movement. If so, they could have found a remedy at the local

---

[1] *Freideutsche Jugend*, 10/11, 1916, p. 322. Max Bondy and his brother Curt continued to play a leading role in the German youth movement after the First World War.

[2] Franz Rust, *op. cit.*

[3] Even earlier, in late 1913, the Zionist youth organization sent a cable to the *Freideutsche* youth, saying that while Jewish like German youth would work for the physical betterment of their people, co-operation with the representatives of the Aryan race would be of doubtful value. Quoted in *Im Deutschen Reich*, January 1914, p. 14.

level without much fuss and without the countrywide open discussion in which so many outsiders joined, and which was in the end embarrassing to the movement itself. What really mattered, however, was that by 1912 the period of comparative calm that had prevailed in Wilhelmian Germany for almost twenty years had drawn to a close. In the general climate of discontent and unrest, the radical right wing and the extreme antisemites who had been out of the limelight for two decades again came to the fore, and it was one of their declared aims to make the *Wandervogel* politically aware and conscious—as they understood these terms. Since the Jewish question was not *only* a political problem, the antisemites did not find it difficult to raise the issue by various indirect means, or to find converts, for with the romantic *Weltanschauung* that was so strongly embedded in them, the youth movement had also implicitly accepted the profoundly anti-Jewish attitude of German Romanticism.

The outbreak of the World War temporarily put a stop to discussions on the Jewish question, but not for long. The Jewish members of the youth movement were now called to arms, and they expected that the cessation of party strife proclaimed by the Kaiser would affect their status too. In this, however, they were frequently mistaken: the antisemites soon complained that few if any Jews were to be found in the front line. The Jewish members of the youth movement tried to counter this by pointing to the number of Jewish war heroes and fallen, which was a futile way of arguing, because it was based on the assumption that facts and figures were relevant in that kind of discussion. It so happened that the first member of the Reichstag to be killed was a Jew (and a leader of the Socialist youth movement). The only comment made by the antisemites was that Jews always had to jump the queue.

The line-up on the Jewish question that emerged during the First World War among the youth movement was as follows: on the extreme right there were the radical antisemite circles around the *Führerzeitung*, then edited by Fulda's successor Dankwart Gerlach, and a new group that came to be known by the name 'Greifen.' There was also a group around Otger Gräff, who published a private newsletter from the front, *Jungdeutsche Führerrundbriefe*, which made a considerable impact on some sections of the movement.[1]

Their attitude was relatively uncomplicated. It was based on what they regarded as the insights of a new science, race theory, and they demanded the expulsion of all Jews from the German youth movement and a relentless struggle against Jewish influences in general.

[1] Hermann Bohm, *Hitlerjugend in einem Jahrzehnt* (Hamburg, 1938), says that the founder members of the Hitler Youth regarded themselves as the pupils of Gräff (p. 38).

The radical antisemites, though highly vocal, were not a majority. More numerous were those who defined themselves as 'asemites' at the 1916 meeting in Naumburg. It was not a very happy term, as one participant pointed out: 'asemite' meant (if it had any meaning at all) somebody who wanted to take no sides on the Jewish question. But the 'asemites' obviously had certain views, though these happened to be much less definite than those of the radical antisemites. As one of them put it: 'The *Wandervogel* wants the Jew and then again does not want him. For the individual he has now and then love and appreciation, but he is opposed to the Jews in general.[1] The 'asemites' disliked the rowdy behaviour of the extremists; they thought that the Jewish question was far more complicated than some wanted to make them believe, and that the lessons of the new science (or pseudo-science?) were by no means as certain as the extremists claimed. Some 'asemites' suggested that special regulations should be applied to the Jews in the youth movement, and that only a small percentage should be accepted. Others preferred a more radical separation and proposed the establishment of Jewish groups in the framework of the *Freideutsche* youth.[2] Lastly, there was a group that believed the complete assimilation of Jews was possible and desirable, and that Jews who met the standards and requirements of the *Freideutsche* youth should not be subject to discrimination. Among the few non-Jews who reasoned on these lines in the 1916 debate was a friend of the youth movement, Friedrich Wilhelm Foerster; as a pacifist and anti-Prussian he was an outsider.

Nevertheless, the number of Jews in the youth movement grew considerably during the First World War. So many of them were soldiers that even the 'asemites' found it difficult to refuse them admission. But the main reason was undoubtedly the progressive radicalization (towards the left) of the youth movement after 1916 under the influence of socialist, quasi-socialist, and internationalist ideas, and in particular after the reconciliation with Wyneken. During this 'leftist' phase, which lasted for several years after the end of the war, there was, for obvious reasons, no Jewish problem.

The attitude of the youth movement towards the Jewish question has here been examined in what may appear excessive detail. It was, it might be argued, in retrospect, only a marginal issue in view of the small number of Jews.[3] Such an interpretation is mistaken,

[1] Werner Schabert in *Freideutsche Jugend*, 10/11, 1916, p. 310.

[2] One proponent of this line was Knud Ahlborn, who headed the moderate right wing in the German youth movement at the time.

[3] According to an antisemitic source 92 per cent of the *Wandervogel* groups had no Jewish members before 1914 and 84 per cent excluded them as a matter of principle under the Aryan paragraph. Louise Fick, *Die deutsche Jugendbewegung* (Jena, 1939), p. 65.

though there was of course some demagogy, especially among the more extremist antisemites. But many were sincerely worried by what they regarded as the judaization (*Verjudung*) of German public and cultural life. They regarded this as a central issue in German politics, and it was in effect a German rather than a Jewish problem. For such an attitude, stemming from a deep-seated uncertainty and feeling of inferiority, would have been unthinkable in a West European nation. There was antisemitism in France and other countries, but it is difficult to imagine there a discussion in the middle of a world war in which the participants expressed the view that the Jewish question was the central issue of the times, and its solution the commandment of the hour. This had something to do with the German national character, the delay in the emergence of a German nation, and the fact that the national movement in Germany had been taken over and monopolized by the reactionary groups. In these circumstances the Jews were bound to be rejected regardless of their German patriotism. As Dankwart Gerlach said: 'A Jew is not suitable for us even if he is baptized ten times over.'[1]

[1] *Wandervogelführerzeitung*, 4/5, 1914, p. 84. The same article argued that the great majority of those of mixed Jewish-German blood were not suitable either.

PART THREE

PART THREE

Ten
THE FIRST WORLD WAR

I

A PRODIGIOUS wave of enthusiasm swept over German youth at the outbreak of the world war in 1914. 'We had not known the reason of our existence . . . youth had seemed to us a burden and a curse,' wrote Ina Seidel, in her poem ending: 'O holy fortune, to be young today!'[1] Those who had previously found no dominant aim in life now felt that they knew the meaning of their destiny—total identification with the Fatherland in its hour of uttermost peril. 'How stupid it is to ask what is our attitude to the war! Anyone who finds time to think about it shows that he does not know how to feel with his people, and is shutting himself up against the blessing that fate intended for him.'[2] If any explanations were needed, they were to be found in the first appeal by the *Wandervogel* leader Neuendorff; the war had come 'because the other peoples could no longer hold their own in peaceful competition with German power, German industry, and German honesty . . . they perfidiously sought to defeat Germany by brute force and weight of numbers.'[3]

But German youth had been hearing for years past how jealous enemies and rivals begrudged the German people its rightful place in the sun. When the storm broke, it should not have found them altogether unprepared. Yet it struck them like a bolt from the blue, for despite all the warnings and the mounting tensions of the preceding months, there had been a general, persistent belief that everything would somehow at the last moment be settled.

To the members of the youth movement, war was so incredible as to seem unreal; their world had been one of carefree rambling, dreaming and singing—a joyful world of utter peace, in the greatest contrast imaginable to the ravages of war. To many, as to Rupert

[1] *Führerzeitung,* November 1914, p. 205.
[2] *Wandervogel,* I. Kriegsheft, p. 259. [3] *Ibid.,* p. 257.

Brooke in England, the sense of liberation, of an awakening out of torpor, was the most memorable experience of those days of high patriotic emotion. But this was a reaction against spiritual emptiness and material frustrations that was perhaps more acutely felt by those outside the *Wandervogel* than by its members. For the youth movement was one of active idealism, in less need of an external moral stimulus; at any rate, it was so in the Reich, though conditions in Austria and the German regions of Bohemia were different. There, the possibility if not the desirability of a world war had been loudly discussed for years past.[1] The youth movement in those parts had also been much more involved in politics; more than once it had been said at their conventions that they were fighting a losing battle against Slavonic encroachment. Many of them seemed to think that the only way to stem this tide was a victorious war in alliance with Germany, leading to the eventual emergence of a *Grossdeutschland* in which foreign elements would be put in their place.

Many group leaders were called up in the very first days of the war, others volunteered, and the girls put themselves at the disposal of the Red Cross. Some of the younger ones feared that the war would be over before they saw any fighting, and a few even tried to reach the front line without having enlisted. Meanwhile groups of younger boys and girls went to the countryside to help with the harvest. Regular youth movement activities, needless to say, were disrupted for many months: some members, assuming that the war would soon be over, argued that no particular effort should be made to resume normal activities, that all energies should be directed towards the war effort. Others thought the time had come for a *rapprochement* with other youth organizations such as the Boy Scouts and the para-military *Jung Deutschland*.

As the months went by, however, and a certain war-time normality was established, the meetings and outings were resumed, albeit on a smaller scale. Girls frequently took over the leadership of groups, and after a few months were reinforced by soldiers who had been wounded and invalided out of the army.

In 1915 the youth movement resumed its longer expeditions despite the strict rationing of food and clothes; there were now enough prisoners of war to help with the harvest.[2]

One of the most important tasks was to maintain contact with those serving in the forces. The soldiers related their adventures and impressions in long letters that often were published, while the groups sent greetings and parcels to their leaders and members on the

---

[1] Luise Fick, *op. cit.*, deals at considerable length with conditions in Austria before 1914.
[2] *Wandervogel*, 5, 1916, p. 98.

field of battle. Gradually an organizational network was established in the various army units; there were unofficial clearing houses, and eventually the *Wandervogel* soldiers even had their own circular letters and little newspapers on both the Western and Eastern fronts, and in other major theatres of war. Two hundred of them held a convention in Brussels at Whitsuntide 1917, and there were other, smaller meetings elsewhere.[1]

How did the individual *Wandervogel* soldier face up to the great patriotic challenge? In the first immense wave of national enthusiasm all petty quarrels were forgotten; all that was best in that generation was demonstrated: unselfishness, comradeship, the readiness to sacrifice. They had not the slightest doubt of the rightness of the cause they were fighting for, and the first great victories appeared to promise an early triumph. 'We are chasing the enemy like a herd of sheep,' Johannes Ilgen wrote on 2 September 1914 from Chalons-sur-Marne. But the German advance was soon halted, and the writer of the letter was killed the very same month; what then followed was grim-visaged war unrelieved by any great advances or triumphs, or by the hope of an early victory. At Langemarck in November 1914 thousands of German students, including many members of the youth movement, stormed the enemy lines and were mown down in swathes, singing 'Deutschland, Deutschland über Alles'; the lists of 'Fallen for their country' became longer and longer. Different undertones began to appear in letters from the front: 'The war is not beautiful. I would thank God if it were over today, and if I could return home unscathed.'[2] It was not only the war itself that was ugly; it soon transpired that the *Wandervogel* soldier had often to face serious difficulties within his own unit. After the first flush of excitement had ebbed away, there was not much left of the comradeship and understanding that he had expected. Max Sidow had been one of the most enthusiastic during the first weeks of war,[3] but five years later he wrote about the *Fronterlebnis* in a very different vein: 'One was alone among the many. The uneducated hated every cultured soldier. Every conversation began and ended with obscenities.'[4] Another wrote of the 'sad days and the heavy nights among vulgar and mean people, the first terrible impressions, and the great ideas of fatherland and world history that made their impact only

[1] There is a vast literature on the *Feldwandervogel*. See for instance *Rundbrief* on the Eastern front; R. F. Heiling, *Feldpachanten* (Glogau, 1918); *Zwiespruch*, the *Wandervogel* organ at the Western front; 'Cölner'; 'Der Feldwandervogel' in *Wandervogel*, 12, 1929; J. H. Mitgau, 'Der Feldwandervogel', in Will Vesper (ed.) *Deutsche Jugend*, Berlin, 1934.
[2] *Wandervogel*, 11/12, 1914, p. 284.
[3] See his poem in *Wandervogel*, 9/10, 1914, p. 259.
[4] *Krieg, Revolution und Freideutsche Zukunft* (Hamburg, 1919), p. 27.

much later—and sometimes not at all.'¹ What had caused the shock and disappointment? Rudolf Piper thought the assumption that the youth movement had really come to know 'country and people' during its perambulations had been no more than an illusion. On such excursions they had seen only the best side of their people. Even the provincial inns, for instance, had been outside their experience; hence their 'terrible disappointment in the army barracks.'² Robert Oelbermann, an army lieutenant and future leader of the *Nerothers*, said that 'horror seized us. Were we human beings? Or animals? Duty alone upheld many of us until the end.'³

In the early days of the war it had been commonly assumed that its moral effect would be that of a great purifying fire; it would destroy everything that was rotten and decaying. But gradually it became apparent that the war was bound also to destroy many real values and achievements; that it was bringing in its train a general brutalization which could be nothing less than an immense cultural and moral catastrophe.⁴ 'When they return home, they will no longer want to dance . . . and their faith is broken,' wrote one *Wandervogel* poet.⁵ Not that all of them were so sensitive; not everybody was affected in the same way by their experiences at the front. Of the generation of Langemarck only a minority became convinced pacifists. Another small group came to believe in war for war's sake; their ideal figure became the *Landsknecht*, and they shared Ernst Jünger's belief that it was inward unrest and the fascination of danger that were the prime motives of war, not the defence of the Fatherland or any other pious appeal to aspiring youth.⁶ The *Fronterlebnis* did have considerable influence on the youth movement between the First and Second World Wars, in particular among the younger members of the right-wing organizations, but the feats of heroism they recalled and venerated were almost always those performed by an individual in isolation—a Bölcke or an Immelmann, von Richthofen or Weddigen, airmen or submarine commanders—not the deeds of the nameless infantry soldier in the trenches or at Verdun.

The great majority went on fighting mainly because they had no alternative, and for that reason, as well as from a sense of patriotic duty, preferred not to question the purpose of the war. In 1914, *Wandervogel* spokesmen, like many others in Germany, had talked idly and fairly openly about territorial annexations: 'After the war

¹ *Wandervogel*, 2, 1916, p. 35.   ² *Ibid.*, 10/11, 1916, p. 211.
³ *Ibid.*, 6, 1919, p. 156.
⁴ See for instance Johannes Müller in *Grüne Blätter*, quoted in *Freideutsche Jugend*, 7, 1917, pp. 223-4.
⁵ Kurt Schulze, *ibid.*, p. 212. See also the replies by Karl Rauch and Wilhelm Hagen in *Freideutsche Jugend*, 10/11, 1917, p. 381.
⁶ *Der Vormarsch*, 1927, p. 289.

we shall again ramble over a greater homeland,' wrote Neuendorff, in his first appeal to the movement after the war had begun,[1] and F. W. Fulda declared that peace should not come unless it would serve the greater glory of the Reich.[2] There were circles within the youth movement which openly joined the annexationist camp, but the majority avoided attachment to a political party, and so far as their opinions are on record they merely echoed official views. The emergence of the right-wing extremist group around Otger Gräff will be related elsewhere; but something must be said here of its direct impact upon the movement. There were not many members in this group—perhaps one hundred to one hundred and fifty at first—but their influence was out of all proportion to their number. They demanded, among other things, that the German language should be cleansed of all foreign influences ('Aufwiedersehn' instead of 'Adieu' was one of the more logical and innocent examples), and they pressed for a reintroduction of the old German names of months: *Hartung, Hornung, Lenzmond* instead of January, February, March, etc. Experts pointed out that these names were of more than doubtful historical authenticity, and the editor of the *Wandervogel* monthly subsequently regretted that he had been rushed into advocating this reform.[3] But meanwhile Otger Gräff and his friends urged that all 'non-German' type faces for printing (such as Antiqua) should be discarded, and pressed for various other reforms. Demands for the strict application of the Aryan paragraph also reappeared, and some went very far indeed in this direction, arguing that the presence of a single member of alien blood (Jewish, Slav, or Mongolian) would thwart the work of the entire community.[4] Nor was Aryan blood always a sufficient criterion, for in the far north of Germany the exclusion of pro-Danish elements was demanded by four *Wandervogel* branches.[5]

Such opinions did not pass without contradiction, and, on occasion, those who were most exposed to the opposition they excited lost patience with the more extreme demands. Kötzschau, the editor of *Wandervogel*, wrote after the movement's yearly convention in 1916 that 'among the "Greifen" (Gräff's group) in Naumburg I hardly saw a German; most were of mixed Slavonic blood.'[6] Family names may not always be reliable guides to racial origin, but for the Nordic purists it must have been somewhat disconcerting to

[1] *Wandervogel*, Kriegsheft, 1, p. 258.
[2] *Führerzeitung*, Kriegsheft 3, p. 209.
[3] *Wandervogel*, 3/4, 1917, p. 80.
[4] *Ibid.*, 2/3, 1919, p. 89.   [5] *Ibid.*, 4, 1919, p. 116.
[6] *Ibid.*, 10/11, 1916. In the twenties, on the other hand, some of the ideologists of the youth movement demanded a 'gradual penetration of German with Slavonic blood' as a prerequisite for a German renascence. *Der Weisse Ritter*, vol. VII, 10/12.

find that many, perhaps most, of their spokesmen had names that had not been in use either in Valhalla or in Midgard.[1]

II

These and similar political issues were of great interest to some—though by no means to all—of the older members of the *Wandervogel*, but they were not often the principal problems thrashed out at local or regional meetings of the movement.[2] The younger boys and girls were, naturally, preoccupied with very different problems, paramount among them the clash of the generations in the movement. Leadership of groups before 1914 had been in the hands of adults, some of whom were nearer sixty than twenty. With the outbreak of war their juniors took over, and it appeared that those between fourteen and eighteen were perfectly well able to take charge of all group and branch activities; it was only at the regional level and in the central leadership that the experience of the older generation was necessary.

In consequence, less than a year after the outbreak of war, voices were raised for the first time to demand the rejuvenation of the movement and the retirement of all those above a certain age limit (eighteen to twenty). But was not this an act of treason to the *Wandervogel* soldiers fighting at the front? Any final decision had to be postponed until after the war; but would not the older members be the first to understand that the tasks facing them in the future could only be tackled from within a new and different framework?[3] Such views were soon heard from many parts of Germany and were to lead to a revolution in the youth movement shortly after the end of the war. Nobody wanted to exclude the 'old boys' *in toto*, but the younger members wanted charismatic leaders chosen by themselves, rather than social workers imposed from above.[4]

What then was to become of the older members? The war had brought the conflict between the generations to a head, but it had been latent for several years prior to 1914. The *Freideutsche* youth

[1] The leaders of the Austrian and Bohemian *Wandervogel*, the most extreme pan-Germans, were named Kutschera, Moutschka and Morocutti. Among those favouring the Nordic orientation of the youth movement in the Reich, names like Luntowski, Konopacki-Konopath or Pudelko were frequent.

[2] It would be tedious to retrace in detail the developments within each of the countrywide *Wandervogel* organizations. It ought to be recalled that the *Wandervogel*, on which the present account is mainly based, was the largest but not the only movement in existence. But conditions in the *Altwandervogel* and *Jungwandervogel* were not at all dissimilar.

[3] G. Weisser, in *Wandervogel*, 7, 1915, pp. 183–87.

[4] See for instance A. Kurella, in *Wandervogel*, 5/6, 1918, p. 138.

had been one of the bodies created to provide an organizational framework for older members of the youth movement. But by no means all the older *Wandervogel* joined it; many rejected it as 'too intellectual,' and on the other hand the *Freideutsche*, mainly students, included some who had never been members of the *Wandervogel*. There had been other such attempts before. In 1913 a group of ex-*Wandervogel* school teachers in Saxony constituted themselves as a 'Landsgemeinde,' an association of young men and women in different walks of life, united in their endeavour to carry on the same work for a German renascence which, on a different level, the youth movement had started. There were long discussions on these lines, and various other 'Landsgemeinden' were established during the war, but none of them lasted, with the exception of the 'Kronacher Bund of the Old Wandervogel,' a less ambitious, looser group, which was formed in 1920 and maintains some cohesion to the present day (1961).

The reasons for the failure of the 'Landsgemeinden' are manifold; the most obvious was perhaps the one that negated their very *raison d'être*. The fact that various people had belonged in their youth to a group of ramblers was more or less accidental; there was really no good reason to perpetuate this in later life, for their interests would undoubtedly broaden and differ—and so would their political, cultural, and social orientation.[1] Only a clear common purpose would hold a group of adults together, but did such a common platform exist? Some, on the extreme left and the extreme right of the political spectrum, saw such a purpose in the establishment of communal settlements, preferably in the countryside, but neither radical socialist fervour nor the National Socialist belief in blood and soil sufficed to give a lasting impetus to the settlements that came into being in 1919–22. More promising were the attempts to establish 'guilds' constituted by people *within* a given profession; some of them, such as the Social Workers Guild uniting educators, social workers, etc., continue to exist to this day.

The associations of the older *Wandervogel* failed, in brief, because they were too ambitious in their conception and because the individual members had not enough in common to make such projects work. Which does not mean that these attempts were altogether misplaced. It would have been a great achievement, if it had indeed been possible, to establish a German Fabian Society, as some left-wing and liberal circles proposed in 1918–19, and again after World War II. The right-wing extremists around Otger Gräff and

[1] Cf. the discussion in Georg Schmidt, *Randbemerkungen* (1917), pp. 12 *et seq.*

Luntowski, with all their crackpot ideas about 'Germantik'[1] and a racial and religious German rebirth, had eminently sensible ideas about the need for adult education and the extension of *Wandervogel* activities to non-middle-class youth.[2]

III

The place of girls in the youth movement had been defined by the compromise of 1911 according to which, after strong initial resistance, girls' rambling groups had been accepted. But mixed rambling spread, especially among the older members, and the resistance of some German *Länder*, such as Catholic Bavaria which put a ban on all such activities, only strengthened the belief in co-education in the movement. As a result of the war the importance of the girls in the movement grew even more; in some branches boys were now a minority, and the girl leaders had assumed a leading position on the regional (*Gau*) level.

Against this state of affairs the younger boys began to revolt as the war years went by, and 'Girls, out of the *Wandervogel*' became a frequently heard war cry. It was argued that the presence of the girls was damaging to the movement; it inhibited the boys, who became either effeminate or obstreperous, and teased the girls in an attempt to get rid of an unwelcome tutelage. Others, advancing a more sophisticated or more devious explanation, argued that the *Wandervogel* was not good for the girls; their participation in war games, for instance, was unseemly. According to yet another opinion, mixed group activities were bound to fail, for by the nature of things the older boys would be mainly interested in the girls of their own age, and the younger boys would feel neglected, and therefore revolt and cause mischief.[3]

The girl leaders replied that the arguments used against their presence in the movement were not really sound. The girls needed it as much as the boys did, and there were practical difficulties which sometimes made separate rambling difficult.[4] Nor was it all a one-

[1] See for instance Kurt Gerlach, *Germantik, das Rechte Leben, das ist ein Büchlein deutsch*, Leipzig, 1913, or Willibald Hentschel's books *Varuna* and *Mittgart*, also published by a *Wandervogel* publishing house.

[2] Such suggestions were, however, usually rejected with a variety of arguments, including the one that 'we are not a rubbish heap for all kinds of riff-raff,' *Wandervogel*, 9, 1916, p. 184.

[3] See the letters in the 'Girls' Number' of *Wandervogel*, 1/2, 1918; also some of the replies in *Wandervogel*, 5/6, 1918, pp. 140–1.

[4] Before the war, the girls had been a comparatively small minority in the *Wandervogel*, but in 1918 there were 243 girls' groups (in comparison with 326 boys' groups) and 98 mixed groups. In some regions, such as Berlin-Brandenburg, the number of girls and boys was equal (*Wandervogel*, 7/8, 1918, p. 177).

sided affair, either, for the *Wandervogel* needed the girls; how could anyone seriously intend to reform German youth and plant the seeds of a new way of life while limiting this movement from the very beginning to one sex only? These were undoubtedly valid arguments, but they did not in the end prevail over the deep-seated instinctive dislike of the younger boys who wanted to keep to themselves. The drive to restrict girls to groups of their own gathered momentum, and there were some who demanded that they should be excluded altogether. No decision was taken while the war lasted, but at the convention at Naumburg in 1920 some regional organizations seceded from the movement because their demand for an unmixed *Bund* had not been accepted.

These were the natural birth pangs of a youth movement, symptomatic of real problems to which no easy solutions could be found.

The heated debate about antifeminism, on the other hand, which went on at about the same time, strikes one as somewhat artificial. It had started with some publications of the ubiquitous Blüher on 'bourgeois and spiritual (*geistig*) antifeminism.'[1] There was a tradition of 'spiritual antifeminism' in Germany, the last and most famous exponents of which were Nietzsche and Weininger, and there was very probably more to be said on the subject. Whether there were not more pressing problems during the First World War, and whether the *Freideutsche* was the ideal forum for a debate so inconclusive by nature and necessity, is a different question. But the young women and some of the young men of those circles thought differently, and so we find them in the fourth year of the war fighting about the Gothic and the Dionysian man, about Amazons and Hermaphrodites, about Socrates and Diotima, and about the limits of the emancipation of women. It was, as one of the more sober observers put it, a struggle against a ghost which had been conjured up by the *Freideutsche* themselves.

IV

The *Freideutsche* youth was hit more severely than the *Wandervogel* by the war, for a greater proportion of its members were of military age. It took several months before a rudimentary form of organization maintaining some contact between its members was re-established. During the first year of the war most of its members wholeheartedly supported the policy of the Kaiser and his government;

[1] Published in Berlin, 1917. Previously a shorter essay by Blüher, 'What is Antifeminism', had appeared in the August 1915 issue of *Aufbruch*. The discussion continued in *Freideutsche Jugend*, 8/9, 1916. There were five articles in reply (*Freideutsche Jugend*, 3, 1917).

if they had any reservations they kept them to themselves.[1] Gradually, however, a change set in; the movement became more political, more critical in its attitudes towards society, the German government, and its policy. This reflected the gradual realization that politics did matter; but the majority long resisted the efforts of the right- and left-wing factions to compel the movement to adopt a clear political position or to collaborate with existing political parties.[2] A motion by Max Hodann and his Berlin circle in support of Professor F. W. Foerster, who was in difficulties with the authorities because of his anti-Prussian and pacifist publications, was rejected; and so were the appeals of the racialists on the right. Some outsiders, such as Professor Nelson of Göttingen, joined in the debate, accusing the *Freideutsche* of inertia and cowardice and its leaders of senility and effeminacy[3] for abstaining from any form of political action that might possibly endanger their internal unity. Would working-class youth have acted so? asked Nelson, somewhat rhetorically. The *Freideutsche* spokesman replied that, since practically all the older members of the movement were in the army and could not take part in the debate, and since the majority of those at home were boys and girls under the age of eighteen, was it not rather demagogic to ask them for decisions for which they were so obviously not ready?

The discussion continued so long as most of the leading figures of the movement were in the army; it created widespread confusion and led to much talk about the decline and fall of the youth movement. On yet another front a not very edifying polemic between the *Freideutsche* and Wyneken continued.[4] Wyneken, it will be recalled, had been ousted shortly before the outbreak of the war and, not without reason, felt deeply offended; but even from afar his personality was strongly magnetic, the more so in a time of confusion and crisis, and a gradual *rapprochement* was effected; in August 1917 Wyneken was invited to a West German youth meeting at the Loreley and, according to one eye-witness, 'absolutely dominated the meeting'; he was loudly acclaimed by the seven or eight hundred participants, including about one hundred soldiers home on leave. Some of the leading *Wandervogel* and *Freideutsche* leaders may have had their

[1] The only exception was the *Aufbruch* circle, on which more below.
[2] Cf. *Freideutsche Jugend*, 1/2, 1917, a number entirely political in content, in which, however, most authors opposed political engagement and merely emphasized the need for political education: 'We are looking for a political direction, but cannot find it in any of the existing parties because none of them conforms with our wishes and ideals . . .' *ibid.*, p. 11.
[3] *Die Tat*, 11, 1916, p. 760.
[4] For the polemics see *Freie Schulgemeinde*, 1/2, 1916 and 4, 1916; the answers in *Freideutsche Jugend*, 3/4 and 10/11, 1916.

doubts, but they too were swept off their feet. The alliance between the youth movement and Wyneken was thus renewed: 'The Loreley can be compared to the Hohe Meissner,' wrote another participant, not originally a Wyneken sympathizer; 'two mountain peaks (in the history of the movement) divided by a plain. We were all carried away by him.'[1] Optimistic views prevailed again; fresh impetus was given to the movement and everything seemed to point to a new, great upsurge after the end of the war.

V

About fourteen thousand *Wandervogel* had seen military service during the war, most of them in the front line. Of these, one in four never returned, among them some of the most central figures of the movement: Hans Breuer, who had written the *Zupfgeigenhansl*; Hans Wix, who had founded the Academic *Freischar* at Marburg; Walter Illgen, leader from Saxony; Christian Schneehagen, who had organized the festivities on the Hohe Meissner; Rudolf Sievers, the painter of the movement; Frank Fischer, who had taught the ramblers not merely to walk record distances but to have an eye open for their surroundings and for the beauties of nature. Otger Gräff, the head of the extreme right wing, did not return, nor did Kutschera and Moutschka, the leaders of the *Wandervogel* in Austria and Bohemia. Blüher rhapsodized about the idea of a German nation from Berlin, and some of the ideologists of the racialist right wing, who had taught the youth to live perilously, found their presence at the home front indispensable and never fired a shot in anger; but Ludwig Frank, Jew and pacifist, leader of the Socialist youth, volunteered and was killed in a skirmish the very first week of the war—the only Reichstag deputy to fall in battle. Stefan George, whose work had inspired the young German *élite*, the bard of an heroic life to whom sacrifice and death meant nothing, decided that his place was not, after all, among the shouting mobs. But Richard Dehmel, aged 51, a plebeian poet if ever there was one in the eyes of the George circle, volunteered and spent the war years in the army.

More than ten thousand *Wandervogel* soldiers returned home after the armistice in November 1918, but less than half continued to show any interest in the youth movement; the others were no longer interested in rambling, camps, and group activities.[2] Nor had

[1] *Freideutsche Jugend*, 9, 1917, p. 329. Dr Wyneken told the present writer that German youth had two great opportunities: 'The emergence of a youth movement, and the fact that this movement met me' (interview at Göttingen, 25 April 1960). It sounds presumptuous, but there is a grain of truth in it.

[2] The figures are taken from *Wandervogel*, 4, 1919, p. 111, based on an enquiry carried out in December, 1918.

the 'generation of 1902' (following the publication of a successful novel this was to become a catchphrase) much use for the returned soldiers. Things had turned out very differently from what most of them had expected, and the writers of the patriotic poems of 1914 could offer little guidance or consolation five years later, apart from apocalyptic visions and presentiments of cosmic catastrophes.

Eleven
1919—LEFT v. RIGHT

I

NOVEMBER 1918 saw the downfall of Wilhelmian Germany and the instalment of a Republican government. The Social Democrats who thus came to power were hard pressed in their turn by the Communists on one hand and by the right-wing extremists on the other, both equally eager to supplant the new regime. This struggle for position took place against a background of political chaos and economic breakdown; and the latent social forces at issue were fairly accurately represented by the emergence of distinct trends in the youth movement, which during the war years had become more and more political.

The *Freideutsche* youth provided the main forum of controversy between left and right advocates of the younger generation, and also between the moderates and the extreme left among them. This politicization of the movement was deplored by some, who predicted dire consequences if it were not checked in time.[1] Yet upon closer examination, did not this anti-political attitude itself imply some sort of political line? That of ignoring or belittling the revolution, for instance, or of resisting the growth of Socialist and internationalist opinion among the *Freideutsche* youth? Some of the younger members, it is true, were complaining that the barrage of political literature made them dizzy—was it really the Jews, or the anti-semites, or the alcoholics, who should be made responsible for Germany's ruin? 'I think there is still too much paper in Germany,' grumbled one distracted *Wandervogel*.[2] But that was not the view of the older members: Their sense of the need to take sides had become

---

[1] See Dankwart Gerlach's reasons for ignoring the revolution, in his *Führerzeitung*, 3 (1919) p. 36, and the appeal against politicization signed by (among others) Ernst Buske. *Ibid.* pp. 37, 38.

[2] *Wandervogel*, 5, 1919, p. 144.

overwhelming and so had their desire to take action on their decisions.

The left and the right wings of the youth movement did not, of course, suddenly come into existence in November 1918; in one form or another they had been active for several years before. We shall have to retrace their development up to 1914, to gain a fuller and more accurate picture of the tug-of-war that went on for three years after the end of the war, brought about so many schisms and splits, and finally led to the dissolution of the *Freideutsche* youth.

II

The *Wandervogel* was officially neutral in politics and religious questions; most of its members regarded politics as outside their own scope and sphere of interests—or even as positively harmful. In 1913, however, some discordant voices were heard, claiming that political and social issues could no longer be left to the elders and administrators of the established order. These fresh impulses came from various circles, places and age groups; among them were the young storm-petrels of *Der Anfang*, a monthly magazine written mainly by boys and girls of the upper forms of secondary schools in Germany and Austria. Their revolutionary enthusiasm was as yet mainly directed against the school authorities, and it took them some time to realize that a radical school reform without a revolution in society was highly unlikely. In that group, however, there were the sparks of a much more radical critique of society than elsewhere in the youth movement.[1] Karl Bittel and Ernst Joel, both students at the time, were two other critics who thought that the youth movement ought to lean towards Socialism. It is doubtful whether either had read Marx at the time—and if they had, they certainly rejected his theories. They were in no way tied to official Social Democracy. They were influenced by Tolstoy, by the British "settlement" movement, by Gustav Landauer and other representatives of an ethical socialism. Karl Bittel, a native of Wurttemberg, propagated the idea of co-operative associations among students; and Ernst Joel, a native of Berlin, was the theoretician of the group.

The war nipped these beginnings in the bud. If such political enemies of the Kaiser as the Social Democrats could so wholeheartedly support the war, as they did during its early stages, one could hardly expect a dissenting voice from the youth movement; even such a radical critic of Wilhelmian society as Wyneken was at first in favour of the war. Only a very few sympathizers of the youth

[1] 'It is not at all in the interests of the State to have people coming out of its schools who are able to think independently in politics.' *Der Anfang*, August 1913, p. 109.

movement among the older generation, such as F. W. Foerster or Hans Paasche, did not share the general enthusiasm of August 1914, but professed a pacifism which was a matter of principle rather than party politics. It took the left wing about a year to rally again; then, in early summer of 1915, prospectuses were sent out announcing the publication of a new journal, *Der Aufbruch*, edited by Ernst Joel in collaboration with a few friends.[1] They stood for an avowedly social attitude (the word 'Socialist' was as yet considered too provocative or ambiguous) and their grave misgivings about the war can be read between the lines. They could not voice their opposition openly, but the military censorship did not like roundabout criticism either, and after four issues the *Aufbruch* was compelled to discontinue publication.

The ideas of the *Aufbruch* provoked hostility among some youth leaders. Younger members ought not read it, said Walter Fischer, editor of the *Wandervogel*,[2] though among the older members it was hardly likely to cause much damage—'But hardly anybody will be missing anything if he does not read these articles by Joel and Blueher, written in an esoteric language rich in slogans and foreign words, the vulgarities (*sic!*) of Kierkegaard, or if he does not enjoy the so-called poems of Walt Whitman.' Culturally and politically *Der Aufbruch* was well above the intellectual level of the average *Wandervogel*. It was also verbose and unnecessarily vague. The main merit of Ernst Joel's two long programmatic articles published at this time[3] lay in their attempt to explain why youth would have to take an active part in political and social life, and that no one could isolate himself from society and politics. Joel based much of his argument on Fichte ('the first German Socialist'), while Gustav Landauer quoted some of the utopian socialists and prophets of land reform in support of his ideas about the building of socialism through the establishment of agricultural settlements of a new type. Most interesting, perhaps, or at any rate, most relevant to the youth movement, was what Friedrich Bauermeister said about the 'class struggle of youth.'[4] This writer certainly knew that youth was not a class, but he was convinced that youth had a special mission in the world of tomorrow. The Socialist movement, including Marx and Engels, he regarded as 'eudaimonistic'; they wanted, quite rightly, a just social order and higher

[1] Including Gustav Landauer, Friedrich Bauermeister, Karl Bittel, Hans Blüher, Kurt Hiller, Bernhard and Hans Reichenbach, as well as the editors of *Der Anfang*.
[2] *Wandervogel*, I, 1916, p. 30. The 'so-called poems' by Whitman were translated by Gustav Landauer.
[3] *Die Jugend vor der sozialen Frage*, Jena, 1915, based on a lecture given shortly before the outbreak of the war, and *Der soziale Bourgeois* (*Der Aufbruch*, October 1915).
[4] *Der Aufbruch*, July 1915.

living standards. But would the revolution make a better type of man, would it release the human being from its 'bourgeois and proletarian distortions,' would it liberate the spirit of man? That, according to Bauermeister, was the decisive problem to be tackled, the specific challenge for the young generation. 'The class struggle of youth' remained a highly controversial slogan for several years, until in 1920–21 some of its proponents matured into adult class strugglers, while others retreated into what was somewhat contemptuously called 'civilian life.' Other left-wing initiatives were made in Berlin and South-West Germany. Alfred Kurella, a student and prominent *Wandervogel* leader, met with a few of his friends in August 1917 and formulated a vaguely leftist programme that was published only after the end of the war.[1] Here, too, the idea of collective settlements came up; those who subsequently attempted to establish such settlements in Bavaria soon found themselves in trouble with the authorities who were not willing to tolerate such dangerous and subversive experiments.[2] Some of the leaders of the left wing, notably Kurella and Bittel, joined the Communist party of Germany soon after it had been founded. Nevertheless, Kurella still defended the 'bourgeois' youth movement against criticism from the left in 1918; he acclaimed *inter alia* Stefan George as the greatest living German poet. And at the end of 1918 the leader of the *Wandervogel* right wing stated that he was in full agreement with what Kurella had just written about German politics and the part the youth movement was to play in it.[3]

In November 1918 Karl Bittel developed some curious theories. He was then in charge of the department that was to give advice to members of the movement with regard to the choice of a profession: some professions, Bittel said, were 'without value for our future community and its plans to conquer the world—physicists, chemists, physicians and the engineering professions in general were not needed.[4] Amazing opinions for a twentieth century revolutionary! Or did Bittel want to turn the youth movement into a group of professional revolutionaries? The *Wandervogel* left wing continued to regard the development of the personality as the supreme task. Most of the left-wingers were strongly influenced at one time or another by religious socialism, and Kurella's advocacy (in 1918) of the study of the religious wisdom of the East was in accord with the spirit of the times. There was, however, at least one mitigating circumstance for what may otherwise appear an unpardonable lack

---

[1] F. Bauermeister, Hans Koch and A. Kurella, *Absage und Beginn*, 1919.
[2] For the trial of the Blankenburg settlers in September 1919 see *Freideutsche Jugend*, October 1919, p. 469.
[3] *Freideutsche Jugend*, I, 1918, p. 45; *ibid.*, 11, 12, 1918, p. 423.
[4] *Ibid.*, 11–12, 1918, p. 425.

of precision in all the statements and appeals of the left wing; a strict military censorship was in force during all the war years, which made any open statement in favour of revolutionary Socialism quite impossible.

Among those who had written for the *Anfang* and *Aufbruch* some became well known later on in left-wing literary circles, such as Walter Benjamin, Wieland Herzfelde and Rudolf Leonhard. Of the leading figures, Ernst Joel, who had meanwhile graduated as a physician, soon dropped out of politics.[1] Friedrich Vorwerk, who had been with Bittel one of the leading spokesmen of the pro-Communist faction, reappeared several years later as the secretary of Germany's most influential and fashionable right-wing political club, the 'Herrenklub'. Karl August Wittfogel, a former head of the *Wandervogel* branch in Lueneberg, became a Communist youth and student leader. Subsequently he took up Chinese studies, spent some time in the Far East, and is now a professor, well known in his field, at a leading American university. In his publications since the late thirties he has been extremely critical of Communism.

Both Karl Bittel and Alfred Kurella remained faithful to the cause they first espoused around 1920. Bittel, an economist by profession, became an expert on municipal affairs, edited a Communist newspaper and was ultimately appointed the leading party expert on co-operative societies—his hobby-horse from the *Wandervogel* days. In 1933 he was imprisoned for a year or so, but subsequently released and permitted to publish several books (on non-political themes) in the Third Reich. After 1948 he found his way to East Berlin, where he served for a while as president of the East German Press Association and director of the state institute for contemporary history. All in all, a slightly disappointing career for a man for whom most of his contemporaries had predicted a great political future. Of all those mentioned, Alfred Kurella was the one most deeply involved in *Wandervogel* activities. The son of one of Germany's leading experts in forensic medicine, Kurella, at the age of eighteen, wrote a little book on lute playing which became the standard primer. He was one of the editors of the *Freideutsche Jugend* almost until its demise; and after joining the Communist party he worked for many years as a writer, translator and lecturer at the central party school. He spent several years in France, lived in Moscow from 1934 to 1954 and became a Soviet citizen.

---

[1] According to Blüher's autobiography Joel committed suicide soon after the First World War because he could not survive Germany's defeat and humiliation. Like so many of Blüher's statements this is pure fantasy; Joel, who had not been in good health for many years, died about 1930.

1919—LEFT V. RIGHT

After his return to East Berlin from Moscow, Kurella was made president of the East German writers' union and subsequently head of the cultural department at the party central committee. He became virtually the highest authority on all cultural problems despite, or because of, his ultra-orthodox views. Others from that group who joined the Communist party were less fortunate; Heinrich Schmückle, for instance, after serving as a staff member of the Marx-Engels Institute, disappeared later in the big purge. So did Heinrich Kurella, Alfred's brother.

In that little world of the youth movement in 1918, however, Kurella and his friends were better known as lute players and authors of essays on the sexual question than as party politicians. A considerable section of the *Freideutsche* moved during the later part of the war to a somewhat leftist and internationalist position, but all this was still very indistinct and vague. The real swing to the left came only during the months following the revolution of November 1918. Thousands of young men and women were then drawn into politics. It was a revolutionary situation when the moderates of yesteryear adopted extremist programmes and those who had been indifferent were ready to adopt politics as a vocation. The struggle to determine the political character of the new state had begun and it was reflected, on a smaller scale, in the fight for predominance in the republic of youth that came under way in 1919.

III

A strong right-wing group developed within the youth movement even before the left wing had emerged. Nobody would have considered the *Wandervogel* Socialist in character, but a good many people thought of the youth movement as part of the *Völkische* camp, although it did not identify itself with any political party. Those who regarded the youth movement as an ally in the struggle for the regeneration of the Fatherland argued that nationalist aims and activities—unlike those of the left—were not really political in character; patriotism and faith in the destiny of the German people were causes altogether above party politics.

The first youth organization explicitly dedicated to these causes was founded by W. Cichon before the First World War; it had three branches[1] and did not attain to much importance until after 1918.

---

[1] Nürnberg, Coburg and Berlin. It was known as *Wandervogel V.B.* (Vaterlaendischer Bund, afterwards Völkischer Bund). There were other right-wing youth organizations in existence before 1914 which cannot, however, be considered to be part of the youth movement; for they were directly sponsored and controlled by political parties.

1919—LEFT V. RIGHT

Of much greater significance were the factions within the *Wandervogel* and the *Freideutsche* which first became prominent in 1913, and gradually led to an alliance of all the right-wing forces. The debates on the Jewish question in 1913 and 1914 for the first time made it clear beyond all doubt that the youth movement could not always refrain from taking a stand on the burning political and social issues of the day. On that occasion a compromise was found and the differences between the various camps were temporarily disposed of. The war years, however, exacerbated old passions and created fresh tensions; by 1916 it was estimated that about one-third of the youth movement had adopted a *völkische* position. Many who were of this persuasion still hoped that the whole youth movement would eventually come over to their side, and they were therefore reluctant to provoke a split. Among them was Dankwart Gerlach, who had succeeded Fulda as the editor of the *Führerzeitung*.[1] More extremist was Otger Gräff, a young *Wandervogel* army lieutenant who, in a series of short leaflets written at the front in 1916–18, developed political ideas that served as the basis of a new organization, the *Jungdeutsche Bund*. After Gräff's death at the front in 1918, Frank Glatzel took over the leadership, and helped to make it for a while into the leading right-wing group of the youth movement. Otger Gräff, according to the testimony of his friends,[2] was a man of outstanding personal qualities and great integrity. It would probably be unfair to judge him on the basis of his published leaflets and articles; he was certainly no great thinker. His political ideas were similar to those of other right-wing extremists at the time; he was wholly in favour of annexations and German expansion, particularly towards the East. Gräff also proposed that an order should be founded after the war to continue the work of the medieval German knights in the East: he denounced Jewish capitalism and advocated monetary and agrarian reform. For these opinions Gräff came to be regarded in certain circles of the Third Reich as the greatest leader that the *Wandervogel* ever produced.[3]

The left wing, too, often displayed a weakness for half-baked ideas, but even at their very worst the leftists were hardly as confused as Gräff and his friends. When pressed for an explanation or definition

---

[1] During the war, Gerlach and his paper supported the most extreme rightist party, the *Vaterlandspartei*, but at the same time opposed the politicization of the youth movement. When asked to explain this contradiction, he countered with the well-known argument that in his eyes the Vaterlandspartei was unlike all other parties inasmuch as it stood for the unity of all patriotic forces, etc. (*Führerzeitung*, Lenxing, March, 1919, p. 37).

[2] Cf. the writings of Guntram Erich Pohl, Adalbert Luntowski and others.

[3] Luise Fick, *loc. cit.*, p. 110; for Gräff as a precursor of the Bünde see Werner Pohl *Bündische Erziehung* (Weimar, 1933) p. 69.

of their Germanic and Aryan mission, or when confronted with the evidence that a pure Aryan race had never existed, least of all in Germany, they invariably replied that this did not disturb them in the least; they would create such a race in the future.[1] They were against Christianity because Christianity had failed to improve the German people, which had actually deteriorated, they said, since pagan days. They believed instead in a German deity (*deutsches Gottum*) but failed to make it clear whether they would pray to Wotan or, following Houston Stewart Chamberlain, to an aryanized Jesus Christ. The Kingdom of God on earth became synonymous in their eyes with the superior empire of the Germans (*das hoehere Reich der Deutschen*).[2]

The problem of religion continued to plague the racialists in the youth movement for many years. Some, such as W. Hauer (a former member of the *Koengener*) helped later on to set up their own sect by inserting a few Christian terms and Indo-Aryan concepts into the Nazi ideology. Others went further and, following Alfred Rosenberg, rejected the Old Testament *in toto*, demanding also a reform of the New Testament and a new fifth evangelium, according to which national honour should take precedence over Christian love as the supreme moral aspiration. Others, again, rejected Christianity *in toto* and joined one of the many new religions and occult sects whose prophets grew like mushrooms in the *völkisch* camp between the First and Second World War. Of such were Mathilde Ludendorff's *Tannenberg Bund*, Arthur Dinter's group, the Asgard Circle or Gustav Müller's sect which believed that the human soul was an amalgamation of three or four animal souls ('according to reliable reports from the beyond'), and that the planet Mars was the place where man first appeared. Those who tended towards National Bolshevism declared that they regarded the nation as an 'idea of God,' but that they were quite willing to call the supreme being 'absolute spirit' or 'will to power' instead. It ought to be added that some of the more intelligent leaders of the right-wing extremist camp (such as Otto Strasser or Friedrich Hielscher) and their allies in the youth movement, realized the logical and practical difficulties involved in applying racialist categories, and developed more sophisticated ideas about a German cultural mission, and concerning the Reich as a spiritual conception.

Whatever their disagreements about Christianity, Otger Gräff and his successors had no such doubts about the Jews; there was no room for them in the youth movement, nor indeed any future for them in Germany. 'We do not see any possibility of forming our life together

---

[1] Otger Gräff in *Freideutsche Jugend*, April/May, 1918, p. 183.
[2] Otger Gräff, *loc. cit.*, pp. 160–2.

1919—LEFT V. RIGHT

with the people of a different race,' the *Wandervogel V.B.* declared, at its annual convention in 1919; other groups adopted similar resolutions. But the Jews were not their only target. They also took a very dim view of the internationalist opinions aired by many members of the *Freideutsche* after 1917 and they rejected foreign influences in general.[1] Walter Flex's dictum that 'the word brother has a deep meaning for me, and I am unable therefore to apply it to a Frenchman from the south or a Cossack' was frequently quoted with approval. The racialists saw their main task in fighting Social Democracy (and, of course, Communism), in establishing a network of adult education—'under the sign of the Swastika' as Otger Gräff put it—in order to bring about the German revival in manners, art, law and every other field that they so ardently desired.

It is unnecessary to analyse in detail the ideas evolved by these circles, for they are hardly different from the politics that had been preached by men of the older generation, such as Theodor Fritsch or Friedrich Lange, and by the leaders of such organizations as the *Deutschbund* for many years before the First World War. Gradually it became evident that the opposition between the two wings of the *Freideutsche* had become irreconcilable; the first clash occurred at the Solling meeting in October 1917, and recriminations continued until, in 1919, the final break occurred. The majority maintained (with Wyneken) that to be German was not in itself a spiritual value; certainly not an absolute value as the rightists claimed. Nevertheless, great efforts were made to avoid actual rupture; today's opponents were after all yesterday's comrades, they had all been members of the same youth groups, they shared the memory of countless conventions and expeditions and many of them liked and esteemed one another. But in the long run common memories and personal friendships were not enough to hold the movement together. At the first great convention of the *Jungdeutsche Bund* on Burg Lauenstein in 1919, its spokesmen argued that they stood in opposition only to the *Freideutsche* reality—not to the *Freideutsche* idea. The leader of the new *Bund* was Frank Glatzel, a young lawyer who has been called the diplomat of the youth movement. He was indeed more moderate than Otger Gräff; and the new executive included respectable rather than radical right-wing figures, such as Edmund Neuendorff and Walter Fischer, former *Wandervogel* chiefs, and Wilhelm Stählin, the future Protestant Bishop. Under this leadership some of the extremist slogans were discarded, while the general right-wing orientation was maintained. There were, however, serious differences

---

[1] This took some grotesque forms, such as the attempt to purge the German language of all words of French or Latin origin and replace them by new, 'purely German' expressions.

as to whether the *Bund* should identify itself with any specific political party; some leading members were opposed in principle to the politicization of the youth movement. In this respect, the right wing and the left were confronting very similar dilemmas in 1919.

While Otger Gräff's successors made a determined effort to weld together their political friends and followers into one big organization, other right-wing leaders were not idle. Wulle, the publisher of the *Deutsche Zeitung,* a representative of the most extreme of the groups of the Right before Hitler appeared on the scene, convened leaders of the youth movement at Potsdam in August 1919 at a 'First German Youth Day.' Wulle, who called himself 'the creator of the German youth movement'[1] was trying to enlist the younger generation for his own faction; he was assisted by Professor Förster and other stalwarts of the former 'Vaterlandspartei' and the Pan-German League. They asked their listeners to collaborate in the struggle against the Left, the Jews and the arch-enemies, France and Britain, and ended by demanding that the young generation should bow to the ripe wisdom and the authority of various *Geheimraete* present. A representative of the youth movement countered by pointing out that youth by its very nature was revolutionary, which provoked a storm of indignation among those present. This proved to be too much even for the leaders of the nationalist youth groups, who had come to Potsdam with great expectations, and the convention ended without any tangible results.

The *Jungdeutsche Bund* was the biggest right-wing organization to emerge after the war, but it was by no means the only one. There was a multitude of small groups, most of them more extremist, such as the *Wandervogel V.B.*, which has already been mentioned, the *Geusen,* who were among the very first to espouse the cause of Adolf Hitler, and the *Adler und Falken,* founded by an aged ultra-*völkisch* writer, Wilhelm Kotzde.[2] Attempts to unite these factions never succeeded for any length of time; they quarrelled about political problems, and accused each other of being 'intellectuals,'

---

[1] Knud Ahlborn called him in his report (in *Freideutsche Jugend*, October 1919, p. 452) a 'typical Prussian gentleman with an impressive appearance, elegant, dashing, with a red face and a harsh jarring voice.' Since gratitude was not among Hitler's outstanding characteristics, Wulle, one of his staunchest precursors, found himself for a while in a German concentration camp. He is reported to have died soon after.

[2] The *Adler und Falken* re-established themselves in 1953 under their old leader Alfred Pudelko as the *Doernberg Bund*. Pudelko had been an adviser on racial questions at the S.S. central office. In 1953 he announced that the new *Bund* was in search of a 'significant middle way for occidental man in fruitful tension between disruptive individualization and the trends towards soulless mass society (*Vermassung*)' (*Das Nachrichtenblatt*, June 1953, p. 11). It was announced at the same time that Kotzde's books too would reappear.

1919—LEFT V. RIGHT

'aesthetes,' and of being too soft towards Jews. To an outside observer all these charges would have seemed unjust.

The emergence of a strong extremist right-wing camp in the youth movement during the First World War was not an isolated phenomenon—it coincided with the general polarization in German politics. The war, and to an even greater extent the immediate post-war years, caused a radicalization both on the Left and on the Right. Among the latter, the official patriotism and national ideology of Wilhelmian Germany was found wanting; state, church and other institutions were thought to be too complaisant, not active and vital enough. During the war the young generation was told by church leaders as well as by hundreds of professors, among whom Scheler, Sombart and Simmel were perhaps the most prominent, that their country had a unique mission in the world, whereas the other nations were systematically denigrated. Similar 'cultural' propaganda went on in France and Britain, but in Germany it fell on much more fertile ground; important spadework had already been done by the Lagardes, Chamberlains and Fritschs. With the German setbacks during the war there was an outcry in these circles against the hidden forces that were alleged to have impeded the German victory—Social Democrats, Pacifists, Freemasons, Jews. The Versailles peace treaty, which was considered unjust, not altogether without reason, by the great majority of Germans, gave an immense advantage to the right-wing extremists. Hundreds of former *Wandervogel* found their way directly from the army into the Free Corps. Most of these joined the Nazi party later on, and such groups as the *Artamans* and the *Adler und Falken* provided many S.S. leaders and officers. None of them attained top rank in the Nazi hierarchy—perhaps their individualism was too marked, after all. The writers who had been the spiritual mentors of the racialist wing of the youth movement (men such as Georg Stammler, Werner Jensen, or Bruno Tanzmann) received some recognition, but were not really considered 'top people,' nor did they reach a much wider public during the Third Reich.[1] Albert Krebs, who rose to be the Nazi chief of Hamburg, managed to quarrel with Hitler and Goebbels and was excluded from the party before 1933. Wilhelm Stapel, also of Hamburg, who edited a pro-Nazi periodical which tried to maintain certain intellectual standards (*Deutsches Volkstum*), also fell foul of Rosenberg and the S.S., and his earlier services to the *völkische* cause and his continued antisemitic propaganda work only just sufficed to keep him out of trouble. Gerhard Rossbach, the commander of a famous Free Corps, had been a very early Nazi stalwart, but after becoming a

[1] There was not much scope for ideologists in the Third Reich—not even of the blood and soil variety. *Vide* Alfred Rosenberg's decline after 1935.

leader of a youth group (*Freischar Schill*) he never found his way back to Hitler's party. Ernst Jünger, another protagonist of the extreme right among the younger generation, and editor of a magazine widely read among them, *Die Kommenden*, did not join the party. Nor did Friedrich Hielscher or K. O. Paetel, another former *Koengener*, who became a political *émigré*.

The number of the extreme right-wingers who ultimately fell out with Hitler, or at any rate did not become militant members of the Nazi movement, is surprisingly large. It would be unjust to disregard this fact, but it is only fair to add that most of their quarrels with the new masters were on secondary issues, not on matters of principle, and that their opposition was frequently (as one of them has put it) 'aesthetical' in character. Their education as a sectarian élite made them revolt against a plebeian mass movement.[1]

[1] The role of the Austrian *Wandervogel* is usually disregarded in this context, despite the fact that (from the very beginning) it was more consistently chauvinistic and racialist than the right wing of the German youth movement, and, according to some evidence, has remained so to this very day. Austria has been a small country since 1918 and the antics of some of Hitler's compatriots have attracted little or no attention.

Twelve
YEARS OF DISILLUSION

I

WHEN the German High Command made its first request for an armistice in early October 1918 most members of the youth movement were still in the army. They were subject to military discipline, and if they had any particular ideas or suggestions concerning the state of the world they were prevented from communicating them to others. But there were other members of the movement who had not been conscripted, or had been invalided out, and they resumed political activities during the final stage of the war.

The first initiative came from Karl Bittel in Esslingen, Württemberg, who early in October published the first number of a political *Rundbrief*, which was soon to gain wide currency. It appeared once and sometimes twice a week, and was to become a unique mirror of the trend towards radicalization among German youth. It began by stressing only the need for political education, and the impossibility in the given circumstances of remaining passive.[1] 'We do not want to make propaganda for any particular party,' it stated on 23 October, 'we merely urge that both domestic and foreign policy ought to be governed by principles of justice.' Information about the organization and activities of the British Fabian Society was given as a model to be copied in Germany. But in November, Knud Ahlborn announced that he had joined the independent left-wing Socialists, and gave the reasons for his decision.[2] On 30 December the *Rundbrief* stated that it was the task of the *Freideutsche* to lead its members 'from bourgeois liberalism through democracy to socialism.' Again, some days later, an appeal was published calling upon every *Freideutsche* to vote socialist; it was signed by Ahlborn, A. Bergsträsser, M. Hasseltblatt, Eduard Heimann, Harald Schultz-Hencke, Rudolf

[1]*Politischer Rundbrief*, 1 and 2, 1918.   [2] *Ibid.*, No. 14.

Carnap, Karl August Wittfogel, and Helmuth Tormin, to mention only a few who were to play an important part in subsequent discussions.[1] The right wing countered with a manifesto of its own, of a diluted nationalism mixed with expressions of support for the socialization of many industries, and even for the League of Nations. The right-wingers had been badly shaken by the revolution and had not yet got into their stride again. They called for support of the candidature of G. Traub, who had been one of the principal speakers on the Hohe Meissner in 1913, and had become a member of the Reichstag during the war. But the Left would not for an instant entertain the idea of supporting an erstwhile liberal who had turned monarchist and pan-German. The right-wing manifesto was signed by Walter Fischer, a former editor of the *Wandervogel*, F. W. Fulda, Albrecht Meyen, and Eberhard König, a writer well known in nationalist circles.

Two camps had thus come into being: the left wing which welcomed the revolution and the right wing which actively opposed it. But soon there were further complications. Bittel, who pursued for a time a 'centrist' socialist line, came under fire from various directions: Eduard Heimann, an economist who knew more about socialism than most of the comrades from the philosophical faculty (who were praising Lenin in the same breath with the anarchists Kropotkin and Gustav Landauer) urged a more realistic approach. Instead of the hysterics of the young Johannes R. Becher, who, like many others (Arnold Bronnen, Max Barthel, *et al.*), was giving a guest performance in the movement,[2] some hard thinking was needed—but where was it to come from?

While such criticism was voiced by the moderate socialists another broadside was fired by the left wing extremists around Kurella, who had already, in January 1919, held up a Communist society as the great ideal of *Freideutsche* youth. In February an open letter to Bittel followed: Karl, are you ready to avow your principles? Are you willing to co-operate in the coming, second German revolution?[3] The Left was involved in a fratricidal struggle. The Spartacists had attempted to overthrow the rule of the Social Democrats by force; and their leaders Luxemburg and Liebknecht had been killed. In the meantime an undeclared war was raging in the East. Frontiers had not yet been exactly defined; the Germans wanted to keep as much as possible of what they considered their own lands, whereas the Poles intended to create as many *faits accomplis* as

[1] *Politischer Rundbrief*, No. 20 (published *c*. 5 January, 1919).
[2] All three flirted with Communism at the time. Becher, after many years in the Soviet Union, became Minister for Cultural Affairs in East Germany.
[3] *Politischer Rundbrief*, No. 22 (16 January, 1919) and 27 (6 February, 1919).

possible prior to any treaty or plebiscite. In these days local self-defence groups were created; they were composed of volunteers, many of them officers or non-commissioned officers of the old army. One Breslau *Wandervogel* lieutenant, Hans Dehmel, called for the establishment of a *Wandervogel* unit to defend the German homeland.[1] Their assignment was 'to defend our homes in Silesia and to liberate the Germans in Poznan province who have already fallen under Polish rule. . . . As soldiers you have perhaps seen what Polish-Russian slovenliness (*Schlamperei*) is like. This is the political action that the *Freideutsche* youth is called upon to take at this time.'[2] There was some response to this call, mainly in east Germany, but Kurella and his Communist friends violently opposed any such initiative and called upon Dehmel to lay down his arms.[3] Silesia was not the only region where some of the *Wandervogel* volunteered again for military service. The leaders of the right wing called upon its members to join the struggle against the Red Army in the Baltic countries. Was there any fight more just, any that could be waged with holier conviction than this fight against Bolshevism? asked Wilhelm Stählin, the theologian and future bishop.

The *Wandervogel* units were dissolved after a few months, but the Free Corps continued to be active for some years in one form or another. They are now usually regarded as precursors of National Socialism, a harsh judgement but one that is not on the whole unjustified. Whether Germany was entitled to defend its borders in the east is a different question; by leaving defence to the right wing extremists, the Socialists committed a major blunder which seemed to make national defence a right-wing monopoly, and ultimately contributed to the downfall of the Weimar Republic.

II

With the revolution a chasm opened in German politics, and violent dissension prevailed between Left and Right in spring 1919. Could unity within the *Freideutsche* camp be maintained in these circumstances? Subsequent events have shown that it could be, but that the price was paralysis. One hundred and fifty members of the movement

---

[1] Dehmel's appeals were published in the youth movement periodicals of the day, and in full in Erich F. Berendt, *Soldaten der Freiheit* (Berlin, 1935), pp. 47–53.

[2] *Ibid.*, pp. 47–50. Dehmel subsequently became one of the leaders of the *Deutsche Freischar* which constituted the democratic wing in the youth movement in the twenties. Dehmel served as a colonel in the German army in the Balkans during the Second World War, was interned in Russian camps for many years, and repatriated only in 1955.

[3] *Politischer Rundbrief*, No. 33 (7 March, 1919).

met at Jena at Easter 1919; this was the first post-war convention, and most of the leading members were present. Everybody was now a socialist, anti-imperialist, and even a pacifist; at Jena, Frank Glatzel's small right-wing group favoured socialism, while the *Wandervogel* Free Corps unit inveighed against the accursed imperialists at Versailles who had been false to their word, and whose devilish crimes were driving the youth of Europe into new and more terrible wars.[1] Friedrich Vorwerk appeared as one of the leading spokesmen of a somewhat unorthodox Communist trend the product of a mood of general despair and pessimism, a nihilistic attitude towards the world in general. Everything would have to be destroyed; then, and only then, could the new constructive work begin. 'Communism will come, whether we want it or not; there remains but one thing for us to do—to go under with this world.' The speech was highly acclaimed, and was followed by the adjournment of the assembly to the local pastry shops where, according to one reliable observer, it displayed remarkably healthy appetites.[2] This was not, perhaps, altogether surprising; these young men had been lucky enough to survive four years of war, and both the apocalyptic visions and the desire to enjoy life were only too natural.

The meeting refrained from dealing with current affairs; instead it devoted its deliberations to ultimate questions of politics, philosophy, and indeed of metaphysics. By what factors should political decisions be affected? Should love or justice be the guiding principle in German politics? These were the portentous issues put before the assembly. One questioner asked whether it was not possible to combine the principle of love (religion) with that of justice (Bolshevism)—would not a religious Bolshevism be the answer to their prayers? After some investigation certain difficulties became apparent, and the idea was regretfully abandoned.

Towards their political foes they were generous to a fault. Already during the war it had been realized that the extreme right wing had only one distinct feature that was truly their own, namely antisemitism; their ideas about agricultural settlements were borrowed. And yet there was strong opposition to any suggestion to exclude them, for the 'pious of the land are needed in the movement too.'[3] The

---

[1] *Führerzeitung*, 6, 1919, p. 96. Similar resolutions were adopted in many German cities. Frank Glatzel subsequently became a member of the *Reichstag*, representing the 'Volkspartei.' After the Second World War he served for a while as mayor of Brunswick.

[2] Elizabeth Busse-Wilson, *Stufen der Jugendbewegung* (Jena, 1925), pp. 39 et seq. See also the Report on the Jena speeches and discussions in *Krieg, Revolution und freideutsche Zukunft* (Hamburg, 1919).

[3] Helmuth Tormin, *Freideutsche Jugend und Politik* (Hamburg, 1918).

Freideutsche did not mind what their members (or opponents) thought so long as the beliefs were sincerely held.

And so it went on. Bittel, who had at last come to heed Kurella's admonition, now supported the Communist line, renouncing his own pet schemes. Establishing settlements had been the right thing to do in quiet times, but in present conditions it was tantamount to shirking the commandment of the hour. Salvation would come only in the wake of world revolution. The settlers, however, were not so easily shaken off: one group in Hesse (under the spiritual guidance of Martin Buber) announced its plans to build collective settlements; and Muck-Lamberty, who was soon to acquire both fame and notoriety throughout Germany, advanced similar plans. Ahlborn, the former right-winger, who had dismissed the *Anfang* in 1914 as a clique of precocious Jew-boys, now welcomed the revolution and declared his solidarity with the proletarian youth movement.

But the radicals demanded more than lip service to the revolution; almost one third of them, headed by Rieniets, a Jena youth leader, and Eckart Petrich, left the convention and established themselves as a new group, one that had already taken its political decision, the 'Entschiedene Jugend.'[1] The rest attempted to work out a credo for *Freideutsche* youth, emblazoning on its banner, as its supreme principles, the 'unchaining of the soul' (*Entfesslung der Seele*) and the 'unfolding of the forces conducive to building the community' (*Entfaltung der gemeinschaftsbildenden Kräfte*). Many curious manifestos were published in the disoriented Germany of 1919 by poets, dentists, and retired postal inspectors, but for sheer lack of meaning the Jena credo was outstanding.

Yet a great chance was missed at Jena. The year before, on Good Friday 1918, all the major youth organizations had decided in principle to join forces with the *Freideutsche* youth, and the way seemed clear to the great *Bund* of German youth. But the Jena meeting, which was to have dealt with the concrete ways and means for accomplishing this merger, failed to come to any clear decision, and left everything in mid-air. All it did was to appoint an *ad hoc* executive to convoke further meetings.

III

'Diseases desperate grown, by desperate appliances are reliev'd or not at all.' Of desperate appliances there was no lack, but like Hamlet the *Freideutsche* could not make up their mind to choose between them. In its early days the youth movement had taken little

[1] Once more no translation can convey the full flavour and meaning of the original. Petrich later became a well-known catholic publicist.

notice of contemporary cultural trends, which was perhaps as well, for that was not really its most urgent requirement. Gradually, however, the demand for a youth culture grew more insistent, even among those who had never accepted Wyneken's specific ideas on the subject. During the First World War the youth movement was exposed to a flood of cultural influences; it had to participate in all the intellectual discoveries, emotional experiences and soul-searchings of the *Freideutsche* students. Hesse, Stefan George, and Carl Spitteler were discovered by or for the youth movement; so were many other poets, writers, and intellectual leaders of the day. The latter were all very sympathetically inclined: Max Weber expressed his confidence in the German youth movement and Max Scheler rejoiced in its 'anti-capitalist mentality.'

But together with these came all the intellectual fashions and fads of the day; and in the atmosphere of crisis they grew more luxuriantly than the healthier influences. In 1917 there was another rediscovery of the wisdom of the East; karma had first been mentioned at the Loreley meeting: soon everybody was talking about Taoism, Zen Buddhism, and *tat tvam asi*, and the *Siddhanta* of the Ramanujas and the *Vishnu-Narayana* were being reprinted. Tagore's gospel of spiritual unity, of 'love, not power,' found enthusiastic disciples. 'Why have we become ripe for the Indian teachings and what is their significance for us?' was the title of a typical article published in those days, when Martin Buber, Rudolf Pannwitz, and other pioneers of the discovery of the Eastern soul had become the intellectual heroes of the day.

What did Chinese philosophy and Indian mysticism mean to the generation of 1918–19? Strictly speaking, nothing at all; but they liked the parables; the fact that these were not at all applicable at a time of political and social crisis to people with an entirely different cultural tradition in the heart of Europe, was a secondary consideration. There was, too, the underlying readiness to believe that not only Germany but the West as a whole had failed—Spengler's *Decline of the West* was published in 1918, and widely discussed in the youth movement—and an awareness of the need for new, radically different ideas. Holzapfel's 'Panideism' enjoyed a brief popularity, and for some time Rudolf Steiner's school of anthroposophy gained a considerable influence in the youth movement.

The mystical streak was not of course restricted to the Left. Naturally, the right-wingers were not ready to take the law from Asiatic avatars of doubtful racial origin; they preferred to rediscover the medieval German mystics, Meister Eckhart, Henry Suso, and the rest. There was one young artisan, Friedrich Muck-Lamberty, who thought that since the urge for a new message was so strong he too would try to do something about it. With twenty-five young companions he went from town to town in Thuringia calling the population to contemplation, urging them to wake up to life, to combat the decay of society, and to be gay. How was all this to be accomplished? By dancing, singing, and lectures on the Revolution in the Soul. His followers, like the early Christians, shared all their worldly possessions, and were vegetarians and abstainers. Muck-Lamberty's favourite word was 'swinging'; 'things were swinging if a community was united in peace and joy.'[1]

Wherever the barefooted or sandalled *'Neue Schar'* (as Muck-Lamberty's group was called) made its appearance, thousands joined in its meetings and dances, there was a triumphal procession, and the clergy had to open the churches for Muck's lectures and community-singing. Nothing like it had been seen in Germany since the days of the Anabaptists; it seemed that the millennium was about to dawn and the New Jerusalem was close at hand.

The trade unionists, the students, and the intellectuals had grave suspicions about Muck; some called him a class enemy, others thought he was a foreign agent. But his appeal was not directed to them. It was all very innocent and touching, and might even have ended well but for some disclosures about Muck's somewhat unconventional relationships with the girls of his group.[2] He regarded it as his duty to 'redeem' any girl or woman in need; but his sincere explanations upon this point did not satisfy his critics. Supposing that a girl had been redeemed once, who would redeem her the second time if the redeemer happened to be engaged elsewhere? Muck was not ready to cope with such sophisms, and the authorities took a censorious view of his conduct. This was in the Germany of 1920, where such mental corybantics were by no means unique; it was the heyday of Dada and occultism, when all kinds of curious sects spread and prophets of the most fantastic causes found a ready response. The antics of certain members of the youth movement can be rightly viewed only against the background of an old order that had been destroyed, of uncertainties and fears pervading every walk of life. Nor were all their discussions restricted to the wisdom of the East or their activities to dancing in the market squares of Jena and Erfurt. There were debates on a fairly high level on such subjects as socialism which are of interest to this day. Many, perhaps most of the *Freideutsche* believed with Karl Korsch, that capitalism was at its last

[1] See Adam Ritzhaupt, *Die Neue Schar in Thüringen* (Jena, 1921), pp. 35–6.

[2] After this, Muck was of course finished as far as the youth movement was concerned, despite the defence of some of his well-wishers who believed in the purity of his motives. He established a wood-carvers' workshop, and is still at work in a small West German village.

gasp and that scientific socialism had become a practical necessity.¹ Alexander Rüstow, then a radical socialist, called capitalism the real enemy of the youth movement; only the overthrow of *laissez-faire* liberalism would make it possible to realize the ideals of the movement. In a bourgeois world the *Freideutsche* could have but one aim—to serve the revolution.² Karl August Wittfogel believed in the victory of the proletariat, and urged that the duty of the best forces among the younger bourgeois was to transmit the cultural treasures of the past to the class which was destined to establish the classless society.³ Paul Tillich thought that socialism and Christianity would become one in a new world order; that nobody could yet know exactly where the two would meet, or whether the official representatives of both streams of thought would still be present when they did.⁴ Eduard Heimann, also a future leader of religious socialism, did not think it necessary to join a proletarian party in order to take part in the struggle for a socialist world, but suggested that the *Freideutsche* should regard socialist education as their main assignment.⁵ Some pondered the implications of historical materialism, while the right-wingers denounced Marxism *in toto*: Marxism had led us into the disaster, they said, only socialism could lead us out of it.⁶ Spengler was soon to provide further ideological ammunition in his *Prussian Socialism*, and Moeller van den Bruck was to show that the Aryan Engels had been a better man than the Jew Marx.

IV

'Ye cannot serve God and mammon,' it is said, and 'the love of money is the root of all evil.' Some of the members of the *Freideutsche* youth, strongly moved by both religious and socialist impulses, thought that endless debates about the politics of the youth movement would lead nowhere, and that it was the business of the individual to make his choice then and there how to live in a sinful world. Those who were of this opinion banded together to settle on the land, sharing all their earthly belongings like the early Christians. *Neuwerk* was the name of this group, whose members were strongly influenced by the theological views of Karl Barth and, to a certain extent, by those of Paul Tillich. Their socialism did not fit in with that of any existing party or movement, for they rejected all ideol-

---

¹ *Die Tat*, January 1920, p. 740.
² *Freideutsche Jugend*, 5/6, 1920, p. 196.
³ *Ibid.*, p. 209. Both Rüstow and Wittfogel, as readers of their books will know, subsequently moved far from what they probably now regard as a youthful aberration.
⁴ *Ibid.*, p. 170.   ⁵ *Ibid.*, p. 166.
⁶ *Jungdeutsche Stimmen*, 1919, pp. 38–9.

ogies and theories and set out to realize social justice practically, in their own lives. They criticized the established churches for not adopting the struggle of the working class as their own cause, for not being radical enough, and for condoning the iniquities of the world as it was.[1]

Members of this group established two settlements, the Habertshof in Hesse and the Bruderhof in the Rhön. The Habertshof survived until 1934, when the government made its further existence impossible; but even before that, most of its initial enthusiasm had been spent and much of its early communist practice had been discarded. In the Bruderhof, however, the moving spirit was a remarkable man, Eberhard Arnold. He realized at an early date that the impetus carried over from the youth movement might not last, and that the group would need the experience and support of similar religious-socialist settlements if it was to hold out in its fight against the root of all evil—the love of money and property—which had found its supreme expression in the capitalist world. After careful investigation Arnold and his comrades decided to affiliate to the movement of the Hutterite settlements in America.

The story of the Bruderhof community is a remarkable epic of the power of faith prevailing over all adversities. From a small group of seven pioneers their number has grown to over a thousand. After Hitler came to power they were compelled to leave Germany and had to start anew on a Wiltshire farm in England. When German nationals were interned in England during the Second World War, the Bruderhof had to move again—this time to Paraguay, the only country that was willing to accept them. Inspired by the example of these founder-members, three more flourishing communities had come into existence (in Shropshire, England, in the State of New York, and in Uruguay); in the middle fifties part of the Paraguayan community decided to return to Germany and to continue their work in the old homeland.[2]

Like the Kibbutzim in Israel, the Bruderhof, while of course undergoing important modifications in their scope and structure since the early days, have successfully resisted any major concession to private property. The attitude of the members of the youth movement (and indeed of everyone who has come into contact with members of the Bruderhof) has been one of respect and admiration mixed with a disbelief in the relevance of this experiment to the modern world. The original intention of the founders of 'Neuwerk' had been not only to live an exemplary life but to provide a working

[1] *Neuwerk*, 1922–24, *passim*.
[2] For the history of the group see Hans Blöcker, 'Dreimal Neuaufbau in zehn Jahren', in *Der Pflug*, 1, 1953 (Bromdon, Bridgnorth, England).

model for others as well. But how could a whole people resettle in small communities of peasants and artisans?[1] What practical lesson was to be learned from the Bruderhof experiment for a modern industrial society? Be that as it may, of the many collective settlements established by members of the youth movement in the early twenties, the Bruderhof is almost the only one to have survived. The only other such experiment that has been a partial success is the settlement of Schwarzerden in the Rhön, founded by a group of young women of whom Maria Buchhold, a prominent member of the *Freideutsche* youth, is the best known. This settlement, too, was still in existence in the middle fifties, but has greatly changed in its internal structure, and is now mainly known as a centre for training physical instructors and the seat of a well-known children's home.[2]

All the other enterprises of this kind undertaken by various political, religious, and social groups from within the youth movement failed long ago. Once the youthful idealism had been spent, there was no material inducement strong enough to hold these communities together. Only extreme situations or profound beliefs could provide the enduring bond essential for their survival.

[1] See, for instance, Victor Engelhardt, *Die deutsche Jugendbewegung als kulturhistorisches Phänomen* (Berlin, 1923), p. 86, written soon after the foundation of the Bruderhof.

[2] Manfred Fuchs, *Probleme des Wirtschaftsstils von Lebensgemeinschaften* (Göttingen, 1957), pp. 49–51. This dissertation gives a fairly detailed account of the subsequent fate of most of the settlements sponsored by members of the youth movement in the nineteen-twenties.

Thirteen

THE END OF THE BEGINNING

I

NOT everyone had welcomed the revolution; many withdrew into evasive attitudes and some were actively hostile. 'The fox has been set to keep the geese,' said one of the critics, 'the illiterate is now made minister of education, the anarchist is appointed chief of police, and the Jew—a German statesman.'[1] Those who held such opinions watched the leftward development of the *Freideutsche* with growing dismay. Some charged it with 'permanent high treason,'[2] others were altogether sceptical about the unending and fruitless discussions: 'Just look at those *Freideutsche* leaders and their intellectual leap-frogging from Dostoevsky to Chuang-tse, Count Keyserling, Spengler, Buddha, Jesus, Landauer, Lenin, and whichever literary Jew happens to be fashionable at the moment. Of their own substance they have little or nothing.'[3]

This was harsh criticism, though not altogether unjustified. But what did the right-wing leaders have of their own? They knew well enough what they disliked, but the moment they tried to develop some coherent ideas about their own aims they found the going heavy. Elsewhere, it might have been argued that the right, in contrast to the left, is non-ideological by nature and can do very well without an intellectual programme. Not so, however, in Germany, where right-wing groups too can hardly keep their self-respect without a well-defined *Weltanschauung*.

The *Jungdeutsche Bund* had been founded in 1919 as the leading organization of the right, in opposition to the *Freideutsche*. But from the beginning this new movement was beset by difficulties startlingly similar to those facing their rivals on the left. They could not find a

[1] 2. *Führer Rundbrief*, 1, 1919 (Edited by Frank Glatzel).
[2] Manifesto of the 'Wandervogel V.B.', in *Wandervogel* 7, 1919.
[3] Wilhelm Stapel, in *Deutsches Volkstum*, 11, 1920.

political party that was altogether to their liking. Early in 1919 Frank Glatzel had advised his comrades to vote for the German Nationalist Party, for, as he said, this party was headed by a new set of people who had nothing to do with the traditional right, but were both nationalist and socialist. It was soon evident, however, that the new Nationalist leaders were not so new after all, and that none of them took their socialist phraseology very seriously. More and more of Glatzel's comrades therefore opposed any link with them. They were looking for a socialism that was not Marxist in inspiration, but founded on a moral-religious basis. The *völkische* ideology that they wanted was to be neither right-wing nor bourgeois, but something above parties and classes; the supreme ideal was the community of the whole people, the *Volksgemeinschaft*. The ideas of the late Otger Gräff, however, were too extremist for them; his views were rejected as too primitive by the theologians and the men of the world who were now prominent in the leadership of the *Jungdeutsche*. Some even denounced imperialism and said that antisemitism ought not to be the central plank in their platform. *Völkisch* was the great slogan of the day, but what did that mean if, according to Glatzel, the struggle against the foreigner and on the frontier was not to be the main thing, and if even a Social Democrat could be *völkisch*?[1]

Endless discussion ensued; Stählin and Stapel, Gerber and Glatzel, and many others talked about the tasks of the new *Bund*, and in Austria Karl Ursin, who in later years was to play an important part in the right wing of the German youth movement, tried to get support for an attempt to unite all those in favour of *Grossdeutschland*. But this was all rather nebulous; the right in those days was divided into as many sects as the left; some wanted to keep out of politics while others pressed for political activity, and these in their turn were split into half a dozen different factions. Karl Fischer, the leader of the early *Wandervogel*, had returned from a prisoner-of-war camp in China, and found himself in sympathy with this movement, but he had been away for too long and could not find a common language with the younger generation.[2] After three years, all the plans for a great nationalist youth movement had to be shelved; various factions seceded, and there remained only a group of men of the older generation who formed a loose association that was to meet from time to time for exchanges of opinion. The plans for the mobilization of German youth had failed on the right no less completely than on the left.

[1] *Führerzeitung*, 9–10, 191 9, p. 159, and *Jungdeutsche Stimmen*, 1919–20, *passim*.
[2] With Karl Ursin, Heinz Dähnhardt, and Frank Glatzel, he edited the *Neue Bund* for two years.

II

Meanwhile, on the extreme left, among those whose very name—*Entschiedene Jugend*—signified that their decision had already been taken, there was much heart-searching as to what exactly the 'class struggle of youth' was in practice to mean. Dr Wyneken had been given a key position in Berlin by Konrad Hänisch, the new Social Democratic Minister for cultural affairs. Wyneken's main aim was to carry out long overdue reforms in the school system; and as a first step he wanted all pupils from about the age of fourteen to share in the responsibility for the management of all institutions of higher learning. In a special manifesto, written by Wyneken himself, the Minister called upon youth to hold elections and establish students' councils (Soviets of sorts) which were to be instrumental in introducing a new spirit into the German school.[1] A new German school should arise out of the ruins of the old—free of the traditional submissiveness, mutual distrust and mendacity. Such language had never hitherto been heard, nor had a minister ever turned directly to the younger generation. This was a commendable but highly unrealistic project; whether any such scheme of student co-responsibility would have worked anywhere outside such institutions for the training of an élite as Wyneken's own Wickersdorf was an open question. But it was obvious from the very beginning that the German teachers would refuse to co-operate in a project that was diametrically opposed to all their ideas about the aims and methods of education.

Worse still, the great majority of the young people themselves were either indifferent or actively hostile. Elections such as the Minister suggested took place in a few cities, and in many of them the great majority abstained from voting.[2] Some youth leaders of the right said they refused to believe they had been living in an atmosphere of subjugation and fear, and they rejected the reforms which they said would poison relations between teacher and pupil.[3] Wyneken's reforms were unacceptable to all believers in a strong authority; which meant, of course, to the great majority in Germany. Nor did Wyneken receive the support he had hoped for from his liberal and socialist colleagues; after a few weeks he had to resign. The few who wanted to continue the 'class struggle of youth' met together at Jena in August 1919, and established a Central Committee 'to lead the struggle of liberation of bourgeois youth in school and public life.' It included a number of former youth leaders such as

---

[1] The text of the appeal is in *Wandervogel*, 2–3, 1919, pp. 94–6.
[2] See, for instance *Der neue Anfang*, 9–10, 1919, pp. 173–5.
[3] Albert Herhahn, *Wandervogel*, 4, 1919, p. 122.

Willi Kelber and Carl Rieniets, as well as a number of left-wing teachers such as Alexander Schwab and Paul Reiner.[1]

The Jena conference listened to an impassioned appeal by Hermann Schüller to continue the revolution which had begun in November, but had remained unfinished. The *Freideutsche* were bitterly criticized for their Hamlet-like indecision; it was said, not quite unjustly, that they thought the metaphysics of their own souls of more importance than the liberation of youth.[2] The participants were in sympathy with the Communist movement, but the Communist movement was by no means identical in their eyes with the German Communist party. Most of them were unwilling to adopt the party line on all questions, and on this issue discussions were destined to go on for almost two years. The youth movement revolutionaries differed from the Communists on two essential points. The struggle for socialism, they said, would one day be over, but the struggle of youth against age (or rather against the non-youthful spirit) would go on for ever. Communism, the just redistribution of property, would not in itself bring about the liberation of youth. To both Communists and 'bourgeois' critics these ideas were no more than intellectual constructions; youth was not a class and had no class consciousness. But such criticism did not at first deter the youth movement revolutionaries who deplored the narrow preoccupation of proletarian youth with current political problems, which, together with its lack of education, prevented them from realizing that there were grave problems beyond these immediate questions of the day.

There were other bones of contention, such as the old quarrel about whether the end could justify the means. The Communist youth was, of course, in favour of armed insurrection, and generally speaking, of the use of force to establish a dictatorship of the proletariat. Many youth movement revolutionaries, on the other hand, were pacifists, and thought that nothing good could come out of insurrection or from coercion in general, however idealistic the intention. Besides these questions of principle, there were technical difficulties that made a merger with proletarian youth difficult. At its conference in February 1919, the leading left-wing organization, the 'Free Socialist youth,' had wholeheartedly supported the policy of the Communist party and attacked the majority Socialists, as well as the left-wing Independent Socialists. But at the next conference, in October 1919 in Weimar, they were divided, and only a part continued to follow the lead of the Communists. Nor did the Communist youth really want to co-operate with people who, they

---

[1] On the Jena meeting see *Der neue Anfang*, 16 and 17, 1919.
[2] There is an abridged version of Schüller's speech in *Freideutsche Jugend*, 12, 1919, pp. 538–41.

said, were likely to corrupt the young proletarian fighters with their bourgeois ideas about humanism and pacifism. Some of the more moderate left-wingers reacted by stressing the need to retain their freedom of action; an attitude of blind reverence and obedience towards the proletarian youth was not called for; there were certain fields in which the radical bourgeois youth were superior to their proletarian comrades, who had not enjoyed the benefits of a higher education. The *Entschiedene Jugend* went on discussing their great moral problems; some talked about historical materialism, others of the necessity of a child crusade and 'breaking out of our isolation.' Some of the radicals had already moved towards full acceptance of the Communist creed: Alfred Kurella, imprisoned for a short period while on a mission to Willi Münzenberg, head of the Communist Youth International, had already represented German Communist youth at meetings in Vienna and Moscow. The other left-wingers too were moving in the same direction, though at a slower pace. After their convention at Essen in December 1920, they declared that they were no longer a youth movement in the old sense, and that as the result of their co-operation with the proletariat, they had 'found their way to reality.' The next logical step was to join the Communists,[1] which they did in 1921.

Few of them remained in the Communist camp for long. Those who did continued to criticize the bourgeois youth movement for its pacifist illusions and its social and political isolation. 'You will make yourselves utterly and irrevocably ridiculous if you go on remaining *Landsknechte*,' Alfred Kurella wrote in August 1923.[2] But this was criticism from the outside, and his old comrades took no notice.

III

If the Jena convention in 1919 had been a serious setback for the *Freideutsche*, that which followed it in 1920 was a tragicomedy that quashed all hopes for the future of their movement as the great *Bund* of German youth.[3] The convention opened on a Sunday evening in September in the small town of Hofgeismar in Hesse, with a proposal to establish a 'united front of youth.' The Communists present at once protested, arguing that only the revolutionary class struggle could put an end to the crisis. On the following day the discussion really got under way, the chief topics being Russia and Socialism, on which two eminent experts had been invited to address

[1] *Politischer Rundbrief*, 61–2, 1920.   [2] *Ibid.*, 63–4.
[3] The account that follows is based on Wilhelm Ehmer (ed.), *Hofgeismar, Ein politischer Versuch in der Jugendbewegung* (Jena, 1920), and on the articles in *Freideutsche Jugend*, 2, 1921, and *Die Tat* (December 1920) (H. Schultz-Hencke) and January 1921 (Elisabeth Busse-Wilson).

the assembly and to open the debate. Unfortunately, the two guests were more interested in Dostoevsky and the Russian soul than in Marxism and Soviet realities, and the Communists did not find it difficult to prove that such lectures were not the ideal opening for a 'political seminar' and that such an approach to political problems was impractical. They also complained that they had not received the representation due to them in the steering committee. After he had threatened to withdraw, Bittel, their leader, was asked to act temporarily as president of the convention.

Tuesday saw a protracted duel between Harald Schultz-Hencke, who spoke in the name of the non-Communist majority, and Heinrich Süsskind, who represented the Communists. Schultz-Hencke, the future psychiatrist, was a clever though somewhat evasive debater, but no match for his Marxist opponent; for, like most of the *Freideutsche*, he had never been taught to think in political categories. He made great concessions to his opponent but could not be moved to draw the obvious conclusions from his own admissions. Schultz-Hencke was for the dictatorship of the proletariat—in principle. But in practice he was against it because 'the sacrifices that would have to be made would probably bear no relation to the possible achievements of such a dictatorship.'[1] He admitted that Germany's economic and social situation was hopeless, but he preferred to wait and see rather than accept the remedies proposed by the Communists. This shilly-shallying made a bad impression on many of those present, and it was somewhat embarrassing, according to one witness, to see how completely unable the majority of the *Freideutsche* were to cope with the 'scientific arguments' of comrade Heinrich the historical materialist. Forthright comments were made only by the few right-wingers present—Max Bondy, for instance, who said that he disagreed with the Communists about almost everything, and that, if there must be a dictatorship, it had better be a dictatorship of the intelligentsia than of the proletariat. The Communists called him an honest reactionary; they were much more bitter about the lukewarm majority, those who wanted to be 'pink rather than red or white.' Did not the *Freideutsche* realize that their movement had become a 'morass,' that world historical events were bypassing them?[2] Did they not understand that there were but two forces at work, revolution and counter-revolution, and everything in between was bound to perish?

There were declarations and counter declarations, resignations and negotiations to restore unity, but in the intervals the old songs were sung, as well as some new ones about red flags and the proletarian revolution. The Communists accused the majority of having betrayed

[1] Ehmer, *op. cit.*, p. 41. [2] *Freideutsche Jugend*, 2, 1921, p. 59.

the ideals of the Hohe Meissner, and above all that of sincerity, while the majority said that the Communists had forgotten everything about the *Freideutsche* spirit. There were some guests present from England, pacifists and Christian socialists. Miss Parson pressed everybody's hand and talked about the power of all-embracing love. Others walked up and down in the nearby park like so many peripatetic pupils in a Socratic academy, and announced that they liked each other and that no offence was meant. On the last two days there were some more exchanges, but then the time was over and everybody had to return home.

Hofgeismar made abundantly clear what ought to have been obvious before, that the majority of the *Freideutsche* had no intention of joining the revolution (or, more precisely, the Communist party), which was just what the minority did want. The difference could not be glossed over, nor could one side hope to convince the other. In these circumstances a split had become inevitable, whatever attempts were made to postpone it.

The subsequent history of the *Freideutsche* can be related very briefly: after Hofgeismar the movement faded away. Its publications continued to appear for some months, and Knud Ahlborn and Ferdinand Göbel founded in 1922 a *Freideutsche Bund* to carry on the old tradition. It was not a success, and the attempt to hold a second Hohe Meissner in August 1923 was a failure too, although some of the groups into which the youth movement had split sent their representatives. The Communists appeared and did their best to break up the meeting, which was probably doomed in any case. By the end of 1923 the *Freideutsche* youth had ceased to exist. There remained little groups of people dispersed throughout Germany; a few continued to take an interest in the new youth movement that developed in the early twenties. Others retired into private life and into what were destined, in some cases, to become very distinguished professional careers. A few established schools and settlements still continue in the spirit of the *Freideutsche*; probably the best known of these is Klappholttal, on the island of Sylt in the North Sea.[1]

IV

In 1919 the *Wandervogel* too was in a bad way. Those who went to Jena and Hofgeismar to discuss politics and culture were only a

[1] It continues to this day as a holiday camp for children and an adult education centre; the courses range from Taoism to the history of the youth movement, and include an introduction to depth psychology. The settlement, managed by Knud Ahlborn and Ferdinand Göbel, also houses the archives of the *Freideutsche Jugend*. In 1960 Dr. Ahlborn, who had helped to organize the Hohe Meissner meeting in 1913 at the age of 72, still took charge of morning callisthenics.

minority, albeit a vocal and influential one. The younger members were not concerned in these debates, and most of the ex-soldiers wanted only to return to the golden days of the pre-war *Wandervogel*, when there were no intellectual disputes and nobody debated the great problems of the age. They were not going to commit the same mistake as the *Freideutsche*: they were determined to keep politics out of the youth movement. It soon appeared, however, that this was more easily said than done. Three thousand came to the great reunion in Coburg in 1919, the first to be convened after the war. Here they had the great joy of meeting old comrades again after several years; but old acquaintance alone could not save the *Bund*—far too many problems had accumulated during the war years. When a socialist group hoisted the red flag, the right-wingers immediately had it pulled down. If there had been none but political differences, the movement might have survived, but there were many other troubles, such as the demand for the separation of the sexes (some would have excluded girls altogether), and for a membership age limit, which would have meant the exclusion of all the older members. Willi Kelber and Rudolf Mehnert, who headed the strong Central German regional organization, were among the leaders of this faction. Neuendorff, the head of the *Wandervogel* from pre-war days, succeeded in maintaining unity for a while by compromise, but there were basic differences which no amount of skilful diplomacy could overcome. A few months after Coburg, Neuendorff and the other oldtimers had to resign. But the new leaders were no more successful: Mehnert was drowned during a trip to Scandinavia, and Kelber did not find the response he had hoped for. District leaders carried on, like the diadochi after the death of a monarch; occasionally two or more district leaders would co-operate to perform certain tasks, but strong central leadership had ceased to exist, and in many places chaotic conditions prevailed.

The *Jungwandervogel*—that small and somewhat exclusive group—was in a rather more fortunate position; it had kept aloof from the great merger in 1914, and was therefore less affected by the post-war crisis. The *Altwandervogel*, on the other hand, although drawn into the merger, had somehow managed to preserve its cohesion within the united *Bund*. After the war it found an able leader in Ernst Buske, who decided to carry out drastic reforms. Every member over the age of twenty had to leave, unless a group of youngsters wanted him as its leader or in some other capacity. In 1920, the older members established their own organization, the *Kronacher Bund*, which was to provide a new framework for activities that were as yet ill-defined, but were to include, among other things, mutual professional help and advice, as well as economic co-operation if feasible.

Thus the period from 1919 until the middle twenties was an interval mainly of discord, drift, and indecision. Some said that a youth movement was no longer needed, and that attempts to revive it artificially, by activity for activity's sake, were ridiculous as well as ineffectual.[1] Yet even in those years of chaos, group life went on, and new movements were born, though these were small, and many of only short duration; indeed, it was during that time of seemingly moribund existence that the first beginnings of a new style and a new content became apparent. The *Wandervogel* phase, the first period of the youth movement, had indeed come to an end, but the second era, that of the *Bund*, was about to begin.

The *Wandervogel* had been a movement of reform and protest, but the society it hoped to reform and against which it protested—that of Wilhelmian Germany—had been swept away by war. Just as the *Wandervogel* would have been unthinkable fifty years before it appeared, so it was itself out-of-date in the post-war Germany of inflation and permanent political crisis. The old romanticism, the songs with lute accompaniment, the mixed groups—in fact everything in the old *Wandervogel* spirit—seemed totally out of place in this new Germany. It would be difficult to define the new spirit; perhaps it was most clearly exemplified at the mass meeting in the Fichtel mountains, yet another unsuccessful attempt to weld together the various sections of the movement. Some groups turned up in what German military language calls 'Sauhaufen,' the leisurely and disorderly manner in which the old *Wandervogel* ramblers went on their outings. But others, and these were already the majority, marched in with the regular step of disciplined military columns. It was a small but highly revealing incident: the individualistic ('civilian') period of the movement was clearly drawing to a close.

[1] Karl Wilker. 'Anfang oder Ende,' in *Die Tat*, May 1922.

PART FOUR

PART FOUR

Fourteen

THE 'WHITE KNIGHT'

I

FOR A long time the Boy Scouts had been regarded as the poor relations of the youth movement: led by adults, and specializing as they did in para-military education, they were somewhere on the periphery, outside the main stream of the movement. In contrast to the *Wandervogel*, the Scouts were not strictly selective in the recruitment of their members.

After the war the Scouts underwent a minor revolution analogous to that which occurred elsewhere in the movement; the adult leaders were deposed and younger members took over. But, unlike what happened in the *Wandervogel*, their revolution did not stop there. New forms of activity and new ideas were developed which were to have a decisive influence upon the whole German youth movement and, in effect, to shape the whole course of its development between 1919 and 1933.

At their first post-war meeting in Schloss Prunn there were discussions very much like those that went on among the *Freideutsche* and the *Wandervogel:* should the Scouts become the organization of an élite, or should they on the contrary try not to lose contact with the masses? Was a nationalist orientation to prevail, or should internationalist views be given wider currency? What about the place of religion in the life of the *Bund*?

Deliberations went on for some time, and in 1920 the reformers seceded and founded their own group, the *Neupfadfinder*, led by the so-called 'Regensburg circle' (F. L. Habbel, Ludwig Voggenreiter and others) and a young parson from Berlin, Martin Voelkel. The Regensburg leaders were down to earth, mainly interested in education, and they provided some new ideas about 'tribal education'— the tribe (Stamm) was to replace the group as the basic unit. Voelkel, the ideologist, provided the notions of the 'Reich,' the 'knight,' and the 'holy grail,' with their specific meaning for the young. But at the very centre was the idea, and the reality, of the *Bund*. The former scouts found their way into the youth movement; it could be said that they took it over during an interregnum, and under their influence it was to change its character.

In its second, *bündische* phase the youth movement became much more ambitious. The very name suggested a new trend. Whereas rambling had been the central activity before the First World War, in the new era it became only one of several activities, and not necessarily the most important. The *Wandervogel* had been critical of society, but had never assumed that it had a mission to change the world. This was just what the *Bünde* tried to do; it was a romantic attempt to cope with realities. In the *Wandervogel* the group had been a comparatively loose association; the emphasis had been on the individual and his own development; there had been no specific plans for the future of its members, who were expected gradually to grow out of the youth movement. People belonged to a group because they liked it, there was little reflection and no sense of a purpose beyond this activity. But in the *Bund* created by Voelkel and his friends the collective mattered more than the individual; there was stricter discipline, and it was envisaged as an all-embracing bond making total demands upon the individual[1] for the rest of his life. One belonged to a group to serve a cause, and under the surface of all its activities there were magic formulas, or implied hints pointing to the cause itself. After an initial struggle girls had entered the *Wandervogel*, and although all its leading figures were male, it is impossible to think of the *Wandervogel* as exclusively a boys' movement. The *Bund*, on the other hand, had no mixed groups; it was a male society *par excellence*. Illogically enough, many of the *Bünde* included separate girls' groups, but these were merely subsidiaries and played no great part in the movement; there was too much talk about fighting, struggle, and battle, and it was difficult to imagine a female knight. Generally speaking the lyric romanticism of the *Wandervogel* had been replaced by something tougher—a romanticism that had been decisively affected by the First World War. Freedom and unrestraint had been sacrificed to duty and service in voluntary subjection to a greater whole. Whereas the ideal figure of the *Wandervogel* had been the itinerant scholar, an anarchist if not a democrat, the aristocratic tendencies of the *Bünde* were reflected, not only in the exemplary image of the knight who sets himself a

---

[1] Including, according to their draft constitution, the duty to obtain the leadership's consent to marry. The constitution remained a dead letter.

rule of conduct in deliberate contrast to that of the multitude, but also in a strict hierarchy within the *Bund*.[1]

The *Bund* came into being as the result of some collective experience and emotion; its ideas, however important, came only later. What then was the *Bund*, and how did it come into existence?

II

The *Bund* as a social phenomenon intrigued some historians and sociologists for many years,[2] but the central impulse as far as the youth movement was concerned undoubtedly came from Stefan George and his circle, who had developed the concept in their publications even before the appearance of the 'Star of the Covenant' (*Der Stern des Bundes*) in 1914. The George group was in effect a *Bund*, a closed circle that purported to have a meaning in itself, disregarded the outside world, and despised the vile and disorderly multitude with its banal beliefs in equality and progress. It has been said that the entire younger generation of Germany was decisively influenced by George, 'whether or not they had ever heard his name or read a single line he had written.'[3] It is certainly true that George had a considerable influence, but it operated in width rather than in depth.

His style was imitated, and a few quotations were repeated often enough—phrases about he who once has circled the flame and who forever will follow the flame; about the need for a new nobility whose warrant no longer derives from crown or escutcheon; about the Führer with his *völkische* banner who will lead his followers to the future Reich through storm and grisly portents, and so forth. George's Reich, however, was not of this world: his *Bund* was a little group of friends devoted to the cult of certain rituals and aesthetic forms. What attracted the youth movement was the aristocratic element in all this idealism and its disdain for 'arid rationalism.' But these were already prevailing intellectual fashions: George may well have helped to popularize, he certainly did not initiate

[1] These observations refer mainly to the first heralds of the *Bund*, the *Neupfadfinder*. There was a variety of form and content throughout the youth movement, and a more realistic approach generally prevailed in the late twenties, but there was hardly a single group that was not affected to some extent by early *bündische* ideology,

[2] Cf. Hermann Schmalenbach: 'Die soziologische Kategorie des Bundes,' in *Die Dioskuren*, I (Munich 1922). Helmuth Kittel refers to the (unpublished) research of Prof. Eduard Hahn, which according to his evidence was of great importance in shaping the attitude of the 'Neupfadfinder' (*Das Junge Deutschland*, 12, 1929, p. 509).

[3] Hans Naumann, *Die deutsche Dichtung der Gegenwart* (Stuttgart, 1933), p. 398.

them. His work provided the *Bund* with certain symbols, but nothing was more remote from his intention than to gain or guide a mass following. Some of his disciples regarded their master as the uncrowned king of Germany and thought that he wielded magical powers; they had a rude awakening when their world of fancy clashed with the grim realities of the early thirties.

There were countless differences between George's notion of the *Bund* and that of the youth movement, as it was formulated by Martin Voelkel. According to Voelkel the *Bund* had been engraved in the German soul since time immemorial—it might have had something to do with the Nordic skies or the grey winter twilight. The youth movement was therefore to be found only among Germanic peoples of Nordic blood; 'wherever German blood coursed was the heroes' homeland.'[1] But Stefan George, a son of the Catholic Rhineland, was free of North German mysticism and had no use at all for grey winter skies; Hellas and Rome were his great models.[2] The aristocracy in George's poetry was not one of race, and this was one reason why George was regarded as an anti-*völkische* influence by some of the more radical thinkers of the Third Reich.[3] The distrust of him in these circles was perhaps not altogether misplaced; when Count Klaus Stauffenberg was arrested after the attempt to assassinate Hitler in July 1944, a ring was found on him which bore the inscription 'Finis initium.'[4]

George died in 1933, the very year the *Bünde* were dissolved. Fourteen years later some of the former members of the youth movement met again in Altenberg Monastery to discuss some of the lessons of the past. One said that the esoteric secrets had gained daemonic power because they were surrendered to the mass and fell into the hands of demagogues.[5] It was a very unsatisfactory explanation of what had really happened.

III

It is a far cry from Stefan George, the aristocratic, inaccessible poet, to 'White Fox' (John Hargrave) in Kings Langley, Hertfordshire; but these were the two main formative influences on the

---

[1] *Hie Ritter und Reich*, passim.

[2] In later years there was one small Bund, the *Südlegion*, which accepted George's 'Southern orientation.' See Kurd Lahn, *Von der geistigen Heimat deutscher Jugend* (Plauen, 1933).

[3] Max Nitzsche, *Bund and Staat* (Würzburg, 1942), a detailed attack on the George circle and the *bündische* ideology of the youth movement.

[4] The title of a famous George poem. Klaus Stauffenberg and his brother belonged for a while to the outer fringe of the George circle.

[5] *Freideutscher Rundbrief*, 1, 1947, p. 9.

Bünde in the twenties. Hargrave had been commissioner for camping and woodcraft in the British Scouts movement, but seceded in 1920 to form 'Kibbo Kift, the Woodcraft Kindred.'[1] His aims were the development of camp training to 'inculcate pride of body, mental poise and vital spiritual perception,' the encouragement of handicraft training and craft guilds, and also the initiation of a social movement for grassroots democracy, economic reform, and world peace. Hargrave did not have much success in England; 'Of course, it won't work: not quite flesh and blood,' wrote D. H. Lawrence.[2] But in Germany the ideas of tribal education elaborated in *Kibbo Kift* and other books fell on more fertile ground; they taught their readers not only how to build wigwams, make tom-toms, and read a trail, but something of the mental disciplines of solitude and meditation, as well as obedience to the head of the *Bund*. It was yet another protest against the big city, a more ambitious and systematic attempt to escape from modern industrial society and its evils. The infusion of American-Indian motifs and patterns enhanced its attractiveness in a country where many popular writers had produced romances about life in the wide open spaces of the Wild West, and the marvellous exploits of its strong, silent heroes.

Hargrave's imagination was however restrained, at least during those early years, by certain commonsense notions about education. He realized that school could not and would not give what the boys' group provided, and that the romanticism of 'young Indian warriors taking to the woods' corresponded to a deep urge among boys of thirteen to fifteen to detach themselves from the world of imposed authority.

Some of Hargrave's ideas and methods became part and parcel of the realm of ideas of the German youth movement, although it was later discarded when a wave of 'new practicality' modified the style of the younger generation, and a fresh attempt was made to cope with city life rather than to escape it. Hargrave's subsequent career is of little interest in the present context. For a while he was strongly influenced by the ideas of Social Credit and aspired to the political leadership of that movement. In the middle thirties he combined this with a more ambitious political design, and established the 'Green Shirts,' a right wing extremist group. After the outbreak

---

[1] Kibbo Kift in old English is 'proof of great strength.'

[2] Rolf Gardiner, 'D. H. Lawrence and the Youth Movements of the Twenties,' in *Wessex Letters from Springhead*, Christmas 1959, p. 45. Among the members of the advisory council of *The Trail*, Hargrave's magazine, there figured Norman Angell, Havelock Ellis, Maeterlinck, Stephen Graham, Romain Rolland, and Anatole France. Hargrave's books of that period were all quickly translated and published by the *Weisse Ritter* publishing house.

of the Second World War, his name dropped out of even the byways of politics and literature.[1]

IV

Life in the youth movement was almost always richer, fuller, and more rewarding than the ideas, speeches, and publications of its leaders. It is necessary to repeat this caution before discussing Martin Voelkel and the other leading spokesmen of the *White Knight* circle. Clarity, sobriety, calmness were not among their outstanding virtues; they were always excited, almost always engaged in grandiloquent but frequently meaningless talk. In this their behaviour was quite alien to the spirit of the early *Wandervogel* who had abhorred empty phrases.

Voelkel and his friends believed in the destiny of the Reich, 'The Holy, divine Reich of the German vision, which is everywhere and nowhere,' and of its future, 'The next thousand years belong to the Slav soul. But when this is past, the Third Reich will come. It will be neither culture nor civilization, it will be both of these and more than both.'[2] Nobody but the German himself knew in which direction he was moving; between death and perdition the German Reich, devoted to the eternal in man, was emerging.[3] This would be followed by references to the 'German trinity': God, the I, and the weapon; and to the supreme duty of serving the Holy Grail.[4] German youth and the German State ought to prepare for the last struggle. A great people ought to have a beautiful and wise end. With the courage of despair German youth was fighting for its State.[5] The proceedings would be concluded with the recitation of Stefan George's poem:

> Er geisselt die verlaufenen heim
> Ins ewige recht, wo grosses wiederum gross ist.
> Herr wiederum herr, zucht wiederum zucht, er heftet
> Das wahre sinnbild auf das völkische banner.
> Er führt durch sturm und grausige signale
> Des frührots seiner treuen schar zum werk
> Des wachen tags and pflanzt das neue Reich.

[1] Gardiner, *op. cit.*, p. 45.   [2] *Der Weisse Ritter*, 1920–1, p. 43.
[3] *Ibid.*, 1922–3, p. 526.
[4] *Ibid.*, 6, 1921, pp. 210 *et seq.*; M. Voelkel, *Hie Ritter und Reich* (Berlin, 1923), *passim*.
[5] *Ibid.*, 10–12, vol. VII, *passim*. It is extremely difficult to convey to the English reader the full flavour of the style of the period, which was in fact much more ecstatic and cloudy than appears in translation, in which some concessions to clarity and meaning have to be made.

THE 'WHITE KNIGHT'

On other occasions the *Bund* would be discussed. The majority of the people—the burghers and the peasants—needed a castle as a place of refuge and the knight with his sword (the symbol of faith) to protect them. But castles were built only by knights; by an aristocracy such as the *Bund* was to be. The boys were choosing knighthood as their goal; an eternal bond was uniting them, which grew out of their deepest experience and their holiest will. The believers were preparing for the great battle, for their people were in chains, the enemy was swinging his scourge, the thousand-year-old castles had been destroyed, the banners were torn, the shield stained, and the inner sanctum, the holiest of the holy, was profaned. But the time of prayer was over; youth was now storming into battle, knowing that it would again be free, whether victory or death was to be its fate.[1]

If an outsider enquired about the meaning of all this, he would be told that if he did not feel it he would never understand it. It was not something that could be explained to Philistines in rational terms; nor were the *White Knights* concerned about this inability to convey the deeper meaning of their thoughts. These were secrets that belonged to a few, to the new aristocracy, not something that could ever be understood by people who put their faith in democracy and humanism: 'People who preached humanism, the right of everybody to happiness, and the progress of mankind, belonged to the camp of civilization, not the camp of culture, and could not be taken seriously.'[2]

Such talk has frightening undertones; it has indeed been argued that the *White Knights* anticipated some of the basic concepts of the S.S.,[3] but this is to credit them with ideas and intentions which it is unlikely they ever entertained. Voelkel and his friends were good citizens and the reality behind their heroic speeches was a pretty tame one. As one contemporary right-wing critic pointed out, their new Reich belonged to India rather than to Central Europe; it was the sect, the last remnant of the German people,[4] which was retiring into the forest to lead a life in the spirit of Hölderlin, without interference. The orations about knights and castles, swords and armour, struggle and attack, victory or death, were no more than flights of fantasy. They did not really think in terms of war, and disparaged the

---

[1] Konrad Praxmarer, 'Von Gral und Reich, von Volk und Adel', in *Der Weisse Ritter*, 1922–3, p. 10–11.

[2] *Der Weisse Ritter*, 1920–1, p. 41. It should be remembered that in German right-wing parlance the word civilization has a derogatory meaning, something vastly inferior to culture; the French had produced a civilization, the Germans had created a Kultur.

[3] Cf. Arno Klönne, *Hitlerjugend* (Hanover, 1960), p. 54.

[4] *Deutschwandervogel*, 6, 1924, p. 144–5.

para-military activities of some of the right-wing *Bünde*. With all their invocation of religious elements and symbols, and despite the presence of a fair number of clergymen in the leadership, the doctrine they professed was areligious, if not anti-religious; as Harry Pross has pointed out, theirs was a theocracy without God.[1] Their historical inspiration was medieval, and of course quite unhistorical; the townspeople in the Middle Ages had hardly ever sought the assistance of the knights; on the contrary, cities had generally been founded to escape the oppression of the nobles. To delve more deeply into these ideas would be unlikely to bring anything more to light; it is of little use to look for a meaning where there was none, but only the intoxication of phrases and symbols.

In practice, the political tendency of the leadership of the *Bund* was comparatively moderate. Martin Voelkel, to be sure, thought it 'intolerable' that a Jew should lead a group in the *Bund*, and another spokesman predicted a terrible fate for German Jews unless they left the country of their own volition.[2] Opinion about Hitler was divided; to some the swastika was a ridiculous, insignificant symbol, to be seen scrawled on the walls of public lavatories; to others it was a symbol for which Germans were prepared to die.[3] As for the right-wing para-military organizations, there was only derision for the barbers' apprentices who were said to be inflated with pride as they marched side by side with their customers on a Sunday morning: 'Germany will not be saved by shooting.'[4] It was a sensible observation, but it left the central question open: How exactly was Germany to be saved?

V

The heart-searching of the *White Knight* circle closely reflected the attitudes of the German middle classes in the nineteen-twenties. There were some sizeable 'islands' of democracy, notably in South-West Germany, Hamburg, etc., but in their majority the middle classes were opposed to the Weimar Republic, even if they voted for parties that were playing the parliamentary game. The great majority of the political writers of the day treated parliamentary democracy as a contemptible joke, a foreign importation that was altogether unsuitable for Germany, a poison injected into it after the military defeat in 1918. The leaders of the *Neupfadfinder* were either students or young men who had recently left the universities, and the German universities in the nineteen-twenties were bulwarks of anti-democratic thought. When the National Socialists were still only a small splinter party in the Reichstag they already topped the

---

[1] Harry Pross, *op. cit.*, p. 86.   [2] *Der Weisse Ritter*, 1922–3, p. 120.
[3] *Ibid.*, p. 118.   [4] *Der Weisse Ritter*, 3–4, vol. VI, *passim*.

poll in many universities, and in some they had an absolute majority. When Helmuth Kittel attacked the parliamentary system and called for an authoritarian regime,[1] or when it was said that 'we are the most bitter enemies of the old State,' the words only echoed those of Spengler, Moeller van den Bruck, Othmar Spann and other rightwing thinkers of the day. But it would be a mistake to attribute the anti-democratic attitude of the *Bünde* solely to outside intellectual influence; the *Bund* itself was an authoritarian, not a democratic institution, one based on the *Führer* principle, and it could not have been otherwise. It was not unnatural therefore to project the structure of the *Bund* on to the State at a time when the parliamentary regime was functioning with great difficulty. But only at a time of crisis and in the general anti-democratic climate of the day could such ideas have been seriously entertained. Some observers have argued in retrospect that the anti-democratic trend in the *Bünde* was not directed against democracy *per se*, but only against parliamentary democracy, the rule of vested interests, cliques, and the party caucus. This may be so, but it opened the way to a dictatorship just as the rejection of humanist ideals and of the idea of progress also had sinister consequences. It could be argued that in view of Germany's political backwardness, its lack of political education and experience, and the absence of that minimum of mutual tolerance and consent that is needed to make democracy work, some form of guided democracy was needed. But the argument of the *Bünde* was a very different one; they thought that in the Germany of 1925 all the prerequisites existed for the making of a better, organic, specifically German political regime that would be much superior to that of the decadent West.

IV

If ideology had been all there was to the *Neupfadfinder* it would be difficult to explain their impact on the youth movement, of which, numerically, they were only a small fraction. Their ideology was their most visible and obvious feature, but a youth movement cannot be wholly concerned with public affairs, and in the long run the extra-political ventures of the *White Knight* circle were of greater significance. Their cultural efforts must be mentioned, however briefly. These were not on the same elevated level as those of the *Freideutsche*; no major thinker, writer, or artist emerged from among the circle.[2] But, in contrast to the early *Wandervogel*, literature and

[1] *Der Weisse Ritter*, 1, 1924; quoted in Will Vesper, *op. cit.*, p. 120.
[2] Werner Heisenberg, the physicist, was a member of the circle. But it is unlikely that he drew the inspiration for his work from the youth movement; of the writers of the *Weisse Ritter* circle, Paul Alverdes is probably the best known.

the arts were not neglected and there were even attempts to find modern forms of expression.

More important was the fresh impulse given to the then stagnant youth movement. The idea of the *Bund* as a life companionship proved unworkable; but it did provide the impetus for the establishment of a series of organizations to cater for different age groups: the *Jungenschaft* (up to about 17 years); the *Jungmannschaft* for those between about 17 and 25, and the *Mannschaft* for members above that age. While the idea of the *Mannschaft* was no more practicable than that of the *Landsgemeinde* developed by a previous generation, the other innovations were quite sensible—perhaps overdue. The old *Wandervogel* had never paid sufficient attention to the fact that young boys and adolescents growing to manhood did not share the same interests. Life in the *Jungenschaft* was not altogether dissimilar to what it had been in boys' groups before, though with more emphasis on discipline and leadership; education of character in group life, the camp, the rambles, and the weekly meetings were the central activities.

The real innovation was the *Jungmannschaft*, an attempt to combine youth movement activities with education for active citizenship. Under the influence of such men as Buske, Götsch, and Dehmel of the *Altwandervogel*, a new content was given to these new forms. The expeditions of the *Jungmannschaft* were frequently directed to foreign countries, and more especially to areas of German colonization outside the Reich. Out of the summer camps grew the idea of the voluntary labour service. These ideas were later taken over by the National Socialists and their spirit perverted, but these subsequent developments were not the necessary outcome of what were originally promising activities.

The *Neupfadfinder* were also the driving force in the early twenties in the quest for unity in the youth movement. Their projects were not accepted; the frequent meetings between the leaders of the *Bünde* did not at first produce tangible results. Nevertheless, these efforts were not all in vain, for eventually some leading *Bünde* merged, uniting some of the most vital forces among the younger generation. Only a few leaders of the *Neupfadfinder* did, however, play a leading part in these later developments; most of them dropped out or remained on the sidelines of the movement.[1]

The era of the 'White Knight' is likely to be seen as a negative

---

[1] Martin Voelkel, for a long time a parson in a Berlin suburb, died a few years after the Second World War. Ludwig Voggenreiter ran the leading publishing house of the youth movement and died in a camp in East Germany in 1945. Karl Rauch, too, became a publisher. Habbel now lives in South Germany, while Helmuth Kittel, Erich Maschke, Joachim Boeckh and a few others are professors in German universities or other institutions of higher learning.

phase in the history of the German youth movement. Youthful idealism, personal integrity, and *élan vital* there were in abundance, but these were matched by an excess of hazy and high-flown word-painting, of extravagant and vaporous romanticism. Never before or since has German youth been led to remove itself so far from realities; seldom have clear thinking and common sense been held in such singular disrespect.

Fifteen

ERNST BUSKE AND THE FREISCHAR

I

THE story of the German youth movement between 1925 and 1933, the year Hitler became Chancellor of the Reich, is an uninterrupted chain of unions, splits, and reunions. The great number of organizations and leaders involved makes it impossible to trace in detail all these complex developments without losing sight of the significant trends. An attempt has been made to summarize these transformations in a graph, but the net result, recalling the labyrinth of the Minotaur, is not very enlightening. In the maze of groups large and small, however, the attention is soon arrested by the *Deutsche Freischar*. This was the largest of all the independent *Bünde* and—which did not necessarily follow—was also the most successful; for it blended the tradition of the *Wandervogel* with the new *bündisch* style, and with a more realistic approach to the outside world.

The *Freischar* came into being in 1926 as the result of a merger between the *Neupfadfinder*, whose activities were described in some detail in the last chapter, and the *Altwandervogel*, one of the earlier groups which had survived the great post-war crisis relatively unscathed. Smaller factions from both Germany and Austria joined in, and it looked for a time as though an old and cherished dream might now come true—the united German youth movement. But it did not last, and was revived only in 1933 in a last-minute unsuccessful attempt by the *Bünde* to forestall dissolution by the Hitler government.

The *Freischar* had about ten to twelve thousand members of whom roughly three-quarters were below the age of eighteen; about 15 per cent of its members were girls.[1] The groups of the *Bund* were scattered throughout Germany and Austria, but it was more

[1] See the statistics in *Deutsche Freischar*, 5, 1929.

strongly represented in the East of Germany (Silesia, Saxony, Brandenburg-Berlin) than in other parts of the Reich. The great majority of its members came from Protestant middle-class families, though there were some Catholics and a very few Jews. Like the *Wandervogel* it was essentially a schoolboys' movement, but there was a gradual increase in the number of the older contingent, those in their early twenties. The average group had about sixteen members (up to twenty-four in Bavaria), and the head of the *Bund* stated *ex officio* that a unit with fewer than ten members did not really deserve to be called a group.

This leader was Ernst Buske, who did more than any other one man at the time to shape the destinies of the *Freischar* and of the youth movement in general. Born in Pomerania in 1894, he had been a member of the *Altwandervogel*. He had studied law, and was the legal representative of a large peasants' association in Northwest Germany. A physical deficiency—Buske was one-armed—prevented his taking part in the First World War; and it was during the post-war crisis, at the age of 24, that he emerged as one of the leading figures in the youth movement. He was neither a great orator nor a long-winded writer like so many of his contemporaries, but surpassed them all in sheer force of personality. He was universally respected; one foreign observer said that he combined what was finest in the German character with the best British characteristics.[1] Everybody in the movement acknowledged his authority and looked up to him; some even called him 'General,' although he was not at all militaristic. He was undoubtedly the most mature leader of that generation, and combined the idealism of the youth movement with tact, modesty, an instinctive aversion to visionary and sentimental declarations, and, above all perhaps, a salutary addiction to plain realism and common sense. His 'rule' marks the end of some of the romantic excesses which were becoming habitual in the youth movement under the influence of the *White Knight* circle. Buske thought in practical terms; instead of talking about a Reich *in nubibus* he preferred to concentrate on the work that could actually be done by young Germans. His sudden death in 1930 was one of the most serious losses ever suffered by the youth movement.[2]

Other leading figures in the *Freischar* were Hans Dehmel, Helmuth Kittel, and Georg Götsch. Dehmel, a native of Breslau, has already been mentioned as the commander of the *Wandervogel* unit in the Free Corps; he served as leader of the *Freischar* for short periods both before and after Buske, and was a pioneer in organizing visits

[1] Rolf Gardiner, 'Ernst Buske', in *Die Sammlung*, 11, Vol. XI, p. 539.
[2] His biography is still to be written. In the archives on Burg Ludwigstein there is a great Buske file containing much of interest.

by fairly large youth groups to places outside Germany. Kittel, a theologian and subsequently a professor of pedagogy, had none of Buske's charismatic gifts, and he had adopted too much of the *White Knight* style to be a great success in the *Freischar*. Götsch's main interest was music, and his impressive achievement was the Frankfurt (Oder) *Musikheim*. This institute was founded in 1929, with the signal help of the Liberal Prussian minister for culture C. H. Becker, to make some of the achievements of the youth movement accessible to a wider circle—to the elementary school teachers who came there for refresher courses, and to many others. Over and above this it became a considerable musical centre in its own right.

Of equal or perhaps even greater importance was the *Boberhaus* centre for adult education, established by the Silesian group in Löwenberg. Here, too, a systematic attempt was made to bring senior members of the *Bund* into contact with other representatives of the younger generation, in courses lasting several weeks or months; and this without regard to social origin, profession, or political orientation. The leaders of the *Freischar* had first given close study to the working of a national labour service in Bulgaria—a country which had been a pioneer in this respect. About ten labour camps were arranged by the *Freischar* between 1925 and 1929, and many more between 1929 and 1933. In these camps between sixty and a hundred young men lived and worked together for at least three weeks and often much longer; four to five hours of work each day provided the material basis, in addition to which there was a rich educational programme, a great many lectures, amateur theatricals, music, and above all discussions. The main topic at the 1928 camp at Löwenberg was the economic crisis in the neighbouring coal-mining district and the social and educational problems in distressed areas in general. In 1929 the depopulation of Silesia to the east of the Oder was the main theme, which led to a general discussion on questions of economic and political planning. During the holiday season there were special courses for young industrial workers and for groups of young Germans from East and South-east Europe.[1] There were Communists as well as National Socialists among the participants, but the political views of the majority ranged between moderate left and right of centre.[2]

The labour camp idea was widely accepted after 1929, when an unprecedented economic crisis made millions of young Germans unemployed. The labour camp could do nothing to solve such a

[1] Kurt Ballerstedt, 'Die schlesische Jungmannschaft', in *Das Junge Deutschland*, 12, 1929, p. 540.
[2] *Das Arbeitslager, Berichte aus Schlesien von Arbeitern, Bauern, Studenten.* Eugen Rosenstock and Carl Dietrich Trotha (ed.) (1931).

crisis, but it occasionally alleviated cases of individual hardship, and, what was more important, it became an effective means whereby the *Bund* could break out of the middle-class isolation that had narrowly circumscribed the activities of the youth movement until that time. Many had talked about the *Volksgemeinschaft*, the community of the whole people, the necessity to bridge the widening gulf between the classes. Now for the first time somebody had decided to do something about it.

It has been said that, given time and a little luck, the *Freischar* might have been the decisive influence upon the younger generation, thereby indirectly changing the whole subsequent course of German history. But the early death of Buske robbed the movement of its one great leader; the promising beginnings of 1929 were not permitted to ripen and develop; and the whole youth movement was soon to be overtaken by the general catastrophe. It is moreover doubtful whether the youth movement could have wrought radical changes even under more favourable conditions. Changes of such magnitude are brought about by political parties or social classes and not by the younger generation as such—least of all by one that was no less perplexed, and hardly less divided, than its elders. The success of the labour camps was only made possible by the economic crisis; in less abnormal conditions such a venture would hardly have been possible.

The achievement of the *Freischar* was nevertheless impressive enough. They made a serious and partly successful attempt to come to grips with the modern world without surrendering the youth movement's traditions and ideals. They did something to prepare young men and women to meet the demands of life in their profession and family, in their education, and in the education of others. As Buske put it, 'the realm (Reich) of youth is no longer an ultimate value to us. For beyond this, as we know, is the hard commandment: that "youth is the preparation for manhood".'[1]

The *Freischar* had its utopians and romantics who said that their *Bund*, in its structure and ideas, had already anticipated the new Reich, that it was the new aristocracy which would replace the bourgeois, materialistic regime. But the majority rejected such a view, and pointed to the vanity and arrogance that it implied; would it not instantly vanish into thin air when they had to face reality? To Buske's almost Spartan style and sober attitude any form of intellectual swagger was anathema. He knew that there was a great élan in the youth movement, but he was also aware of its limitations.

[1] Quoted in Hermann Siefurt, 'Politische Vorstellungen und Versuche der Deutschen Freischar', in *Lebendiger Geist*, ed. Hellmuth Diewald (Leiden, 1959), pp. 177ff.

II

Whenever there were some promising beginnings in the history of the youth movement—as in the early days of the *Freideutsche* youth—there were some members of the older generation, mostly professors from the universities, willing to lend their help to these young men and women seeking to find their way in the world. Some did this because they were invited, but others volunteered in the belief that they had a mission to fulfil; and of those who had a marked effect upon the thinking of the *Freischar* Hans Freyer and Eugen Rosenstock-Hüssy are among the more memorable names. Both stood somewhat to the right of centre, and Freyer's ideas about a revolution that was to come from the right did not have a healthy effect; any suggestion that the non-Nazi right was capable of such a revolution in the Germany of 1930 was fantastic. But there were also liberals like Arnold Bergsträsser, and Socialists like Fritz Borinski, himself a member of the *Bund*; no single party or ideology was allowed a monopoly, for the *Freischar* certainly did not blindly follow any one man's lead. In its later, post-liberal phase, it was influenced for a time by the views of the *Tat* circle (of which more below), one of whose leading members, Leopold Dingräve (E. W. Eschmann), a poet and philosopher, was also a member of the *Bund*. J. W. Hauer, who subsequently became professor of theology at Tübingen, should also be mentioned: he had joined the *Freischar* together with his Protestant Swabian group; later on Hauer became the ideologist of a 'German Faith Movement,' but had little success in converting the *Bund* to his ideas. There were even complaints that 'too many theologians meddle in our affairs.'[1] In the *Freischar* many had a keen interest in religion, but the theologians, as is so often the case, had no religion to offer, only various philosophies of religion, and that was not what was wanted.

In their approach to politics the *Freischar* leaders needed first of all to decide how far they wanted to become involved. That there must be some such involvement nobody doubted, but whether they ought to remain above all a youth movement, or become a definitely political organization, continued to be a bone of contention for all the years of its existence. Some said that the struggle of the parties ought not to be carried into the youth movement; but these were often the same people who argued that the political parties were beyond redemption anyway, and that some new form of political organization was necessary. Others, equally critical of the parties and their narrow policy of economic interest, nevertheless saw no

[1] *Deutsche Freischar*, 9, 1929, p. 14 *et seq.*

other possible framework for political activity, unless it were the recourse to dictatorial adventures which they thought even more reprehensible. They regarded political activity as the main assignment of the *Jungmannschaft*; political experience, not only group experience, was needed, and a new definition of purpose, 'otherwise the Hitler youth with its revolutionary political élan will win over our young idealistic activists.'[1]

Having recognized that politics were vitally important—a verdict more easily reached in 1930 than twenty years before—the *Freischar* made the effort to grope its way through the perplexities of the times. Nationalism and Liberalism, Marxism and Fascism—all the ideologies, all the party programmes and all the slogans of the day—were subjected to close scrutiny. It is difficult to present the conclusions drawn by the *Freischar* on these and other issues, since complete ideological unity was never reached, and the majority was prone to modify its opinion from time to time. By and large, however, certain basic trends emerged.

Buske and the other leaders were of course good German patriots; the 'General' belonged to the right-wing nationalist group during and after the split of 1919-20. He believed that only big peoples had any future in the modern world, hence the great emphasis he always laid upon the necessity to strengthen ties with the Germans living outside the borders of the Reich. But in contrast to many of his contemporaries he thought in practical terms: the *Volksdeutsche* were to be induced to buy German products and thus help to strengthen the German economy which was then in great need of foreign exchange. The other main task was cultural propaganda not unlike that done by the British Boy Scouts, on their trips abroad. Time and again Buske condemned the extremist nationalism that was so fashionable among many youth groups at that time, and he had nothing but scorn for their efforts to outbid one another in nationalistic pretensions. On two occasions this reasonable attitude brought it into disrepute in the nationalist camp: it was attacked as liberalist, and even charged with high treason, because it refused to take part in the demonstrations that were organized by certain circles against the Young plan (the attempt made in 1928 to reach a reduced and final settlement of German war reparations). Still more shocking in the eyes of the nationalist zealots was the song book that the *Freischar* produced in 1929, for it included the national anthems of several other European countries. This may appear innocent enough in retrospect, but in the poisoned atmosphere of 1929 the whole nationalist Press was outraged by the enormity of the crime.

[1] Fritz Boriński in *Deutsche Freischar*, 3, II (1929?), p. 182

The *Freischar* were critical of the Weimar Republic; they said it was a purely utilitarian regime which had no attraction for the younger generation; that the parliamentary regime was bad inasmuch as the electors could not vote for men, but only for lists of partisans; the element of personal responsibility was notably absent. But they continued for a long time to believe that the State could be reformed from within, and supported the great *bündische* initiative of 1930, when leading members of the *Freischar* were prominently involved in the attempt to create a strong party of the Centre. This attempt was not a success; the *Staatspartei* failed to get any substantial number of parliamentary seats in the elections, and, worse still, the members of the *Bünde* within that party were pushed aside and secured no key positions.

After this failure, anti-liberal and anti-democratic opinions gained wider currency.[1] Using the argument advanced by Hans Freyer, they now thought that the political principles of the nineteenth century could give no guidance for the future. The *Freischar* was 'further right than the Right, more to the left than the Left wing; it could either close or break open the circle as it chose.'[2] In this kind of meaningless and vainglorious verbiage the absence of Buske's steadying hand was painfully evident.

Even then, they had doubts about the desirability of dictatorship for Germany, or of the *ständische* order preached by the followers of Othmar Spann. In Russia and Italy, they said, a dictatorial regime might be necessary, but in Germany this would be a retrograde step. They were naturally concerned about the ideas of the extreme left and of the right; Buske and Götsch went to study the Russian scene in the late twenties; 'We think that the Russian people is the freest in Europe despite the G.P.U.,' wrote one leader in 1931. Communism was superior to National Socialism because it had a coherent ideological system; what they did not like about Communism was its lack of culture, its narrow sectarianism, its inability to give a lead to the middle classes which had been impoverished no less than the proletariat by the economic crisis; and lastly its failure to understand that the socialism of a defeated people could only be nationalist in its form.[3] On the other hand, what the *Freischar* disliked in National Socialism was its lack of clear ideas in the social and economic field, as well as its foreign political adventurism. While appreciating the great idealism and élan to be found in the ranks of the Hitler party, which was essentially a 'movement for a German renaissance,'[4] the *Freischar* were shocked to discover the discrepancy between the strength of faith in this movement and its intel-

[1] *Deutsche Freischar*, 4, 1931, p. 148. [2] *Ibid.*, 2, 1931, *passim*.
[3] *Ibid.*, 5, 1931, pp. 204 *et seq.* [4] *Ibid.*, 4, 1931, pp. 124 *et seq.*

lectual equipment: 'A giant in the clothes of a boy going to confirmation.'

If the centre parties were rotten, and the left- and right-wing radicals unacceptable, the *Freischar* had no alternative but to develop a programme of its own. E. W. Eschmann of the *Tat* circle developed certain ideas that were shared by many though by no means all members of his *Bund*. The outstanding fact of contemporary social life, he contended, was the pauperization of the middle classes in consequence of the economic crisis, and their political radicalization. We are therefore Socialists, said Eschmann, but not proletarian socialists; for us, socialism and nationalism are identical.[1] The situation of the white-collar workers was in effect much worse than that of the industrial workers, for the latter had strong organizations of their own, but who was there to take care of salaried employees who found themselves out of work? Eighty per cent of the German people had no property whatsoever; how then could they continue to argue in favour of a capitalist system? How could they resist the demand for national control of the economy?

Everybody was indeed a socialist and in favour of economic planning in the Germany of 1930, just as everybody was against the Versailles treaty. But what did all this mean? There was talk of a Prussian socialism, but Spengler alone may have known what the catch-phrase meant, and if so, he did not disclose the secret. Others opposed 'foreign' capitalism but were quite ready to make an exception in favour of the native variety. Some elaborated theories of autarky, while others only believed, in the simplicity of their hearts, that there ought to be no less social justice in society than in the youth movement. Were not food and drink shared equally on all their outings? A large number of those whose sympathies were definitely right-wing were ready to go the whole way and accept the nationalization of all the means of production. But they too had no clear political conception; they had a beautiful programme, but it made no provision for powers to execute the reforms or administer the new society, for since they rejected all existing political parties, and denied the efficiency of the existing State apparatus, there was a missing link in their train of thought.

Yet if their economic and social concepts were often vague, so were everybody else's, with the exception of the fanatics who had ready-made solutions for everything. More serious perhaps was the ignorance of the youth leaders about the realities and the mechanism of political power. They took part in two political initiatives during the later years of the Weimar period: the first in 1930 as co-founders of the *Staatspartei* and the People's Conservative Party. Their

[1] *Deutsche Freischar*, 3, III, pp. 81 *et seq.*

sentiments were praiseworthy, but the basic idea was impractical, namely that of gaining power and influence through a moderate centre party at a time of crisis. The second attempt was made late in 1932, when many of the *Bünde* lent their support to Chancellor Schleicher. At the time this may have appeared to be a policy of the lesser evil, but it was in fact no solution at all, not even an effective stop-gap measure.

But, we may ask, would the clearest programme and even a full understanding of the facts of political life have been of much help in 1931?

It is doubtful whether there was any opening for the youth movement. Even if they had been able to offer a sound nationalist and socialist programme, nothing could have come of it; the time for sound programmes was past. Members of the *Freischar* had been trained in their camps, their trips and meetings to cope with emergencies of many kinds, but a major political upheaval was not one of them. Can they be blamed for failing to deal with it?

III

A British friend of the youth movement who revisited Germany in the early summer of 1932 was struck above all by the unhealthy atmosphere of urgency louring like a thundercloud over discussions in the youth movement, and by the ever-increasing sense of pressure; men were forever in a demoniac hurry; no one had any time. As Georg Götsch, the *Freischar* leader, said to him, in explanation if not in justification: 'You are speaking in accusation of German inconstancy. Would you blame a harried hare because it runs? Germany cannot go slow at the present time.'[1]

And yet, though the world economic crisis was formidable indeed, much of the pressure the Germans complained of was self-inflicted. The radical trend among youth made rapid progress: 'We do not want to discuss any more, we want only to act.'[2] Opposing slogans took the place of intellectual confrontation with the urgent issues of the day; street fighting replaced political debate, and the appeal to reason was silenced by strident appeals to instinct and emotion.

The *Freischar* strove in vain against the turbid flood; their leaders rejected what they called the two great fallacies of the day—the ideas that a political programme could be all-powerful, and that the primary duty was to win power. What use would it be to have power

[1] Rolf Gardiner, *Letters from Springhead*, Autumn 1948, pp. 170–1.
[2] Josepha Fischer, 'Entwicklungen und Wandlungen in den Jugendverbänden im Jahre 1931', in *Das Junge Deutschland*, 2, 1932, p. 39.

without purpose, or to be rulers without rules?[1] But that, of course, was tantamount to criticizing National Socialism.

It was an uphill battle; in fact a hopeless one. The perplexity that oppressed even the thirteen and fourteen-year-olds is described in an otherwise undistinguished novel of the time. It portrays the strong and silent *bündische* youth against a background filled with the shouting columns of the Hitler Youth and the Communists, both so blindly confident that what their leaders have told them is the truth. The *Bünde*, on the other hand, are depicted as a 'secret army, the quiet reserve force of the future,' which is to create a new Germany, not by the use of hand grenades and machine guns but by the example of their faith.[2] But what was the use of secret armies now, and who was thinking about the future?

As the summer months of 1932 passed and winter approached, the German situation steadily deteriorated, until members of the *Freischar* as well as other sections of the youth movement lost all hope that anything less than some extreme solution could possibly save the country. This was why Hitler's successes had such magical effect; scarcely anyone wanted to stand aside at the hour of victory. What happened fulfilled the prediction made in May 1932 by a Catholic youth leader: 'It can be foretold with mathematical certainty that the hour is approaching when any group of people of weak character will fall a victim to the victory psychosis and climb upon the bandwaggon of the millions.'[3]

In March 1933, several weeks before the *Bünde* came under real pressure, the leaders of the *Freischar* announced that they wanted to join the Hitler movement, and that those who were unwilling or not eligible to join it would have to leave the *Bund*. This was not only, perhaps in some cases not chiefly, a question of weakness of character: they simply had no strong opinions one way or the other. They had not been National Socialists before January 1933, but they had no wish to stand aside in the hour of a great national uprising. Lacking firm convictions of their own and seeing that Hitler had in fact prevailed, they were willing to co-operate with and within his party. For was not January 1933 a moment of incalculable change, the promise of a new beginning? In the words of a poem of Rilke's that was frequently quoted in those days:

Man fühlt den Glanz von einer neuen Seite
auf der noch alles werden kann.[4]

[1] *Deutsche Freischar*, 10, 1931, p. 111; *Der Zwiespruch*, 27 December 1931.
[2] Heinrich B. von Bazan, *Fackeln der Jungen Front* (Plauen, 1932), p. 130.
[3] Else Peerenboom in *Das Junge Deutschland*, 5, 1932, p. 152.
[4] 'One feels the splendour from a new direction/whence anything may still come.'

Thus, somewhat ingloriously, the story of the *Freischar* came to an end.[1] It would have ended in any case, as the new rulers set about destroying all rivals, but this only makes the event seem doubly deplorable; for the historian of a movement which had roused such hopeful expectations would prefer to record a more dignified departure from the scene.

[1] After the end of the Second World War a new *Deutsche Freischar* came into being, mainly in South-west Germany. But it had little in common with the old *Bund* but the name.

Sixteen
PANORAMA OF THE BÜNDE

I

GERMAN youth never produced a Bismarck prepared to bully and cajole all its little groups to unite into one great movement. The *Wandervogel*, which had split into four different streams within the previous decade, subdivided during the twenties and early thirties into at least a dozen major *Bünde* and countless minor ones, each with its own leader, its magazine or newsletter, its yearly camps and its distinctive banner and attire. Even experts sometimes found it difficult to distinguish between, say, the *Deutschwandervogel* and the *Wandervogel deutscher Bund*, or between the *Ringgemeinschaft* and the *Reichsschaft* of the Scouts. Yet this progressive fragmentation may have helped at times to extend its influence.

Before the First World War the *Wandervogel*, tolerated as a curiosity, had little effect beyond its own membership and hardly any upon the school, youth welfare, or other authorities. But after the war had transformed the scene, the whole country suddenly became youth-movement-conscious. Church youth organizations, and even those of political parties, began to model themselves on the pattern of the *Bund*; the youth movement's songs became public property; its group activities, including the camps and the long excursions, were adopted and adapted wherever German boys and girls associated. A network of youth hostels spread over the country, and by the end of the twenties it was often not easy to say at sight whether a party of young people encountered at a hostel belonged to the autonomous youth movement, or to one of the Catholic or right-wing groups, or whether it was just a group of schoolboys on a holiday ramble, led by a teacher who happened to be a former member of the youth movement.

Many a *Wandervogel* had chosen to become a teacher; and it

followed that the youth movement had a great, albeit an indirect, influence upon educational theory and practice: this was conspicuous in the work of such leading pedagogues of the day as Spranger Flitner and Nohl. Both the *Freideutsche* and the right-wingers established adult education centres in the early twenties: others founded private 'progressive' schools, often on the lines of Wyneken's Wickersdorf, which were strongly influenced by the spirit and the style of the youth movement. They ranged from the famous Odenwald school[1] (which still exists) to Schloss Salem,[2] with many variants in between.

One well-known Free Corps leader, having realized by 1925 that the time for bomb-throwing was over, established a successful theatrical youth group, while others specialized in puppet shows, medieval mysteries, and dance ensembles. The musical activities of such men as Jöde, Hensel, August Halm and Götsch aroused interest far beyond the youth movement itself; there was a growing circle of enthusiasts who regarded music as one of the central elements in education, if not its essential basis.

The organization of the *Wandervogel* in the early days had been simplicity itself: to go on an excursion required only the permission of parents; toleration by the school authorities, though desirable, was by no means indispensable. But as the youth movement spread, all sorts of problems made their appearance; legal problems, administrative and financial difficulties, and encounters with the government authorities multiplied. To deal with them an executive committee was established, and by the time this body was dissolved, in 1933, it included delegates from all the major youth organizations and represented many millions of German boys and girls. Of this multitude the autonomous youth movement was only a very small minority; but it was always the vanguard, and the others freely and gratefully admitted that they had learnt much from its example.[3]

To classify the *Bünde* is as difficult as to write their history. It has been argued that the *Bund* has no history, that it was a collective experience without coherent development, and that any attempt to trace its course against the background of contemporary German history is therefore bound to fail.[4] This is an exaggerated conclusion

---

[1] Like Wickersdorf this attracted considerable, and not always fortunate publicity in German *belles lettres* (cf Klaus Mann *et al.*).

[2] Better known now as the institution in which Prince Philip, Duke of Edinburgh was for a time educated.

[3] See, for instance, Erich Ollenhauer, 'Die Roten Falken', in *Das Junge Deutschland*, XX, 3, 1929, pp. 81–87. Ollenhauer, the leader of the German Social Democratic Party after Kurt Schumacher's death in 1952, had been one of the presidents of the central youth executive in the twenties.

[4] Herman Mau, 'Die Deutsche Jugendbewegung, Rückblick und Ausblick', *Zeitschrift für Religions- und Geistesgeschichte*, 1, 1948.

drawn from accurate premises; for although the *Bund* cannot be seen rightly in isolation from its historic environment, it is true that the fact that a particular *Bund* flourished during a certain period, and took up this or that attitude towards a certain problem, does not of itself tell us much about that *Bund's* special characteristics and features. For better or worse, youth groups were less consistent than political parties. Those on the extreme right, for instance, were liable on occasion to take up pro-Communist and pro-Soviet positions, while sections of the Social Democratic youth sometimes lent their voices to ultra-nationalist slogans. Catholic and Protestant groups were prone to revolt against their confessional advisers from time to time; the non-political *Bünde* frequently became involved in politics; while certain political party youth organizations moved in the opposite direction—away from politics. Any classification of the *Bünde* according to political or even confessional categories is therefore little more than an expedient, and subject to reservations and corrections.

II

The existence of a strong right (*völkische*) wing in the youth movement dating back to the period before the First World War has already been noted. After 1918, it split into two camps, moderate and extreme nationalist, which in their turn subdivided into several more factions. Among the extremists were the *Adler und Falken* (Eagles and Falcons), the *Geusen* (the *Gueux*), the *Freischar Schill*, the *Deutscher Pfadfinderbund Westmark*, and some others. The 'Eagles and Falcons' had been founded by the writer Wilhelm Kotzde, 'together with thirteen boys of German blood,' in February 1920 in the Black Forest.[1] Kotzde, himself a literary figure of sorts and extremely active, succeeded in enlisting the help of some well-known thinkers of the Right, such as H. S. Chamberlain, O. Spann, Ewald Banse, Ludwig Ferdinand Clauss, the amateur expert on race and prehistory Gustav Kossina, and the writers Ludwig Finckh and Börries von Münchhausen. Groups sprang up throughout Germany and Austria, fervently trying to combine something of the spirit of the youth movement with a belief in the superiority of the Nordic race and the German people. In such groups there was much sympathy for Hitler, but no inclination to join the Hitler Youth, whose rowdyism and low cultural level were frequently deplored in these quarters. The 'Eagles and Falcons' had more cultural aspirations; and the *Geusen* and the *Eidgenossen*, which were less sophisticated but more radical in temperament, flirted with National Bolshevism in the early thirties.

[1] See W. Kotzde, *Die Geschichte der Adler und Falken* (Munich n.d.), *passim*.

Out of these extreme right-wing groups grew the 'Artamans,' a movement of young men and women who decided to discharge a patriotic duty (that of saving German agriculture from being swamped by Polish labourers) as their contribution to the larger aim of building a new and better German race upon the principles of 'Blood and Soil.' The first 'Artaman' group began its work on an estate in Saxony in 1924; later on, many hundreds of them laboured on farms in Eastern Germany. Naturally, National Socialism took a great interest in this movement; its leader at the time was a Party member, as were the heads of the Bavarian district, Heinrich Himmler[1] and Darré, both destined to fame in the Third Reich. But this movement became divided in 1929 and then disintegrated.[2]

The 'Artamans' originally intended to mobilize 100,000 young Germans, but never succeeded in enlisting more than two thousand. The reasons for this were manifold: for one thing, their leaders quarrelled, as so often happened among nationalist sects, and the more socialistically inclined protested, with indubitable justification, against their exploitation by the big estate owners of East Germany.[3] The difficulties the 'Artamans' had to face were complicated further by the economic crisis; the idealism of these young people from the towns appeared insufficient to pass the severe test of agricultural labour: it was easier to rhapsodize about blood and soil than to buckle down to a working day of ten or twelve hours.[4]

As the political situation deteriorated, some of these *Bünde* were drawn deeper into politics—which by then meant National Socialist politics—while others retreated into the 'Germany of the forests' (Kotzde) and concentrated upon cultural activities, including a campaign against short hair for girls. 'Bobbed' hair was a new Western fashion, and they attributed its importation into Germany to the Jews and the Marxists.[5] One of the extreme right-wing groups disliked the growing influence of the National Socialists upon certain sections of the youth movement and the gradual disappearance of all that had been specifically youthful. Under the influence of its leader Karl Bückmann, the *Wandervogel völkischer Bund* decided to drop the adjective *völkisch* in 1926.[6]

The extreme right-wing groups were numerically small, and the

---

[1] Rudolph Proksch, 'Artamanen,' in *Wille und Macht*, 5, 1939, p. 22; see also *Blut und Pflug*, 1928, and other publications of the Artamans.

[2] In Mecklenburg and Pomerania some remnants continued to exist, and were incorporated, with due honour, in the Hitler Youth in 1934.

[3] Rolf Becker in *Die Kommenden*, 7 March 1930.

[4] Ironically enough, the Jewish youth movement succeeded where the Artamans failed, and made peasants out of several thousand young men and women.

[5] *Die Kommenden*, 13 October 1926.

[6] Hermann Lutze in *Wille und Werk*, 9, 1926, p. 70.

upsurge of National Socialism did not greatly benefit them. Far more numerous were the moderate right-wing organizations, such as the *Jungnationale Bund,* the *Grossdeutscher Jugendbund,* and the *Fahrenden Gesellen.*[1] The two last, which were controlled respectively by a nationalist trade union and a Vice-Admiral who was a friend of Hindenburg, are of no particular interest to us here; they adopted the youth-movement 'technique' but belonged, at most, only to the periphery of the *Bünde.*

The *Jungnationale Bund*—better known as the *Junabu*—had a capable leader in Heinz Dähnhardt; it was staunchly nationalist, but refused to identify itself with any particular political party, and regarded political activities as the business of adults, not adolescents. During the twenties this was undoubtedly one of the more effective *Bünde,* and it was remarkably free from the cultural narrow-mindedness that was so prevalent in German right-wing circles. Towards the end of the twenties, however, with the aggravation of the political crisis, such moderation failed to attract or hold the younger generation. Even earlier, a small 'activist' group under Hans Ebeling had split off and veered towards National Bolshevism; far more serious were the mass defections to the Hitler movement in 1929-30, when the *Junabu* lost the important Berlin area and some other districts. 'The youth movement is simple and straightforward while the National Socialists are blustering and brash,' Dähnhardt wrote, commenting on the permanent disputes, and adding that there was nevertheless much in National Socialism that attracted the boys.[2]

It is difficult to do justice to the various *Bünde* of the moderate and extreme right; Hitler's rise to power overshadowed their development and their very existence, and it is virtually impossible to consider them in their own right rather than in relation to National Socialism. Their attitude towards the Hitler movement was the central political issue for them. Some leaders of the *Junabu* and other right-wing groups had strong reservations about National Socialism and its evasions, such as failing to take a clear stand on socio-economic questions. They commented sarcastically on the petty bourgeois elements who were carried away by party meetings and parades, observing quite correctly that street demonstrations would not save Germany. They also opposed the ultra-nationalist phraseology; but such criticism was all too frequently 'aesthetic' in character, and therefore irrelevant as a reaction to a mass movement.

[1] The *Fahrenden Gesellen* reappeared about 1950 in their traditional strongholds in North Germany.
[2] 'Bündische Jugend und Nationalsozialismus,' in *Das Junge Deutschland,* 8, 1930, *passim.*

III

Strictly speaking, there was no left wing in the youth movement after 1921. Very small groups of the *Jungenschaft* went over to the Communists in 1932, and larger sections came out in favour of National Bolshevism, a school of thought that had little in common with the traditional ideas of the left. The Communist youth was fairly small in number, and, in view of its quality, not exactly an ornament of the party. The Social Democratic youth improved after the great crisis in 1918-9, and held some impressive conventions, such as those at Weimar in 1920 and Nuremberg in 1923. But somehow this movement lacked momentum, élan, and fighting spirit. Its leaders were decent, dedicated men and good democrats, and it was perhaps these very qualities, together with a lack of militancy—if not outright apathy—among the rank and file that proved to be their undoing in a revolutionary situation. Of the minor factions the 'Young Socialists' were perhaps the most significant. Their sympathies were with the working-class movement, but, in view of its 'one-sided rationalist and materialist orientation,' as they put it, they found it extremely difficult not to stray from the party line. At a meeting in Hofgeismar in October 1923 there were pronounced nationalist speeches: some thought the community of the whole people (*Volksgemeinschaft*) rather than class struggle ought to be the supreme aim, others talked about the coming German dawn and the willingness to die for Germany.[1] Whether their practical proposals were suitable for a Socialist party is a moot point, but there is no doubt that their critique of the lack of emotional appeal and of a national programme was very much to the point and touched one of the main weaknesses of the German democratic Socialists.

The Social Democrats did not take kindly to such 'national romanticism'; disciplinary measures were taken against the young rebels and by 1925 they were in full retreat. Some returned to the fold, others went with Niekisch and the National Bolshevists, and a few became active National Socialists.

The party organizations on the Left continued to exist by the force of inertia. They looked with much disfavour upon the small but cohesive and very active sects such as Nelson's little group, the 'I.S.K.,' whose radicalism (in private as well as political life) was rather more than either the Communists or the Social Democrats could stand (they both excluded I.S.K. members). The decline of

---

[1] Karl Bröger, *Jungsozialistische Blätter*, 1922–3; Franz Lepinski, *Die jungsozialistische Bewegung, ihre Geschichte und ihre Aufgaben* (Berlin, 1927), *passim*.

the left wing is somewhat surprising, for many members of the *Bünde* continued privately to prefer the left-wing and left-of-centre parties, despite all their weaknesses.[1] At worst they thought of these as a lesser evil. But the idea that a lesser evil might be worth fighting for did not occur to more than a few.

IV

While many young Germans were drawn into active participation in politics, others stayed imperturbably outside, and still others were firmly resolved to 'postpone their decision,' as they put it. Mention has been made of the *Freischar* and more will have to be said about the *Jungenschaft*, a small but influential offshoot of the former. Of such small *Bünde* there were others, like the *Jungentrucht* led by 'Teut' (Karl Christian Müller, a writer and teacher in the Saar), the *Graue Corps*, even more élitist, which was headed by 'Sebastian Faber' (Fred Schmid, a Swiss professor of chemistry), and a few more. The biggest was the old scouts' organization, the 'D.P.B.';[2] probably the greatest curiosity among them was the *Nerother*. Founded a few years before the First World War, the 'D.P.B.' was not, strictly speaking, a part of the youth movement; after the war, the reformers (such as the *White Knight* circle) split away. But a fairly solid remnant continued to exist, and gradually adopted much of the *bündische* style, eschewing the extravagances of Martin Voelkel and his colleagues. There was less talk and more discipline in the 'D.P.B.' than in the rest of the youth movement—preoccupation with the ultimate questions of philosophy, religion, and politics was discouraged. Its leader for many years was Hartmut (Wilhelm Fabricius), a forestry expert and right-wing nationalist who opposed modern dances, Freemasons, Marxist poison, psychoanalysis, the Weimar republic, *'the new practicality'* (*Neue Sachlichkeit*) etc.[3] He was also a member of Alfred Rosenberg's *Kampfbund* for German Culture years before the National Socialists came to power.[4] At the same time he was a capable educator who fought for the independence of his *Bund* and resisted the encroachments of the Hitler Youth as long as he could. Generally speaking, the 'D.P.B.'

[1] In a snap poll taken among the older members of the *Bünde* in Berlin in 1928, the Social Democrats registered an absolute majority with 53 per cent of the votes. In 1930, the German Democratic Party together with the Social Democrats got 65 per cent of the total. *Zwiespruch*, 14 March 1930.
[2] *Deutsche Pfadfinderbund*.
[3] Wilhelm Fabricius, 'Der Aufstand der *bündischen* Jugend,' in Curt Hotzel, ed., *Deutscher Aufstand* (Stuttgart, 1934), pp. 230 *et seq.*
[4] But in a private letter to Baldur von Schirach, the Hitler Youth leader, he said: 'I am not Hitler's subordinate' (NSDAP Hauptarchiv, file 354—B.D.C.).

was very much alive during all those years despite the earlier defections; because of its neutral character it became the most promising battleground for would-be empire-builders in the youth movement.

The *Nerother* (so called after a small village in the Eiffel mountains) was a much smaller group founded by the twin brothers Karl and Robert Oelbermann, after their return from the First World War. In the eyes of their friends and well-wishers they were the most uncompromising of all the *Bünde*, while their many critics called them the desperadoes of the youth movement. They certainly did not lack originality; they restored the old ruin of Waldeck Castle, which became their operational centre;[1] they were unflinching in their resistance to compromise with society (bitterly opposed to the idea of growing up, said the critics); their adventurous and daring expeditions to far-away continents lasted not weeks, but months and years. Occasionally they worked for their living, but they were the bohemians of the youth movement, who carried the *Wandervogel* spirit to an extreme, refusing to come to terms with the world around them. This in itself would hardly be sufficient reason to pass an adverse judgment on them; there have been similar phenomena in many lands at various times, and it is a moot point whether perfect adjustment to society should be the supreme aim of education. But the other extreme cannot be an educational ideal either; after all, the *Nerother* were not a small band of blood brothers, but a *Bund* including many hundreds of young boys. Hitch-hiking is not a vocation, and in later life only a few *Nerother* became explorers of strange lands and exotic cultures. It was an interesting experiment, though not a very successful one, and it found few imitators.

V

The Protestant and Catholic youth groups[2] were strongly influenced by the *Bünde* in the twenties and were frequently indistinguishable from them, except by the stress put on religious motives in their cultural activities. Numerically they were much stronger, and if some were rather loosely organized, others had as much cohesion as any independent *Bund*. In their respective Churches these youth groups often constituted a radical and reforming wing, but those who controlled them usually succeeded in preventing any serious

[1] Most of the *Bünde* mentioned in this section, including the 'D.P.B.' and the *Nerother*, reappeared in West Germany around 1948 and still exist. But their character has very much changed, and what is said here about the *Nerother* of 1930, for instance, does not apply to the *Bund* of the same name in 1960.

[2] Such for instance as *Neudeutschland, Quickborn* and the *Kreuzfahrer* among the Catholics; *Christdeutscher Bund, Bibelkreise, Bund deutscher Jugendvereine* among the Protestants.

mass defections. With the rise of National Socialism, however, the situation changed, and by 1931 whole groups, especially from the Protestant organizations, went over to Hitler with banners flying. This was not altogether surprising, because the German Protestant Church had never felt itself at ease in the Weimar Republic; it still wanted an All-German empire in which throne and altar were one; it put a strong emphasis on Germanic medieval traditions, opposed the disruptive ideas of the French Revolution, and inveighed against an international (Jewish) capitalist-atheistic conspiracy against German paramountcy in Europe.[1] There was a small democratic-republican wing in the Church, but it never pulled much weight.

Among the Catholics the state of affairs was somewhat different. The Church was lukewarm about the Weimar Republic and by no means committed to defend parliamentary democracy; most of its representatives would undoubtedly have preferred a more authoritarian regime. But comparatively few were actively anti-democratic and a good many of them realized, much earlier than the Protestant clergy, that National Socialism, despite all conciliatory formulas, was basically opposed to religion. As a result, the Catholic youth groups suffered less from the onslaught in 1932-3.

A few individual Jews belonged to the *Freischar*, the *Jungenschaft*, and some other *Bünde* which had no Aryan shibboleth. But the great majority were members of the Jewish youth movement, which was hardly less subdivided than the German movement. There were Zionists and (German) assimilationists, orthodox Jews, Liberals and Freethinkers, those who wanted a selective and those who wanted a mass movement. All had been greatly influenced by the style of the *Wandervogel* and *Bünde*, and they were perhaps closer to them in inspiration than to the Catholic or Protestant organizations, for most of them were not of a religious character: they were organized on ethnic lines simply because the German-Jewish symbiosis in the youth movement had broken down long before 1933; something of the kind had existed only in the days of the *Freideutsche* youth. There had been a strong Zionist contingent from the very beginning, and in the early thirties it became dominant. The Jewish organization received initially a great stimulus from the persecutions after 1933, but ultimately withered away because of the emigration of most of its members and the restrictions gradually imposed on all Jewish activities. Many went in groups to Palestine and established collective agricultural settlements, of which those of Givat Brenner and Hasoreah are today among the largest and best known.

[1] See Manfred Priepke, *Die evangelische Jugend im Dritten Reich* 1933–36 (Hanover, 1960), pp. 35–6.

VI

The largest and most numerous of the *Bünde* in the Weimar Republic were not those of the youth movement, but the para-military organizations, most of which were inclined towards the right. Their inspiration and structure were military in character, and owed little, if anything, to the youth movement, But a few were politically non-committed, and developed ideas and organizational forms of their own. With them the youth movement occasionally co-operated. The largest of these groups was the *Jungdo*,[1] founded by First Lieutenant Arthur Mahraun in 1919 as an anti-revolutionary group of the extreme right. Mahraun and other leading members of the group such as Kurt Pastenaci were former *Wandervogel*, and the movement they envisaged was very different in character and orientation from other para-military organizations. They wanted to be a strictly disciplined order, but rejected political dictatorship; they were strongly nationalist, but became leading advocates of a rapprochement with France; they rejected theories of racial supremacy, but nevertheless excluded Jews from their ranks. This was a sincere if inconsistent attempt to break away from the traditional tenets of right-wing and *völkische* ideology, which involved the leaders of this group, like those of some other *Bünde*, in the unsuccessful attempt of 1930 to create a strong democratic centre party. It is a sad reflection on the German situation in the early thirties that these democratic leanings were the undoing of the *Jungdo*; the chauvinist slogans and the call for a dictatorship proved much more effective.

Oberland was another, smaller para-military group which had seen service as a Free Corps. Its leader, Friedrich Weber, was also a former *Wandervogel*, and in the early twenties the political location of *Oberland* was in immediate proximity to that of National Socialism. Later, however, radical socialist demands were put forward by members who were increasingly dissatisfied with the traditional Right. While the *Jungdo* was extremely anti-Soviet, *Oberland* moved for a while towards the National Bolshevist camp and at least one of its leaders (Beppo Römer) became a Communist.

In the Third Reich nobody had much use for these para-military groups, although the earlier merits of *Oberland* were not entirely forgotten. The *Jungdo* was more suspect, in spite of a belated attempt to integrate itself into the new order. Mahraun, who had been a name to conjure with during the Weimar Republic, spent the

---

[1] *Jungdeutscher Orden*. There is now a detailed, though somewhat uncritical history of that movement: Klaus Hornung, *Der Jungdeutsche Orden* (Duesseldorf, 1958).

Hitler era breeding sheep in Central Germany and died in 1950, a man forgotten by all but the small community of the faithful.

VII

It is impossible to generalize about associations so conspicuously devoid of a common denominator. Some of the *Bünde* pursued definite purposes of a political, social, or religious character; others were, or at any rate aspired to be, purposeless, free of any tie to the world of adults, spontaneous, united only by the bond of comradeship. A *Bund* might be favoured simply as an educational means or as the form of organization most attractive to youth itself and most efficacious from the point of view of its sponsors—the churches, for instance. Others considered the *Bund* to be an end in itself; some thought of it in terms of a life-brotherhood, while others took a more realistic view of the limitations of the youth movement and understood that the *Bund*, like youth itself, was only a transitional stage.

All this was based on the tacit assumption that life in a group, in intimate association, was vastly preferable to life in interest-motivated, atomistic, impersonal society.[1] The *Bünde*, and the youth movement in general, thought that the group was a deeper, more immediate and organic way of living together than that provided by 'mechanistic society.' Such views were very common, and not seriously challenged, either in the youth movement or in German sociology at the time, but since then they have come in for serious criticism.[2]

The youth movement wanted, like Rousseau, to return to nature, to enter into a life free from the restraints of civilization, warmer, more vital and more spontaneous. To justify this aspiration, it unduly idealized primitive society, completely unaware that it is in fact hag-ridden by fears and taboos, and anything but free. Equally unfounded was the assumption that human beings in groups were more sincere and spontaneous than as individuals; for is it not precisely within a group that people learn to adopt mask-like patterns and attitudes? To think and act as exclusively in terms of group and community as the youth movement tried to do is an impossible

---

[1] The youth movement was influenced by the school of German sociologists that made the famous division between *Gesellschaft* (society) and *Gemeinschaft* (community). The *Bund* did not fit into the scheme since it was willed, whereas the community, in theory at least, was organic and free of any ulterior purpose. It followed that a new sociological category had to be created to accommodate the *Bund* in sociological theory.

[2] Cf. the summary of a lecture by Prof. René König in *Erkenntnis und Tat*, VI, 4, n.d. (ca. 1956), pp. 4–6.

undertaking, an attempt to cheat the devil out of his share in this world.[1]

This is legitimate criticism, for the youth movement not only committed excesses, especially during its *bündische* period; there was something mistaken in its basic approach. The mistake of most of the *Bünde* was that they wanted to remedy the discontents of modern society by reverting to the irrecoverable past, instead of seeking by trial and error for new forms of life within modern civilization. For that purpose, the group itself was neutral, neither good nor bad. Whether people were better or worse for belonging to a group is a question impossible to answer. Whether they became more or less sincere in a group likewise depends upon such a multitude of factors as to defy generalization. Psychoanalysts, who as a rule are more interested in the individual than the group, have nevertheless come to adopt group analysis and therapy in many cases, which suggests that they do not necessarily find that people behave less sincerely in groups than as individuals. Group education has its distinct advantages; what the *Bünde* frequently failed to realize was that group life was no panacea, and no absolute value; the deification of the group (or the *Bund*) always had unfortunate results.

The *Bünde* chose to ignore sexual problems; in this respect the *Wandervogel* and the *Freideutsche*, with all their half-baked ideas on the subject, had been more mature in their attitude. The existence of exclusive boys' and girls' groups was probably a necessity during puberty, but the attempt to delay the meeting of the sexes beyond the age of seventeen—to create an exclusively male *Jungmannschaft*— was doomed to failure and, in individual cases, caused or aggravated sexual maladjustments later on.

What were the achievements of the *Bünde*? At their best, they did succeed in finding new and promising forms of community life. The visionaries who thought in terms of a community for life, with all-embracing demands upon the individual, were the least successful. But the less ambitious, who were aware of the limitations of the group, *Bund*, and youth movement, made steady if inconspicuous progress, turning more than one difficult corner before the general disaster overtook them.

---

[1] *Erkenntnis und Tat*, quoting H. Plessner.

Seventeen

TUSK OR THE TRIUMPH OF ECCENTRICITY

AMONG the leaders of the *Bünde* there was one who became a myth in his own lifetime. Eberhard Köbel, better known as 'Tusk'[1] made, for better or worse, a strong impact on his contemporaries which even outlasted the Third Reich; the attempts to revive the youth movement after the Second World War were based more often than not on the traditions established by this man and a handful of his followers in the early nineteen-thirties.

They regarded themselves as the prophets of the third ('hellenistic') age of the youth movement—after the pre-war *Wandervogel* and the post-war *Bünde*. For a short but eventful day the figure of Tusk dominated the scene; some called him the only man of genius the youth movement ever produced, others considered him its evil genius, a charlatan engaged in feverish and purposeless activities. He left Germany shortly after Hitler took over and died in East Berlin in 1955, a lonely and forgotten man. Yet the image of the Tusk of 1930 lives on, and passionate disputes about the man and his place in the history of the movement have by no means come to an end even now.

I

Born in Stuttgart in 1907, the son of a senior government official, Eberhard Köbel joined a *Wandervogel* group as a boy, then became a member of the *Freischar*, and in 1928 was leader of the Wurttemberg region of that *Bund*. Small in stature and rather slim, he was

[1] He was given, or gave himself this name during an excursion in Northern Scandinavia (*tysk*-, German).

full of nervous energy, and if his intellectual interests were limited, he had considerable artistic gifts. He revolutionized the youth movement Press, editing two or three periodicals at a time, radically changing their lay-out, make-up, type and use of illustrations. Until the late twenties, most youth-movement publications were produced in the early *Wandervogel* tradition, stale and stylized, the contents usually dull and the illustrations in unbelievably bad taste. Köbel made them simpler and livelier and immensely more attractive. He had a genius for little inventions and apt innovations. The new form of tent (*kohte*) that he imported from Lapland became very popular throughout the youth movement. The story goes that Köbel once came to the art school in a new blue jacket of military cut designed by himself, and that when his professor asked for an explanation of this singular attire, he declared that one day, probably very soon, this jacket would be worn by every German boy. This sounded like an idle boast at the time, but the prediction came true, for a modified form of this jacket was adopted by the *Jungvolk*, the junior section of the Hitler Youth. Instead of the lute, and in addition to the guitar—which had been the standard musical instrument of the youth movement—Köbel and his friends introduced the balalaika and the banjo. New songs were imported from various parts of the world, and group excursions to Lapland and Novaya Zemlya were reported in a new style of travelogue. There was even the beginning of a youth-movement cinema school.

As the pastor said of Tusk at his funeral, 'He was a man full of love and full of ire.' Certainly few were indifferent towards him. Like a man possessed, he raced all over Germany on a heavy motorcycle, to win adherents to his *Jungenschaft* and his ideas. There was fanaticism and even ecstasy in his speech and behaviour: his boys were to become models of intrepidity, an élite of radiant physique and character; the whole of Europe would be amazed by the daring displayed in their summer camps; they were to dance as no one had ever danced before, in complete rhythmic self-surrender.

Some of Tusk's antics surpassed the worst excesses of the *White Knight* era; emotionalism and moral relativism ran wild. With their glorification of the soldier, of military virtues and even of the 'death wish,' the local branches of the *Jungenschaft* became 'garrisons' and every boy a budding warrior. Finding even the Prussian tradition too mild to serve his turn, Tusk held up the ideal of the Samurai (in his book *The Heroes' Bible*). In an article extolling *harakiri*, he affirmed that the most important virtue was 'demonic, knightly masculinity'; heroic Japan was more akin to the *Jungenschaft* than were any cowards talking German. A little story published early in 1933 in a *Jungenschaft* periodical gave a grim example of the spirit of this 'Order of Tomorrow' (as the story itself was entitled): 'A widowed lieutenant in Tokyo had been unable to find anyone to take care of his little daughter when he went to war. He therefore killed her and joined his regiment before his action became known. Thereafter he sought death upon the field of battle and found it, in order to follow his child upon the way to Maido. His conduct recalls the terrible spirit of the old feudal times when the Samurai, before engaging in hopeless battle, sometimes killed their wives and children, in order to erase from memory the three things which no warrior must recall upon the field of battle—his home and possessions, his beloved family, and his own body. After this act of superhuman heroism, the Samurai was armed neither to give nor to expect mercy in the *shinimono gurni*—the hour of mortal rage.'[1]

Many years earlier, Wyneken had said that youth was mankind's eternal 'chance of fortune.' Tusk tried—as he so often did—to go one better, and argued that youth was the only chance, the supreme value in itself, and that maturity was, almost *a priori*, a bad thing. For did not maturity mean coming to terms with society, being tied down by those hundreds of laws and conventions that it was necessary to destroy? At one time the youth movement had seemed dangerous in the eyes of the powers that be; Tusk wanted it to become dangerous again, to be the vanguard of the new revolt. That was why he wanted his boys to emulate the nomads or the Samurai, and be free from all bonds.

But these boys, like Tusk himself and their other leaders, were youngsters from middle-class families, who went to school at eight o'clock every morning (only a few were as yet students or apprentices), and lived in the homes of their parents upon whom they were more than merely materially dependent. The reality of their daily lives was quite incompatible with the dreams about the Samurai; it was only in the few weeks they spent together in their camps each year that they could try to live that supposedly higher life. Nevertheless, Tusk and his teachings fascinated thousands of them. More than any other contemporary leader of the youth movement he kindled their imagination. Tusk had more charisma and more élan as a leader than Voelkel, whose glorification of medieval knighthood in the early twenties had brought about a similar divorce from reality. But this alone would not account for Tusk's success; he combined wild flights of fancy with a good dose of common sense in practical affairs. He had been a brilliant and inventive student of the applied arts; he had more acute feeling than most of his contemporaries and knew better how to captivate the adolescent mind.

[1] Quoted by Harry Pross, *Die Zerstörung der Deutschen Politik* (Frankfurt, 1959), p. 156.

Playing soldiers was not, after all, exactly a new game, nor was it very original to exploit the charms of distant countries and exotic ideas; *Wandervogel* had been to Lapland before Tusk ever heard of that country. But he realized that a new style was needed for the new generation, that the old romanticism would no longer serve. What he attempted, albeit often in grotesque ways and ultimately without success, was to find adequate expression for the aspirations of youngsters growing up in a modern industrial society. He did not want to oppose the age of technology and the great towns, but only the kind of society that was emerging with them; hence his retreat into a fantastic world of Cossack songs (both White and Red), single-stick fencing, ecstatic dancing, and the Samurai cult. As for the ethical nihilism that went with these things, and the glorification of the 'death-wish'—so singularly out of place in the education of boys of fourteen—these were partly engendered by the moral climate of the time, which was that of the great 'economic blizzard' and the political dismay of a Central Europe whose social system was visibly disintegrating. Everyone was humming the songs of the new *Threepenny Opera* that had just been performed in Berlin.

Originally, the *Jungenschaft* had been one of the most selective of the *Bünde*. But Tusk was realistic enough to understand that, as the leader of a small select group, he could never attain his ultimate aim of forging German youth into the one great army of his dreams; he therefore tried to bring about a merger between the *Jungenschaft* and the other *Bünde*. He was met with a mixture of jealousy and derision; the others envied the *Jungenschaft's* verve and élan and often imitated its innovations, including its attire, but they ridiculed its artificial pathos and its tendency to swank. And of course there were worse allegations. Good looks was one of the qualifications for membership, and many of the pictures in its publications have a barely-concealed erotic undertone. None but the blind could fail to perceive the existence of an erotic quality in the relations between leaders and led and between members of a group.

Tusk's politics before 1932 were fairly conventional. He was a German nationalist, though not an extreme one; he believed in a Greater Germany, and called for resistance to the oppression of the *Volksdeutsche* in the East, for the abolition of the Danzig corridor, etc. His attitude to the Weimar Republic and the political parties was negative, but, unlike the *White Knight* circle, he did not believe in a mythical Reich to come. Tusk's ideal soldier (like Jünger's) was not really sacrificing himself for Fatherland or people, but for the greater glory of the military profession. There was a Russian cult in the *Jungenschaft*, just as there was a cult of the Samurai, but the Russia, too, was mythical; the heroic deeds of both Stalin and Admiral Kolchak, the leader of the White armies, were celebrated with commendable impartiality in the *Jungenschaft's* songs. Wherever the famous Don Cossack choir appeared in Germany after 1933, there were enthusiastic demonstrations by members of the *Jungenschaft* and former members of other *Bünde*, which caused some concern even to the Gestapo.[1] But the Cossack choir was made up of *émigrés* who had no sympathy whatever with Bolshevism, and their songs belonged to an epoch that had come to an end in 1917. Such misunderstandings were typical of the prevailing confusion; the Russophilia that was common in these circles was mainly non-political in character.

There was a sad disparity between Tusk the charismatic leader and inexhaustible inventor of new ways and means, and Tusk the thinker, providing a younger generation with guidance through the perplexities of the time; the one had genius, the other was pitifully incompetent. He played with the idea of becoming the leader of German youth under both the National Socialist and the Communist regimes, both of which distrusted him and kept him at a safe distance, for neither had any use for men with such dynamic impulses. Tusk's place was not in politics, and it was part of the tragedy of the German developments that they drove such a man into situations in which he was hopelessly at sea. If his tremendous ardour and his talents had been applied in the sphere of the arts, there is no knowing what heights he might have attained. In politics there was no opening for him during the thirties and forties, yet he was irresistibly attracted, as though by a magnet, to the very tasks he was least competent to handle.

II

In 1928, when Tusk was a regional leader of the *Freischar*, his energy and impetuosity came to the knowledge of 'General' Buske, the then leader of the *Bund*. Buske tried to provide scope for Tusk's zeal, but remained suspicious of the man's enormous ambitions. He made him editor of one of the *Freischar* magazines, but prevented his elevation to the leadership of the whole South German and Austrian region, which Tusk coveted as the springboard to higher positions. A disappointed Tusk went home to Stuttgart, wrote yet another travelogue, and founded, on 1 November 1929, a small conspiratorial group which set out to transform and rule the German youth movement from within. It called itself the 'D.J.1.11' (*Deutsche*

---

[1] See, for instance, the circular of the Munich political police dated 5 February, 1938, in B.D.C.

TUSK OR THE TRIUMPH OF ECCENTRICITY

Jungenschaft of November 1st), a title which, in later years, was to become as magical for certain circles as the name of its leader.[1]

According to Tusk and his collaborators the youth movement had declined into a lifeless official institution and lost most of its revolutionary character. The 'D.J.1.11' wanted to do everything better than the existing *Bünde*—'to sing better and to be silent better, to carouse better and to fast better, to work furiously and to be lazy without compunction.' What Tusk thought about the rest of the youth movement emerges from a circular letter that he wrote to his lieutenants explaining his decision to join the German Communist Party: 'For me, the "D.J.1.11" *is* the youth movement *par excellence*. Right and left of it there is only cowardice, meanness, and obdurate stupidity . . . this conceited, babbling, too-clever-by-half bourgeois youth movement is simply horrible.'[2]

But in 1929 he was still trying to work from within that bourgeois youth movement. After Buske's death in February 1930, his group came out into the open; but the new leaders of the *Freischar* did not want to have anything to do with Tusk who, meanwhile, had gained sympathizers in Berlin and Austria, and tried unsuccessfully to get control of the Central German region. Shortly afterwards, he and his *Jungenschaft* were excluded from the *Freischar* for persistent plotting and insubordination, and he found himself in the wilderness with a few hundred boys. About the same time he was appointed editor of a new youth magazine, *Das Lagerfeuer*, which was read throughout the whole youth movement; but this was a business venture launched by a commercial publishing house: Tusk's direct participation in the youth movement was at an end.

He was not quite alone in the wilderness. There were a few other leaders with small, élite *Bünde* on the same fringe of the movement. One was Fred Schmid, a Swiss professor of chemistry and an inventor, who for a while was at the head of the Rhineland region of the *Freischar* which later became the 'Grey Corps.' Schmid was less ambitious than Tusk; he did not want to create the great *Bund* of

---

[1] This account of Köbel's activities after 1928 is based on the recollections of some of his contemporaries in Stuttgart, Berlin, and London, and upon Tusk's own writings. Of these a bibliography is given in Kay Tjadden's *Rebellion der Jungen* (Frankfurt, 1958). This does not, however, mention all the writings of Köbel that were published during the London exile and in Berlin during the last years of his life, and posthumously. Of the special Tusk numbers of youth movement periodicals published after his death which contain biographical information, *Der Graue Reiter* (December 1955) is laudatory, while *Das Lagerfeuer* (August 1958) is extremely hostile. Tusk's own recollections of his struggles during 1929–33 were published in *Der Eisbrecher*, 1933, *passim*; others exist in an unpublished manuscript of 1949, 'Rückblick auf die Jugendbewegung.'

[2] Quoted in Helwig, *op. cit.*, p. 373.

German youth, but to be the master of a small group of select pupils.[1] In his view everything was dependent upon *eros*; a boy was either suitable material for his group or he was not, in which case no amount of training and education would help. Karl Christian Müller ('Teut'), a literary historian and teacher from the Saar, was a moderating influence in these circles; he had been strongly attracted by the ideas of the *Jungenschaft*, as Tusk had developed them, but Tusk's extremism remained alien to him, as were the esoteric rites of the 'Grey Corps'.

The *Jungenschaft* joined forces with Teut and his group, but the Grey Corps did not want to become involved in any mass activities. It was not enough for Tusk merely to unite the small *Bünde*; he meant to break up the entire youth movement, and either win over the sections he wanted, or establish some new formation that would serve as the rallying-ground for a great new movement. He tried to do this both from within and without the camp; the 'Red Grey Action' was to attract the best elements from all the *Bünde* to membership of the *Jungenschaft*. But for a little while Tusk also tried working from within one of the largest of the uncommitted *Bünde*, the 'D.P.B.,' the erstwhile scouts' organization.

All these efforts ended in splits, exclusions, and mutual recriminations. The leaders of the *Bünde* had become extremely distrustful of Tusk (the desperado, the highwayman of the youth movement, as his enemies now called him). They saw clearly enough that he did not come to help them but to make proselytes for his own group and its ideas. Meanwhile Tusk had moved to Berlin, and here at last, in the winter of 1931–32, he appeared to have found the rational conviction that might give intelligible purpose to his activities. Rumours spread that Tusk had become a Communist, was studying Marx and Lenin, and had acquired a scientific world outlook. Even his critics, who were now ready to believe almost anything about Tusk, were astounded. Could this be the same man who had introduced the most militaristic practices into the youth movement, who had ordered his boys 'to salute every commander ten times more smartly than in the *Reichswehr*?' Tusk himself repudiated the rumour in April 1932, as one more malicious attempt to smirch the reputation of the 'D.J.1.11,' which, he declared, was a school of character; there

[1] Schmid entered the annals of the German youth as the owner of a private aeroplane—an almost unheard-of possession in those days, although the Socialist Adolf Reichwein also had one. Schmid was also involved in the activities of the national-revolutionary camp in the early thirties. Under the pen-name 'Sebastian Faber' he published two political pamphlets and also financed *Der Gegner*, the periodical of one of those groups. The editor of the paper was Harro Schulze-Boysen, executed by the Nazis in 1943 as the leader of the 'Rote Kapelle,' a Communist espionage network.

could be no question of identifying it with the political judgments of some of its leaders.

This declaration was dated 11 April, 1932. But almost simultaneously Tusk's closest collaborators received a circular letter in which he announced his intention of joining the Communist Party. He was retiring from the leadership of the 'D.J.1.11' because continuance in that position would not only harm the *Bund*, it would also damage his own political career ('joining the Communist Party is, of course, merely the beginning . . .'). Tusk said he regarded this as a step towards manhood and maturity: 'You ought to have men you can look up to. Men *are* in politics at a time like this. We have never abhorred manliness.' The tie between him and his boys would never be broken: 'Your messengers will find the way to me even if I am sitting somewhere in a cave. My words will be the same, whether I am in Moscow or in Stuttgart, talking to you or to other people.'

What induced Tusk to join the Communists at that moment? Was it merely a 'lack of political instinct' as some of his foes later alleged? Many people more sophisticated than Tusk were attracted to Communism in that crisis, and it was not unnatural that the perpetual oppositionist should turn Communist just when the majority of his contemporaries were moving in the opposite direction, towards Adolf Hitler.

Tusk's guest performance with the Communists did not last long; they had no intention of using his talents; he never found a place in the party, and dropped out, or was dropped, after a few months. The *Jungenschaft* split apart after the resignation of its leader: a few hundred at most stayed on with the successor whom Tusk had designated. Older members—mainly in Berlin—joined a Communist cultural association in which Tusk was active at that time. Teut and his friends disapproved of Tusk's political decision, seceded, and founded their own little *Bund*, the *Jungentrucht*, which, owing to a fortunate set of circumstances—its main concentration was in the Saar, which was not then a part of the Reich—was to survive longer than most of the German *Bünde*.

Yet it was just at this time of the *Jungenschaft's* swiftest decline (the summer and autumn of 1932) that it did most to energize the youth movement as a whole. This was the last great wave of youth-movement enthusiasm before Hitler; it swept not only through all the *Bünde* but powerfully affected the religious youth organizations and even the political party groups. The example of the *Jungenschaft* spread like wildfire, the dress of the 'D.J.1.11,' their songs and their general behaviour with all its eccentricities were copied throughout Germany and even beyond its frontiers. After the National Socialists had come to power, the Hitler Youth noted quite rightly in one of its internal magazines that 'all the *Bünde* are directly or indirectly influenced by Eberhard Köbel, the leader of the "D.J.1.11." '[1]

Tusk's attitude in 1933 was somewhat inconsistent, even if given the benefit of all possible doubts. He continued to write for the youth magazine he had founded, *The Icebreaker*,[2] and to edit a new cultural-political organ, *Die Kiefer*, which displayed much interest in Far Eastern culture and religion, particularly in Zen Buddhism. All in all, this phase was a curious ideological sequel to his recently announced conversion to the Marxist-Leninist world outlook. Members of the 'D.J.1.11' were advised to join the Hitler Youth and try to gain positions of command, which some did—temporarily, at any rate. This, as Tusk subsequently explained, was in order to subvert the Hitler Youth from within; but any such action presupposed a clear political purpose, which was of course conspicuously absent among former members of the *Jungenschaft*. Secretly they clung together, but all they knew for certain was that they detested von Schirach and hoped that Tusk would somehow be made Führer of the Hitler Youth: Tusk himself seems to have nursed illusions on that score for months. It was quite unthinkable, of course, that the new rulers would give a position of power to a man whom they regarded as an adventurer and a 'cultural Bolshevist.' But there was so much talk in the air about a second, more thorough revolution, that Tusk's large expectations may not be quite inexplicable.

Legends have grown up around Tusk's departure from Germany in 1934. According to some of these stories he had become one of the most wanted men in the Third Reich, was arrested by the Gestapo, wounded in a successful attempt to escape, and hidden by friends until sufficiently recovered to flee abroad. He was, indeed, arrested in January 1934 and brought to Berlin for interrogation; he tried either to escape or to commit suicide while in the notorious Columbia House and suffered a fracture of the skull in the process. Released by the Gestapo—the evidence against him being apparently insufficient—he recuperated in his native Wurttemberg and finally left Germany in June 1934 as an ordinary passenger on the railway ferry to Sweden. If there were police agents trying to stop him, they did not try very hard.

Small groups of former *Jungenschaft* members continued to exist within the official youth movement or outside it: occasionally they would meet to sing the old songs, to take part in a semi-private

[1] See also the circular letter issued by the Bavarian political police (BN 23571 (35)), dated 4 June, 1935 in B.D.C.

[2] It continued to serve as the rallying ground for remnants of the *bündische* youth until it was suppressed by the authorities in 1935, when even the fact that it had carried a swastika on its title-page and had been repeatedly banned in Austria and Czechoslovakia for its propaganda, did not save it.

excursion, or to indulge together in wistful memories of the good old days. A few distinguished themselves as soldiers in the German army; others were involved in some form of resistance.[1] One of these was Helmuth Hirsch, an *émigré* Jew who was executed in June 1937 (although he was an American citizen), after having been found guilty of the attempted assassination of the Führer.[2] Some received long prison sentences for maintaining political contact with *émigré* circles in Paris, while others had their homes searched or were placed under short-term arrest. Inge Scholl states in her book that her brothers, the Munich students sentenced to death in 1943, were profoundly influenced by the *Jungenschaft*.

III

Exile is a bitter fate for any man; for Tusk it was a time of almost uninterrupted physical and mental suffering. His health was broken, and chronic sickness disabled him for years. In England nobody knew him or cared for his ideas; to be a writer in a foreign country is bad enough, but what could a youth leader do without the youth to accept his guidance? His presence awakened no interest whatever. In his German years he had known no rest from strife and crisis, but at least there had been occasional periods of achievement that enabled him to relax for a while. In London there was almost nothing but the naked struggle for existence that absorbed most of his energies; weakened as he was, he could hardly provide a living for his wife and children. He tried his luck as a photographer and studied Far Eastern languages without gaining proficiency or success in either. Even for his family and his closest friends he became more and more impossible.

A small group of young *émigrés* in London, Communist-led, under a neutral, popular-front disguise, provided Tusk with at least a symbolic framework for his activity. The Communists, unlike the National Socialists, were now willing to make use of him, but they never trusted him, and he must have felt deeply insulted by being held at arms' length as a fellow-traveller when he wanted nothing more than to be active within the party. Tusk now came to reject in public most of the ideas he had propagated. It had been a mistake,

[1] Of the two principal leaders of the *Jungenschaft* who emerged after 1945, one, characteristically enough, was a *Ritterkreuzträger* (roughly comparable to a British V.C. or a Congressional Medal of Honor), while the other, formerly a political prisoner, had spent the war years in a State penitentiary and a punitive battalion.

[2] The whole affair was allegedly staged by *agents provocateurs*; it is difficult to understand how even the most simple-minded persons could have been enticed into taking part in such a 'plot.' See the *Deutsche Rundschau*, 8, 1956, pp. 843–7.

he said, to apply selective criteria in the *Bünde*; the youth movement had failed because of it; those who were thus arrogantly excluded had streamed away to Hitler.[1]

In August 1944 Tusk expressed the hope that the former members of the *bündische* youth would fight as partisans against Hitler in the imminent, final phase of the war.[2] After the war he denounced the tendency towards small *Bünde* in the German youth movement and demanded one unified State youth organization: 'In the autumn of 1931, a wise man told me that the unity of German youth will never be attained without the suppression of the small splinter organizations. There are always splitters who will find a certain following among the stupid. . . . The tragedy of our people is that it has never learned to think politically. We now have to make up for this.'[3] What a fitting epitaph upon Tusk's activity before 1933! He certainly tried hard to make up for his own past political mistakes; he obeyed the party line to the point of arguing, in 1940, that the war was a disruptive factor in the struggle of German patriots against Hitler.[4]

Tusk tried to maintain contact and influence with his surviving followers, and with some new adherents, in circular letters from London during the first years after the war, but their effect was very limited. A *Jungenschaft mystique* had indeed survived the war, and many of the little *Bünde* that sprouted in West Germany after 1945 were modelled on the pattern of the 'D.J.1.11.' But most of their leaders were dubious about Tusk's political propaganda and, generally speaking, were more interested in the legendary Tusk of 1931 than the real man of 1947.

Nor did he fare any better in East Berlin, where he ultimately settled. He was given work in the East German broadcasting service, and published occasional articles in literary magazines; but his suggestions for the re-establishment of units of the *Bündische* youth within the framework of the Communist State youth, which he pressed in countless memoranda, some of them of great length, were dismissed out of hand. He was advised instead to concentrate on economic problems and questions of the class struggle; and indeed at the time of his death he was working on a book about the German electrical trust.[5] He might possibly have written good books on bird watching; instead, he had to analyze the prices of shares and the trends of capital exports. There were unpleasant charges laid against

[1] 'Aufruf an die bündische Jugend,' in *Freie Deutsche Jugend* (London), 9 January 1940.
[2] 'Bündische Jugend,' in *Free German Youth*, August 1944.
[3] *Freie Tribüne*, London, 12 January 1946.
[4] *Freie Deutsche Jugend*, 9 January 1940.
[5] Published posthumously under the title *A.E.G.: Energie-Profit-Verbrechen* (East Berlin, 1958).

him, followed by investigations; those who met him during this period were struck by his pathological sensitivity. He even went back to his native Stuttgart, still praising the Communist youth to a new generation of West German boys who stood in awe of this legendary figure but could not make head or tail of what he was trying to tell them. He died in East Berlin in the summer of 1955, not yet fifty years of age.

IV

A dispute promptly ensued in West Germany about what, if anything, of the Tusk tradition should be emulated. Some admirers were weary of his politics, especially of the last phase, but still thought that the impulse he had given them 'had survived the times.'[1] They wanted, in other words, to continue in 1958 where Tusk had left off in 1931. Others saw Tusk's enduring example as one of non-conformism, of intransigent opposition to society and the 'barbaric existing order.'[2] The engagement of the younger generation in politics, they argued, was now more than ever necessary. And lastly, there were many who thought Tusk had been no better than a great seducer, a pied piper luring young boys into a senseless 'children's crusade,' an unstable character who had no message at all for the young people of the nineteen-fifties and whose legacy was best buried with him.[3] This was all very well, but it so happened that many of the attacks on Tusk after his death were made by people who had supported Hitler, either from conviction or opportunism, with dubious qualifications for passing judgment on Tusk's political aberrations.

Some of his successors in present-day West Germany have strong opinions about the political engagement of the younger generation. But instead of trying to introduce an element of political responsibility their impact has been almost entirely negative. They found the Germany of the fifties horribly oppressive and the *Wirtschaftswunder* utterly vulgar; their libertarian ambitions were limitless, but, unfortunately, in inverse ratio to their political maturity and ability to live in freedom.

Such reflections lead one far beyond Tusk and his *Jungenschaft*, who were essentially products of the late Weimar Republic that made sense, if at all, only in that specific context. There were perhaps a few points of resemblance between that period and the Western Germany of the fifties, but the 'D.J.1.11' was not one of them; and all the attempts to conserve or revive its style were bound to fail.

[1] *Feuer* (Cologne), 19, *passim.*   [2] Kay Tjadden, *op. cit.*, p. 6.
[3] *Das Lagerfeuer*, 48, August 1958, *passim.*

Eighteen
NATIONAL BOLSHEVISM

THERE were five million unemployed in Germany in 1931; industrial production had dropped by one-third in two years. During the same period the membership of both the Communist and the National Socialist youth organizations doubled, a political symptom not in itself mortally dangerous to the Weimar Republic, for the extremist youth organizations in Germany never played an important part in politics; but it was an alarmingly true reflection of the flight into extreme political opinions and, above all, of the radicalization of the middle classes. Other countries were hardly less affected by the world economic crisis, but they had richer reserves of political strength. In Germany large sections of the middle classes believed that political democracy was a foreign importation unsuited to German conditions, and there had been signs of anti-liberal and anti-parliamentarian unrest since the very first years of the Weimar Republic. To say anything in its defence was decidedly unfashionable, especially among the younger generation, who never identified themselves with the regime; if it failed to cope with a situation, or if, as a 'system,' it seemed irresponsible, rotten, and doomed to fail, why should they care? They hardly ever thought of it as their own State. Long before the crisis reached its climax one of them wrote that dictatorship suited the style of leadership (*Führerstil*) of the younger generation, because it took responsibility away from anonymous society and transferred it to a man of flesh and blood.[1]
As for liberalism, there was no greater abomination: 'German youth turns away from liberalism with nausea and especial contempt, for there is nothing so contrary to their world outlook.... In the liberal man German youth sees the enemy *par excellence*.'[2] Moeller van den

[1] Tiedemann Ulrich Lemberg in the *Deutsche Allgemeine Zeitung*, 31 March 1929.
[2] *Das Dritte Reich* (Hamburg, 1931), p. 68.

Bruck was perhaps overstating their opinions, but not much. Many of this generation were, or became, anti-capitalist and to some extent also anti-Western; 'the West' was their synonym for the American way of life, of which a largely distorted picture was current among them, and for the Versailles Powers who meant to keep Germany enslaved for ever.

The origins of authoritarian and anti-democratic thought in Germany have often been studied, and need not be reviewed here. But the unwillingness shown by large sections of the younger generation to follow the lead of any political party had also something to do with the structure of the *Bünde*; their '*élite*' character unfitted them for finding their way into any mass movement. There were genuine political disagreements which led many of them to pursue the forlorn hope of finding some synthesis between Communism and National Socialism. They agreed with Hitler's radical nationalism, though not with his anti-Bolshevism; they were quite willing to join in the Communist attack on bourgeois society, but not to accept the theory of Marxism-Leninism.

I

The first initiative came from a small group of members of the extreme right-wing *Bünde*, who ventured for the first time into the no-man's land believed to lie at the far end of the political scale. Somewhat to their surprise they found that the range of political ideas took the form of a circle, not a straight line. 'We, the lost battalion of the extreme right,' reported Rolf Becker, one of the leaders of the 'Eagles and Falcons,' 'suddenly realized that the fight for social revolution on the left and the right is one and the same fight, the struggle of the whole people, *the* revolution.' Nor did they regard this as merely a tactical position. As Heinz Gollong, a leader of the *Freischar Schill*, put it: 'If we take our place in the great phalanx of proletarian and oppressed peoples of all countries, as Lenin— one of the greatest of us—commanded, we do it out of sincere conviction, not for tactical reasons.'[1] They appealed for an 'anti-capitalist front of youth from Right to Left,' and a few years later the central organization of the German youth movements, the *Reichsausschuss* (which also included the Protestant and Catholic groups), officially adopted an 'anti-capitalist' platform at its meeting in Söest in November 1932.

Such a very general declaration might have been taken with a pinch of salt, but the extremist slogans of the National Bolsheviks aroused some alarm both in the traditional right-wing parties and in Hitlerite circles. Alfred Rosenberg, the principal ideologist of National

[1] See *Die Kommenden*, 10, 1930.

Socialism, was set to work to demonstrate that the pro-Soviet enthusiasm of these young men was either due to a misunderstanding or was a very dangerous deviation.[1] But his remonstrances had little effect upon zealots who not only believed in the certain victory of the Russian national element in Soviet Bolshevism but were already talking about the '*Bündische* character of the marching columns of the Communist party of Germany.'[2]

Their revolutionary language—asking, in 1929, for nothing less than an anti-capitalist State of the workers, peasants, and soldiers—made the traditional right-wing spokesmen groan that not even the *Rote Fahne*, the German Communist organ, could be worse.[3] The conservative old guard was willing enough to support these boys in their campaign against liberalism and 'Jewish capitalism,' but reacted with horror against their attack on capitalism *per se* and the entire social order. These extreme ideas had not originated inside the youth movement, but had developed independently during the twenties and had only been carried to their extreme—or, as some said, their logical—conclusion by the more reckless members.

Of those external sources of ideas, the most prolific was the works of Moeller van den Bruck. He was already dead when the wave of National-Bolshevism surged up in the youth movement at the end of the decade. A man of a bohemian style of life, he was originally better known as the German translator of Dostoevsky; it was only during the First World War that he turned to politics and gained a small following. The world at large took little notice of his jeremiads against liberalism and 'the West,' or of his appeals for a policy identified with the cause of the young, exploited, and oppressed peoples such as those of Bolshevist Russia and Fascist Italy.[4] But with the great economic breakdown there was a recrudescence of all sorts of formerly neglected ideas and proposals, and in 1931, when a popular edition of Moeller's *The Third Reich* was issued, it was a great success.

The idea of an anti-Western and anti-imperialist 'front' of the

[1] 'Rebellion der Jugend,' in *Nationalsozialistische Monatshefte*, 5, 1930, pp. 50, *et seq.*

[2] Werner Lass in *Der Umsturz*, 1, 12 (1931–32), pp. 4, 5. Lass, an old *Wandervogel*, had been head of one of the smaller extreme right-wing *Bünde*, together with the former Free Corps leader Rossbach. In 1933 he became chief of the Hitler Youth Central German region, but remained suspect and was ultimately removed.

[3] Quoted in Karl O. Paetel, 'Die heutige Struktur der nationalen Jugend,' in *Das Junge Deutschland*, 6, 1929, p. 235.

[4] There is a great deal of German literature on Moeller van den Bruck. His ideas are discussed in Roy Pascal's essay in *The Third Reich* (London, 1955) and Klemens von Klemperer's *Germany's New Conservatism* (Princeton, 1957), pp. 153 ff.

'young' and 'proletarian' peoples was not solely Moeller's, but was quite fashionable in many countries during the twenties; it was shared even by the radical pan-Islamists of Russia (such as Sultan Galiev), by Kemal Ataturk, and by certain pre-fascist thinkers in Italy. During the First World War certain German sociologists had done useful spadework in a similar direction. Some of them accepted Lenin's theory of imperialism but rejected the class-struggle (which they replaced by a theory of solidarism); they regarded Bolshevism as, at bottom, only á national liberation movement and refused, or were unable, to understand its vast ambitions, either on the ideological or the international levels. Such a profound misreading of the facts might not be altogether inexcusable among, for instance, Asian or African political leaders, who could reasonably think of a political alliance with Soviet Communism as a practical (albeit temporary) possibility. But Germany was not in that position; any alliance between the German right and the Soviets could not possibly last. It is not at all easy, in retrospect, to see why Moeller was ever taken seriously in his own country, even at such a time of crisis. Perhaps it was his cocksure manner that made such an impression upon a generation hungry for certainties and impatient of any instructions seasoned with buts and ifs or any qualifying clauses whatever.

Even more confident in his own wisdom was Ernst Niekisch, who also had many followers in the youth movement and maintained close contact with some of the *Bünde*. His influence on German youth was calamitous, but he deserves some credit for his brave stand after 1933. He refused to climb on Hitler's bandwaggon and suffered imprisonment. Niekisch had been a Social Democrat, but left the party because it did not take a strong stand against the Versailles treaty and the West in general, and because he rejected Marxist socialism. Niekisch called upon German youth 'to spit out' all 'Roman' influences: for him Paris was the centre of all the enemies of the white race; it would cease to be the *de facto* capital of Germany only when it went up in flames.[1] He praised Rosenberg, the leading National Socialist ideologist, as 'much more profound' than Hitler, published antisemitic propaganda, advocated a totalitarian régime, and rejected the ideas of 1789 and of humanism, adding that even the most barbaric means were justified if they were necessary in the national interest.[2] Niekisch's eastern orientation was based on his assumption that the 'spirit of Potsdam' (and of Sparta) had found its reincarnation in present-day Russia. After 1933 Niekisch reverted to historical materialism and ridiculed his former allies for believ-

[1] *Widerstand*, 6, 1931, *passim*; 12, 1931, p. 372.
[2] *Politik deutschen Widerstandes, passim*.

ing that Old Prussia had been a Socialist State, when its real character had been feudal and patriarchal. After being freed from prison in 1945, Niekisch became a Professor in East Germany.

It has been argued that concepts such as 'the spirit of Potsdam' and the 'totalitarian State' were used by Niekisch as symbols of moral behaviour, and that they meant something quite different from what Hitler believed in.[1] Since Niekisch, unlike Hitler, never became Chancellor of the Reich or had the opportunity to put his ideas into practice, we have no material proof of this; but it is not easy to give him the benefit of the doubt.

Niekisch's circle attracted some of the older members of the *Bünde*, but his influence was largely indirect; his attempt to unite all the nationalist groups into one great front—the 'front of the young'— was not a success, and Niekisch, in his autobiography, has little good to say of the leaders of those *Bünde*.[2]

Ernst Jünger, the novelist and hero of the First World War, was widely read and admired in the youth movement, but his authority as a thinker was limited, although he was 'protector' of one *Bund* and the co-editor of a widely circulated youth magazine. Most of his contemporaries thought of him as a member of the National Bolshevist movement and he was, indeed, fascinated by the Soviet regime; but in fact he had no very deep interest in politics either national or international. His influence was largely destructive; and though young people are sometimes attracted by an attitude of nihilism, what Jünger had to offer was too much of a bad thing. His own ideological position became more and more 'above the battle,' until it was beneath his dignity to contribute anything to such minor contemporary issues as the future of Germany; his was an appeal to philosophy, to which few were willing to respond—least of all the philosophers.

More representative was the *Tat* circle, a small group of young political journalists who had been, or still were, members of the youth movement. In 1930 they made *Die Tat* (an old-established and staid monthly magazine) into the most interesting and representative mouthpiece of the younger generation. They were anti-Western, but not to such a fanatical degree as Niekisch; and they thought in terms of a strong Central Europe (with German economic and political expansion to the south-east), rather than of pro-Soviet orientation. It was mainly German domestic affairs upon which they commented every month, with considerable sarcasm and an unconcealed satisfaction at the deterioration of the situation, for they expected, and

[1] Hans Buchheim, 'Ernst Niekischs Ideologie des Widerstands,' in *Vierteljahreshefte für Zeitgeschichte*, October 1957, p. 352.
[2] *Gewagtes Leben* (Cologne, 1958).

indeed desired, a general catastrophe. In their view the Weimar Republic was moribund and doomed, and they would lend it no support; in fact, their anti-liberalism was second to none, and it transpired that they were in favour of an authoritarian regime, of economic autarky and of some sort of state Socialism. As one historian has said, the remarkable success of this group and of its publication is something of an enigma to a later generation;[1] but, like the homage paid to Niekisch or Moeller van den Bruck, it can be understood only against the peculiar background of Weimar Germany as it neared its end.

Like Niekisch, the *Tat* circle showed amazing ineptitude in their estimate of the real political forces of the day. They thought that National Socialism would never attain power because it lacked brains. In 1930, when it was still possible to do some useful work, they advised the youth movement not to get involved with any of the existing republican parties; but in the winter of 1932–33, when it was already too late, they called for a *bündische* initiative in support of the unpopular Schleicher cabinet. They did not welcome Hitler's victory at first, but subsequently some of them became prominent party propagandists.[2]

While Niekisch's influence was restricted to the right-wing *Bünde*, the *Tat* circle appealed far more widely both to right and left—the *Freischar* included. This was partly because of their personal contacts; in contrast to Niekisch they themselves belonged to the young generation of the day and some of them were playing important parts in the youth movement. While Niekisch was engaging in grandiose historical speculations, they were making a more sober and matter-of-fact study of social and economic problems; people who were repelled by Niekisch's fanatical pathos were attracted by the seemingly much more reasonable ideas of the *Tat* publicists. But with all their sincerity and good intentions, they were intellectual pacemakers for National Socialism, labouring under a strange illusion of their own political importance.

II

Though the leading conceptions of National Bolshevism had been arrived at outside the youth movement, its protagonists in the *Bünde* did not slavishly follow the instructions issued by Niekisch and

[1] Kurt Sontheimer, 'Der Tat Kreis,' in *Vierteljahreshefte für Zeitgeschichte*, July 1959, p. 257.

[2] The leader of the group, Hans Zehrer, did not, however, adjust himself to the requirements of the new masters of Germany; he withdrew to a North Sea island, to emerge again after 1945 as the editor of a leading West German newspaper.

others. Their ideas were developed in countless groups and sub-branches, each with its own ideology and programme. The *Aufbruch* circle, for instance, consisted mainly of former National Socialists or other right-wingers, and served as a half-way house on the way to Communism, at which some of them finally arrived. Among the members of this circle were Beppo Römer, a leader of the *Oberland* Free Corps; Scheringer, the famous Reichswehr lieutenant who was jailed for National Socialist activities and became a Communist while in prison; Bruno von Salomon, brother of the well-known author; the writer Bodo Uhse, the former parson Eckert, and others. The *Jungnationalisten* (Ebeling), the *Gruppe sozialrevolutionärer Nationalisten* (Paetel), the *Eidgenossen* (Werner Lass), and the *Bündische Reichsschaft* (Kleo Pleyer), were almost all members of the *Bünde*. There were many other small groups and magazines propagating national revolutionary and National Bolshevist ideas; some were even more radical than Niekisch, whose pro-Soviet standpoint was then based mainly on considerations of foreign policy. Paetel and his friends stood for the socialization of the means of production and the class struggle, and they accepted local soviets as the basis of revolutionary organization. The *Aufbruch* circle taught its members, not always with success, the rudiments of dialectical materialism. Yet another faction included dissident National Socialists such as Pleyer, or Peter Berns, the leader of the *Geusen*, who had some difficulty in deciding whether to support Hitler or the more radical, socialistically-inclined Otto Strasser.

Thus 'National Bolshevism' or 'German Leninism' were really misnomers for a multitude of small factions whose intentions could not possibly be brought under a common denominator. Most of them preferred to be called 'national revolutionaries,' regarding the title 'National Bolshevism' as both inaccurate and offensive, although it was willingly adopted by some who wanted to shock the bourgeoisie. Many had sympathized with Hitler's party in the middle twenties, but had been disappointed by his lack of consistency—his readiness to collaborate with the traditional right wing of Hugenberg (and with 'bourgeois parties' generally) and his support of Mussolini and Italian fascism—implying the suppression of working-class organizations.[1]

Moscow and the Comintern were in an intransigent mood in 1929–30; there was less willingness than ever before to co-operate with non-Communist parties, and the campaign against Communist deviationists was at its height. However, since the 'National Bolshevists' could not be regarded (like the German 'National Communists' of 1919–20) as a group of deviators from the Communist

[1] R. Rudolf in *Die Kommenden*, 14, February 1930.

Party line, but were defectors from the extreme right who were moving eastwards, Moscow was inclined to take a more lenient view of their activities. The Soviet spokesmen welcomed Paetel's and Gollong's demands for a revision of the programme of the Hitler movement and their insistence on more socialism, praising them as the 'most progressive group of the national-revolutionary movement.' Ebeling's critique of the German conservatives who mouthed nationalist phrases while co-operating with Western trusts was also commended, and approbation was extended to some others who had proposed a pro-Soviet orientation of German policy—Professor Friedrich Lenz of Giessen, and some members of the 'Junabu.'[1]

But it is only as the expression of a mood or tendency that National Bolshevism is of interest; politically it was never of much account. Its attempts to link up with other groups, such as Strasser's 'Black Front' or the *Landvolk* movement of rebellious peasants in North Germany, came to nothing. And when Hitler came to power some of the former national revolutionaries made their peace with his party; Franz Schauwecker, who like Jünger had been a widely-read writer of the *Fronterlebnis* of the First World War, became one of the leading lights of the new literature; while Kleo Pleyer, having become a professor of history, specialized in anti-French and anti-Jewish propaganda.[2] Werner Lass's mixed fortunes as a Hitler Youth leader have already been mentioned; Paetel and Ebeling emigrated and continued to attack Hitlerism from abroad.[3] Niekisch was sentenced to life imprisonment for carrying on anti-Hitler activities after 1933, and Richard Schapke, a *Wandervogel* leader who became Otto Strasser's lieutenant, was executed. A great and growing amount of autobiographical literature, by writers ranging from Scheringer, Uhse, and Salomon to Hielscher and Jünger, records in detail what became of the National Revolutionaries and National Bolshevists who survived. As human documents these memoirs are often fascinating; politically they are of little importance.

III

National Bolshevism was not an exclusively German phenomenon; there were similar developments in other European countries about the same time with, of course, local variations. In Poland, for instance —a country from which a pro-Russian tradition was conspicuously absent—some leading representatives of the younger intelligentsia

---

[1] *Rundschau* (Moscow), 27–28, 34, 1929.
[2] He was killed in battle in 1942.
[3] Ebeling returned to Germany after the war, while Paetel is now an American citizen living in New York.

were then moving from the extreme right to the extreme left. Like their German contemporaries, they realized that the old conservative forces were quite incapable of coping with the disastrous situation, and that a revolutionary programme of some kind was indispensable and inevitable. As Paetel points out, this swing to the left in Germany and elsewhere was a natural consequence of their common experience—of unemployment and of the proletarianization of the middle classes, and the young intellectuals in particular.[1] That experience is enough to account for the rapid drift of youth into the Communist or the National Socialist camp, and their attempt to create a 'third force' out of the ideologies of both. But the young German radicals had to work through their own factions because of their belief in the *Bünde* as effective means to the re-shaping of German politics; they mistrusted all political parties and resented the coolness with which their ideas and suggestions had been received on both the extreme left and right.

Their political conceptions—even allowing for their youth and lack of experience—were immature; and they misjudged the major political forces of their time: their political appeals and declarations bore at their worst a fatal resemblance of style to those of the National Socialists. Yet the great majority of them never became closely involved with that party; some even actively resisted Hitler. In that respect their record is certainly no worse, on the whole, than that of the neutral *Bünde*, which were originally far more critical of Hitler and his movement.

Obvious as were the blunders and self-delusions of the National Bolsheviks, in retrospect it is not so easy for even the most relentless critic to point to a practical policy they should have espoused; for a sensible and detached policy it was probably already too late. Any political platform in the Germany of 1930 had to be nationalist and Socialist in essence and radical in approach to attract the younger generation. What was clearly wrong with the national revolutionaries from the very beginning was their incontinent eagerness to get rid of democracy in Germany, their implicit assumption that whatever might come after the Weimar republic, it would be better than that detested 'old' regime. Clearly they lacked imagination.

[1] Karl O. Paetel, 'Der deutsche Nationalbolschewismus,' in *Aussenpolitik*, 4, 1957, p. 11. See also O. E. Schüddekopf: 'Linke Leute von Rechts' (Stuttgart, 1960), *passim*.

PART FIVE

PART FIVE

Nineteen

IN HITLER'S SHADOW

I

NATIONAL Socialism came to power as the party of youth. Its cult of youth may have been less pronounced than that of Italian Facism, whose very hymn was called 'Giovinezza'; but Hitler lost few opportunities of declaring that his movement was *inter alia* a revolt of the coming generation against all that was senile and rotten with decay. Yet for all their claims to represent youth, the National Socialists never succeeded in establishing a strong youth movement of their own before 1933. All through the twenties the Hitler Youth remained a negligible force, and in 1933, when it became part of the State apparatus, it lost whatever spontaneity or independence it may ever have had.

The establishment of a separate youth group dates back to February 1922, when Hitler demanded this in a circular letter to his Party and in a manifesto published soon afterwards in its newspaper.[1] The head of this initial group was a man named Lenk, who soon faded out of the picture—perhaps because he was charged with embezzlement. An interregnum followed, in which the Schill Youth, a right-wing extremist *Bund*, became for a time the official youth section of the party. Kurt Gruber, who was appointed to succeed Lenk, even announced in a letter to Rossbach, the former Free Corps leader, that he wanted to unite his own young Hitlerite groups in

---

[1] *Völkischer Beobachter*, No. 19, 1922. No history of the Hitler Youth has yet been written, though some short sociological studies have appeared in recent years (cf. Arno Klönne, *Hitlerjugend*, Hanover, 1960). The N.S. *Hauptarchiv*, now partly in American hands in the Documents Center (B.D.C.) in Berlin-Dahlem, contains very interesting source material that has not hitherto been used, including unpublished manuscripts by Lenk and Gruber, the first and second leaders of the Hitler Youth, and letters written to and by Baldur von Schirach, who became *Reichsjugendführer* in 1933. The name 'Hitler Jugend' was coined by Julius Streicher, the editor of *Der Stürmer*.

Saxony with the 'Schill Youth;'[1] apparently the National Socialists did not feel confident of an independent success in this field. Nor did the Hitler Youth make much headway under Gruber. As late as 1929, Baldur von Schirach, who had been very successful as a students' leader and was later to become Gruber's successor, told Rossbach that 'the Hitler Youth is badly led and its discipline is indifferent.'[2] To the leader of the *Geusen*, another extreme right-wing *Bund*, Schirach wrote that he was the friend of both the official party youth organization and the *Geusen* and that 'the youth movement and the Hitler Youth cannot be divided.'[3]

Indeed, for many years there were close contacts between some leaders of right-wing *Bünde* and leaders of the Hitler Youth, while Baldur von Schirach, who was something of a poet in his spare time, played the role of *arbiter elegantiarum* in these circles and offered advice on literary topics.

However, the leaders of the right-wing *Bünde*, sympathetic though they might be to the principles of National Socialism, came to realize that the National Socialist professions of sympathy for the youth movement were not very sincere. While, in 1932, the Hitler Youth leader in Berlin was complaining that proletarian groups distrusted youth leaders with a *bündisch* past, the *Bünde* were growing no less suspicious of the Hitler Youth, whose rowdy and brawling behaviour repelled them. Even members of the National Socialist party were critical of the human material collected by the Hitler Youth. Holfelder, the first leader of the 'Artamans,' wrote a long letter to Hitler in 1925, urging that local National Socialist leaders should be instructed to refuse membership to former members of the 'Artamans' who were on the 'wanted' list of the police for robbery, murder, or living on the earnings of prostitutes. (This throws a revealing light not only upon Hitler's party but also on the more 'élitist' 'Artamans.') Prominent members of right-wing *Bünde* made repeated complaints of drinking orgies among the Hitler Youth and, in general, of the lack of appreciation of the youth movement shown by National Socialism. One of them wrote that if Hitler's companions would only show a greater measure of under-

---

[1] Letter dated 16 July 1925. Rossbach replied that the 'Schill Youth' preferred to remain an *élite* organization. Gruber was playing a double game; a little while before, he had told Hitler that 'it would be quite impossible to get a single working-class child into the *Schill Jugend*' (25 May 1925). All these letters are in file 335, B.D.C.

[2] Letter to Werner Lass, dated 5 January 1929; *ibid.*, file 354.

[3] Letter to Peter Berns, dated 5 June 1930, *ibid.*

standing of the psychology of the youth movement, they would count many more members of the *Bünde* in their ranks.[1]

As time went by, the leaders of the Hitler Youth tended to assume a more and more hostile attitude towards the youth movement, even towards the *Bünde* whose ideology was closely related to their own. Gruber wrote, in the *Völkischer Beobachter*, that the *Bünde* had 'played a dishonourable part,' and that they had ridiculed the Hitler Youth as no genuine part of the youth movement (*Unjugendbewegt*). Even more unfriendly was Baldur von Schirach, who said that 'the youth movement had trained cowards and egoists to hunt after chimeras.'[2] 'Empty phrases' and 'nationalist philistines' were among the epithets hurled at the *Bünde* by spokesmen for the Hitler Youth, who attacked them as unteachable sentimentalists indulging in moonlight romanticism, aristocrats of the youth movement who would never soil their hands to support the proletariat in its struggle, indifferent to the sufferings of the working class, etc.[3] For in the early days such anti-capitalist, quasi-revolutionary language played a great part in Hitler Youth propaganda; they found it necessary in order to compete successfully with the left-wing groups during that decade of acute economic crisis: indeed, their official title in those days was 'Hitler Youth, *Bund* of German working-class youth.' All the same, they were never very successful in left-wing centres such as, for instance, Berlin. Before 1933, their main strongholds were in Austria (Carinthia and Upper Austria), and in North Germany (Hanover, Schleswig-Holstein, Lower Saxony).[4]

The Hitler Youth leaders' enmity towards the *Bünde* is easily understood, for to a certain extent they were competitors. The attitude of the party leaders (as distinct from leaders of the Hitler Youth) was more complex and ambiguous. None of those nearest the top had been members of the youth movement in their early days, though some of the second rank had belonged to the *Wandervogel* or the

[1] See letter of Georg Anton, one of the leaders of the '*Geusen*,' 19 April 1929, in B.D.C. file 370; also Holfelder to Hitler, letter dated 22 June 1925, *ibid.*; and V. von Lichenow in *Die Kommenden*, 27 December 1929.

[2] *Völkischer Beobachter*, 22 October 1931. Typewritten script of speech by Schirach, undated, probably summer of 1933, B.D.C. file 336.

[3] Hermann Bohm, *Hitler Jugend in einem Jahrzehnt* (Hamburg, 1938), pp. 38–41.

[4] They were weakest in the traditionally Catholic strongholds of the Rhineland, the Saar, Lower Bavaria, and the left-wing bastions (Berlin, Hamburg, the Ruhr). See the secret Hitler Youth *Rundschreiben* dated 1, 32, Anlage 4 in B.D.C. file 335; on the situation in Berlin see 'Report on the Organizational Situation,' 12 January 1932. At that date, when the National Socialists were already the strongest political party in the country, the Hitler Youth had fewer than 1,000 members in the German capital!

Bünde.[1] Hitler himself had no use for the youth movement; he had the same contempt for it as for the *völkische* splinter groups. For him, 'Wandervogel' was a term of derision: he called Otto Strasser a 'political Wandervogel' after his defection in 1930. Goebbels took more interest in the youth movement; so did Hess, and also Rosenberg, the principal ideologist at that time, who eulogized the 'beautiful romanticism' of the *Wandervogel*—now to be replaced by a new romanticism 'of steel.' Some National Socialist spokesmen used lofty terms in commendation of the youth movement; one of them called it a 'child-like, creative movement' very much like their own party: 'National Socialism is the forum of political struggle for all sincerely German youth *Bünde*.'[2]

These and other friendly declarations produced, among members of the youth movement, a mistaken impression that the party leadership, in contrast to von Schirach and the Hitler Youth leaders, was amicably disposed towards them. They therefore tried—needless to say without success—to obtain help from Hess and even Hitler, over the head of von Schirach, after National Socialism had come to power in 1933.

II

The Hitler Youth adopted many of the outward trappings of the youth movement, but differed from the *Bünde* in essential respects. It adopted their uniform and organizational structure (group, tribe, and *gau*); it had its banners, sang many of the movement's songs (as well as some of its own), and played war games. But whereas the primary concern of the *Bünde* was with group life and the education of individual character, the Hitler Youth was mainly a training centre for future members of the S.A. or the S.S. While the *Bünde* retreated into the seclusion of woodlands, or went on long and adventurous journeys abroad, the principal task of the Hitler Youth was to impress the public by ostentatious parades through the streets of big cities. The youth movement engaged in mock fights and war games; a knife was part of the scout's equipment, but it was not to be used to wound or kill. The Hitler Youth, on the other hand, took part in frequent street fights in which weapons were freely used. Opponents were attacked and sometimes killed in these brawls, which occasioned some casualties among the Hitler Youth them-

[1] Such local leaders as, for instance, Krebs, Terboven, von Gregory, Haake, Haverbeck and Brückner. Of the National Socialist intellectuals, many had belonged to the German Academic *Gildenschaft*, a students' association which combined youth movement and right-wing extremist elements.

[2] A. Rosenberg, 'Rebellion der Jugend,' in *Nationalsozialistische Monatschefte*, 5, 1930, pp. 50 ff; Winfred-Kiel, 'Der Weg der Jugendbünde zum Nationalsozialismus', *ibid.*, p. 59.

selves, including the twenty-one 'martyrs' of the 'years of struggle.' The overwhelming majority of *Bünde* members were high-school students, whereas, according to their own statistics, only twelve per cent of the Hitler Youth were from secondary schools; the bulk of them were of working-class origin and many were unemployed.[1] Middle-class youth who joined Hitler's party were more likely to have belonged to the National Socialist *Schülerbund*, and some of them were group leaders in the *Jungvolk*, the junior section of the Hitler Youth for those between ten and fourteen years of age.

The leaders of the Hitler Youth were greatly irritated by what they regarded as a patronizing attitude in those circles of the *bündische* youth which professed *sympathy* with National Socialism. These sympathizers were always saying that the Hitler Youth were of course doing a useful and necessary work, but that it was 'not our work.'[2] Other *bündische* critics even deplored the Hitler Youth's total involvement in politics and its utter submission to the party, and one of them cast doubt upon the party's dogmatic omniscience, quoting Cromwell's remark that 'he who knows not whither he goes, goes furthest.'[3] They accused Gruber and von Schirach of trying to destroy the *Bünde*, and blamed them for the bodily violence practised against their members.[4] But what infuriated the Hitler Youth most of all was the calm expectation of the right-wing *Bünde* that the key positions in the coming Third Reich would be theirs by right, for had they not paved the way and trained an élite for the new dispensation?

There were leaders of the *Bünde* who went over to the Hitler Youth in the twenties; but not all of them stayed the course, and some came to grief in the Third Reich.[5]

The Hitler Youth undoubtedly had its share of misguided idealists, but the boys who were induced to join it (there were very few girls in it before 1933) had neither the makings nor the aspirations of the 'ideal *bündisch* type'; it therefore attracted comparatively few of the members of the *bündisch* élite, who looked upon it as a collection

---

[1] Günter Kaufmann, *Das kommende Deutschland* (Berlin, 1943), p. 19. There are no means of checking these figures, but there is good reason to believe that a fairly high proportion came from lower middle-class families who had been 'proletarianized' during the years of inflation and economic crisis.

[2] W. Fabricius in *Die Kommenden*, 13 December 1929.

[3] G. Rebsch, *ibid.*, 28 March 1930.   [4] W. Müller, *ibid.*, 19 July 1929.

[5] According to a National Socialist source, 400 members of the *Bünde*, and 300 former members of the Socialist and Communist youth organizations (including the former secretary of the Communist youth), joined the Hitler Youth in 1929. *N.S. Monatshefte*. 5, 1930, p. 59. These figures cannot, of course, be checked.

of uncouth upstarts.[1] It appealed most of all to mass organizations on the fringe of the youth movement, such as the gymnasts and the Protestant youth groups. Leopold Cordier, one of the leading figures in the Protestant youth movement, estimated that in 1931 about seventy per cent of the members of the 'Bible Circles' were already under National Socialist influence, and an even higher figure was put forward by another Protestant observer. Many leaders of the Protestant *Bünde* attempted to resist the rising flood, but were soon swept aside, and the groups which tried to oppose it by declaring that membership of the Hitler movement and of their own confessional body were incompatible had as little success.[2]

It was National Socialism, not the Hitler Youth, that made such a powerful appeal to young Germans, above all by its activist character.[3] In vivid contrast to the interminable discussions of the *Bünde*, elaborating ideals that were to be realized in some indefinite future, Hitler affirmed that the hour had already struck; the day of national salvation had arrived. The *Bünde* had wanted their members to understand that all the different aspects and facets of the political problem had to be studied, each from its own angle, before a political judgement could be valid and comprehensive. Commendable in itself, this relativistic approach was also their weakness, and made them an easier prey to the fanaticism and one-sidedness of National Socialism. While the *Bünde* were talking about sacrifice, their rivals were demanding, and getting, immediate action.[4] Facing the rising tide of National Socialism, more and more of the *bündische* youth feared that history would pass them by, and felt incapable of remaining inactive. The cry for political engagement awakened a profound response in such a period of disarray and desperation. It must be remembered that the middle classes were hardly less seriously hit by unemployment than the working class; everything seemed undermined by the general economic decline and the spectre of academic and white-collared poverty was becoming a grim reality. Choosing Hitler was not an act of political decision, not the choice of a known programme or ideology; it was simply joining a quasi-religious mass-

[1] The chief exception was the *Junabu*, some sections of which went over to Hitler in 1930.

[2] Leopold Cordier in the *Evangelische Jugendführung*, 3, 1931, p. 70; Manfred Müller, quoted in M. Priepke, *op. cit.*, p. 17.

[3] 'The *Jungmannschaft* of almost all the *Bünde* and the Protestant youth are in their majority either members of the NSDAP or its storm troops and youth sections, or about to join the party' (Werner Kindt in *Das junge Deutschland*, 12, 1932, p. 397).

[4] For a critique of the relativism of the *Bünde*'s thinking as the source of their weakness in confrontation with National Socialism, see G. Rebsch, quoted in *Wille und Werk*, 1, 1930, pp. 6–7.

movement as an act of faith. Rational misgivings about the relevance of Hitler's professions to the solution of Germany's real problems cannot have been entirely absent from the minds of many, but they were perfectly willing to surrender their own critical judgement. It meant abandoning democracy and freedom as impotent and discredited ideas and trusting the Führer, who would know best what to do.[1]

III

Did the youth movement contribute to the victory of National Socialism in January 1933? And if it did, to what extent?

If one takes the view that all the romantic movements of the last 150 years were precursors of National Socialism—as a whole line of thinkers from Plato to Luther and Proudhon have actually been included in a list of the precursors of Fascism—then one can, no doubt, make out a good case for not excepting the youth movement. More specifically, large sections of the German youth movement belonged to the *völkische* camp, even if they were not among the most extreme of its devotees. They were also great believers in order, authority, the *Führer* principle, and a *Grossdeutsches Reich*. Most of the *Bünde* did not like Jews, and if many of their members were not pronounced racialists, they did contribute their share to the mystique of 'blood and soil.' Hitler's régime was certainly no sudden break in the continuity of German history, not as unprecedented as some would like to believe; nor was racial antisemitism thinkable without the different kind of antisemitism that preceded it. The sources of National Socialism are deeply rooted, and can be traced far back in German history.

In truth, the youth movement bears a share of responsibility in the same sense as, with but very few exceptions, do all other German movements and parties. But such a generalization is of little value, for if all are responsible no one is really guilty. A more discriminating approach is imperative if degrees of guilt and responsibility are to be established. In the case of the youth movement, its sins were those of omission rather than of commission. It had too little political influence to have decisively affected the course of events, but it did less than it could have done to develop an ethos of individual political responsibility. Thus, while some of its leading

[1] A leading member of the *Bünde* complained bitterly about the 'shocking lack of independence among our older members' who preferred to be fellow travellers rather than to think for themselves. 'They trust one man who is to be in charge of everything' (*Der Bund*, 12, 1932, p. 169). Erik H. Erikson, an American psychoanalyst of German origin, touched the very kernel of the problem, observing several years later that Hitler had replaced the complicated conflict of adolescence with a simple pattern of hypnotic action.

members had been intellectual pace-makers for National Socialism, and a small number actively resisted it, the majority did very little one way or the other.

If there was not much collaboration of the youth movement with the Hitler Youth, there was a great deal of wavering, hesitation, and plain opportunism in their attitude. Leaders of the *Bünde* showed no great concern about the growth of the Hitler Youth when, after years of stagnation, it began at last to grow apace in 1932, after having been banned by the Government for a little while in the spring of that year. Illegality seems to have acted as a stimulus and gained it new adherents, for at its Convention in Potsdam in the autumn, the Hitler Youth assembled nearly 100,000 members and sympathizers. Impressive as this was, one of the biggest youth demonstrations in Weimar Germany, the *Bünde* were far more impressed by the Hitler party's seemingly inevitable march to power. Some were ready to support General Schleicher's attempts to stem the tide of National Socialism by a dictatorship of the *Reichswehr*. Others, including even leaders of the Catholic youth organizations, demanded a coalition government that was to include the National Socialists.[1]

The leaders of the *Bünde* did not take sides, and their perplexed, temporising attitudes were no protection against such a political storm. One has only to glance through some of their more representative publications for 1932 to see how they drifted with the prevailing winds. One of these journals, which served as a platform for several of the neutral *Bünde*, was now specializing chiefly in biographies of war heroes of the past, such as York, Andreas Hofer, Lützow, and Moltke. We find it quoting *in extenso* one of the most chauvinist documents in German literature, Kleist's *Catechism*, and dwelling at length upon the heroic stand of the Nibelungs or of the last Goths. It prints poems to the effect that 'We will never retreat before the lash of the Polacks'; it attacks Lithuania, and calls for re-militarization: 'A people without arms is a people without honour.'[2] A scouts' magazine reprints a fireside speech by a Leipzig professor on New Year's Eve, 1933, expatiating upon 'faith in the aristocracy of Germandom' and 'the destiny of our people as willed by God.'[3] These were all fairly typical symptoms of the general climate of approved opinion in the *Bünde*, as the German *annus mirabilis* of 1933 was rung in.

[1] *Junge Front*, 7 August 1932. [2] *Jugendland* (Plauen), 1932–33, *passim*.
[3] Prof. Felix Krüger, *Bund, Volk und Reich* (Berlin, 1933), p. 27.

IV

In the eventful spring of 1933 a truncated and terrorized *Reichstag* voted to give Hitler unlimited power. The governmental system was metamorphosed; the first concentration camps were established, and the first steps taken towards the systematic extermination of the Jews in Germany. Dr. Goebbels was made Minister of Propaganda, and all political parties except that of Hitler's creation were dissolved. The State was being re-modelled upon a totalitarian plan, a State in which there could be room for only one youth organization, though as yet the *Bünde* hardly realized it.

The first proofs they had of this were pin-pricks compared to what was to follow; some groups were attacked by the Hitler Youth in their camps, on excursions, or in their town centres. Then, on 5 April, a Hitler Youth commando descended on the central office of the Executive of German Youth Movements in Berlin (the *Reichsausschuss*), seized the premises and the documents. The Jewish and the Socialist youth movements were expelled from the executive, the Communists having been banned already. Hard upon this raid, von Schirach announced that the 'tremendous material' which had now fallen into the hands of the Hitler Youth had proved that German youth was in mortal danger from the continued existence of the *Bünde*. (The statement is ridiculous enough to suggest that the Hitler Youth itself did not yet feel too sure of its position.) All the *Bünde* were now on the defensive, and many of their leaders endeavoured, with almost indecent haste, to secure seats on the bandwaggon. Leaders of the *Freischar* had already notified their intention of joining the National Socialist party in an open letter dated 8 March, and they expected their comrades to follow suit. On 3 May, Helmuth Kittel, who was the head man of the *Freischar*, announced in a circular letter that all those members for whom there was no room in the National Socialist movement (i.e. Jews and 'Marxists') must leave the *Bund* forthwith, and the regional leaders were made responsible for the execution of this order. Ludwig Voggenreiter, a former stalwart of the *Weisse Ritter* and head of the biggest publishing house of the youth movement, wrote a confession of conversion to Adolf Hitler,[1] and the periodicals of the movement were full of similar documents.

Still, while so many suddenly professed allegiance to the *Führer*, they did not admire von Schirach, and last-minute efforts were made to save the *Bünde* from extinction and incorporation in his following. The *Freischar* again approached Admiral von Trotha, who had

[1] *Die Spur*, 1 May 1933.

headed the short-lived merger of some of the *Bünde* in 1930. At that time the *Freischar* had reservations about von Trotha's authoritarian leadership and his right-wing politics, and the Admiral had complained of their lack of military spirit and their inclusion of some Jews and Social Democrats. But now, in March 1933, the *Freischar* was only too willing to seek shelter under the mantle of a man who was believed to be a close friend of President Hindenburg. Some other *Bünde* took the same course, including even the *Geusen*, who had been in close contact with Hitler's party for many years, but who could not bear to accept von Schirach's authority.

And thus at last, on 30 March 1933, the old dream seemed to have come true—the great union of the German youth movement was achieved. But alas! this *Grossdeutsche Jungenbund*, as it was called, was very different both in structure and in essence from anything that the unionists of the *Bünde* had imagined. The executive of the new *Bund* decided, on 15 April, to integrate it with the National Socialist movement.[1] Before May was out the *Grossdeutsche Jungenbund* was already marching under the banner of the swastika to its regional meeting in the Berlin Grunewald.[2] High party dignitaries had been invited but could not be present; a resolution was passed committing the *Grossdeutsche Bund* to march under the orders of von Trotha and in accordance with their *bündisch* tradition into the new, emerging Reich.

Disagreement persisted, however, between the Hitler Youth and the *Grossdeutsche Bund*. Some of the National Socialists in the youth movement, such as Küsel and Peter Berns, who had opted for von Trotha rather than von Schirach, complained bitterly that the Hitler Youth were assailing them as 'Communists.' In a letter to Göring they stated that the situation had become so tense that violence might break out at any moment, and asked for a guard of honour.[3]

The leaders of the *Grossdeutsche Bund* soon began to despair of its chances of survival as a separate entity; and during the month of May their anxieties crystallized into a demand that they should join the Hitler Youth as a body. This proposal was rejected both by the Hitler Youth and by Hitler himself, who announced on 1 June that the *Grossdeutsche Bund* could continue to exist or not at its own discretion,[4] but that its members would be accepted as individuals only.

[1] The present account is based on the documents in file 334 of the B.D.C.: 'Bericht über die Arbeit des Herrn von Trotha in der bündischen Jugend' (*Report on the Activity of von Trotha in the Bündische Youth*), dated 14 October 1936; and on documents in file 220, also in the Berlin Document Center.
[2] *Grunewaldtreffen* 1933, Berlin, n.d.   [3] Document in file 220, B.D.C.
[4] File 334, B.D.C. This was of course sheer hypocrisy; it was already obvious that the *Bund* was going to be banned.

Events now moved very quickly. At their Whitsun camp in June, the outraged *Bünde* sang in a spirit of defiance, 'Lever dot as slav' (*Better dead than a slave*, an old Lower German battle song), and 'Ein feste Burg ist unser Gott' (*A Safe Stronghold our God is Still*), the famous Protestant hymn. At the same time the Press was informed that the German youth movement had sworn allegiance to Adolf Hitler, the Führer of the new Germany.[1] But to no avail. On Whit Monday, police and stormtroopers surrounded the camp, and its 15,000 participants were sent home. Admiral von Trotha made one final effort to prevent the dissolution of the *Grossdeutsche Bund*; he wrote to Hitler, and tried also to enlist the good services of his friend von Hindenburg. But the aged *Reichspräsident*, now in the last year of his life, had very little influence in the Third Reich. Von Trotha's effort only irritated the National Socialists, who searched his house. Hindenburg had, indeed, tried to do something for his old friend, but he got nothing from Hitler beyond an assurance that he had given von Schirach instructions to see von Trotha, and the *Führer* had made it clear that he was not to be bothered any further with this affair; for there was 'a great desire for unity among German youth, and to have done with the wretched disunion and fragmentation of Germany.'[2] What von Trotha had written, about the unhappiness of German boys who were longing to join in the building of the new Germany but were not allowed to do so, had obviously left Hitler cold. The *Grossdeutsche Bund* was dissolved on the day that von Schirach was appointed supreme youth leader (17 June 1933). Not till three years later, when von Trotha was compensated with honorary membership of the Marine Hitler Youth, did he receive von Schirach's private assurance that the ban had not been directed against him personally.[3]

During the following months most of the remaining *Bünde* were dissolved; a few, such as some of the Scouts' organizations, were permitted to exist until 1934, perhaps on account of their international contacts. The activities and publications of this remnant became virtually indistinguishable from those of the Hitler Youth, but their imitative zeal did not save them from eventual dissolution. When the *Reichsschaft* of German scouts was banned in June 1934, the Gestapo tried to justify the ban by saying that 'more and more individuals hostile to the National Socialist State and movement have joined the *Reichsschaft*, till it has become in effect a haven for

[1] *Niedersächsische Volkszeitung*, 6 June 1933.
[2] Letter dated 15 July 1933, in file 334, B.D.C.
[3] Letter dated 26 June 1936, *ibid*. Von Schirach wrote in 1938 that von Trotha had become one of his most faithful collaborators, who had really regarded the Hitler Youth as the fulfilment of his own wishes. *Revolution der Erziehung*, p. 39.

young men hostile to the new State, who dispute the Hitler Youth's monopoly as the guiding political force.'[1] This was a gross exaggeration of the influence of this surviving *Bund;* but then *any* separate activity is suspect in a totalitarian State, and none can be tolerated.

The Protestant youth organizations were incorporated in the Hitler Youth in December 1933; few of the leaders protested, and that to little purpose. German Protestantism was a house divided against itself, and the majority now urged voluntary dissolution. The Catholic youth organizations were a harder nut to crack; some of them managed to survive, despite official duplicity and persecution, until 1939.[2] The gymnasts were merged in the Hitler Youth without much difficulty; the youth hostels were taken over by the State; and if some of the former periodicals published by the youth movement were permitted to exist, it was a concession for which they had to pay a high price in conformity.

V

Corruptio optimi pessima. Most of the leaders capitulated ignominiously. 'They got positions, titles, uniforms,' as one of the recusants recalled long afterwards; 'they left us younger ones behind, lonely and helpless, and admonished us not to persevere in our mad, useless, and dangerous opposition, but to collaborate. ... But then we should have lost faith in all we had held great, holy, and inalienable: in freedom, humanism, clean-mindedness, law; and in the Socialism that we ourselves were living.'[1] For these young men it was a great dilemma, and a great temptation. 'If only a few took up a clear position and maintained it, this was not because resistance was so impossible; the fact was that National Socialism offered all that a young man in his most secret and proudest imagination would desire —activity, responsibility for his fellows, and work with equally enthusiastic comrades for a greater and stronger fatherland. It held out official recognition, and careers that had been unthinkable before; while on the other side there were only difficulties and dangers, an empty future and doubts in the heart.'[3]

---

[1] Circular letter of the Bavarian Political Police, 21893/34, dated 19 June 1936, in the B.D.C.

[2] It should be noted, however, that some of the official Catholic historians writing since 1945 have exaggerated the extent of Catholic resistance. And some Catholics, including former leaders of their youth movements, such as Stonner, went very far in their efforts to accommodate Catholicism to National Socialism.

[3] Johannes Georgi, in the *Freideutscher Rundbrief,* 3, 1948. Such frank admissions were quite often heard in the years immediately after the war, but have become more infrequent since.

IN HITLER'S SHADOW

In April 1933, a younger member of the *Bünde* described, in the third person, what it felt like to be in this personal dilemma: 'There was a torchlight parade in honour of the new government: the *Bürger* were shouting "Heil Hitler." Was it not his duty to be marching in those columns rather than standing aloof? He felt almost like a traitor to his own people. His own *Bund* had always talked about service, and sometimes about struggle; they also sang soldiers' songs; but where did it all lead to? . . . Here came another column, they were marching badly, stooping and out of step—his own group marched far better than that! Both the Hitler Youth and his own *Bund* were nationalist—they with their many slogans, sonorous parades and numerous badges; his comrades through service. Of course it was much harder to undergo training in the woods than to be received with acclamation in the streets.'[1]

What they resented was not so much the principles or the aims of the new government, but simply that their own *Bünde* were doomed to disappear; all their work was to come to nothing, their old friendships were to be forgotten. In one district the order for their dissolution, after stating that the Government had destroyed the *Bund*, went on to say: 'It has grown dark around us. But the invisible *Bund* (*bond*) that unites such people as we are should survive in order that it may strengthen the Germany of the future. This invisible *Bund* is no secret organization but the common obligation of service.'[2]

Objections like these do not, perhaps, amount to a deep critical rejection. Had the new marching columns been less vulgarly ostentatious and better drilled, above all, had they taken the *Bünde* into their ranks, and acknowledged their merits and their prior claim to be builders of the German future, perhaps no such resentment would have been expressed. Mental resistance to National Socialism in the youth movement was based on instinct rather than on moral or political principle. But could more than that have been expected? In 1933 there were no extermination camps; only a few people in Germany—or elsewhere—understood and foresaw that National Socialism was heading inevitably towards barbarism and a new war. Many groups of the *Bünde* went over to Hitler with colours flying, only a minority refused to be swept off their feet. Whatever their arguments were, their instinct was right: it was not just the deportment of the marching columns that was lamentable; there was something very wrong with what the *Bünde* called the 'innere Haltung' (the inner attitude). It showed no mean insight in a young German to have spotted this in the spring of 1933. Unfortunately, there were but few of them.

---

[1] Rolf (Dresden) in *Jugendland*, 4, 1933, p. 67.
[2] Owtas in *Jugendland*, n.d., *ca.*, June 1933.

Twenty

THE ROAD TO RUIN

EVERYBODY and everything, in 1933, had to be 'integrated' or 'co-ordinated.' *Gleichschaltung* became the universal order of the day and, for a time, the most important word in the German political dictionary. Those who sought or accepted place or position in the new Germany or, more precisely, joined the Party, the S.A., the S.S., the Hitler Youth, or another group of the same allegiance, did so from various motives. Many members of the youth movement did so with considerable enthusiasm; they had been in general sympathy with National Socialism for some time, and for them, joining the movement was simply the logical thing to do. Others, whose approval had been more reserved, were either swept into the movement by the huge tidal wave of nationalist emotion, or thought it necessary to join because everybody else did, or because abstention might have damaged their professional prospects. Of these opportunist or reluctant converts the motives again varied, as did their subsequent behaviour. Some became opponents of the regime at an early date; some discovered the value of democratic principles after 1945; and there are some who are still of the opinion that National Socialism (barring some regrettable errors) was the best political regime Germany ever had. Many argue now that National Socialism was a perversion of the youth movement; in 1933 it was the great wave of the future.

I

The history of the *Bünde* comes to an end in June 1933. Some of the members joined the S.A., others the S.S.; and a few became *aides-de-camp* to Hess and other dignitaries. Like immigrants in a new and unknown continent, they tended to flock together in certain parts or places of the new order: *Volkstum und Heimat*, one of the many Party subsidiaries, the *Kulturgemeinde*, and Professor Hauer's 'German Faith' movement were institutions with a high percentage of *bündische* members.[1] For the behaviour of individuals and groups in this crisis various explanations have subsequently been advanced; it has been said that they had to compromise with National Socialism in order to save some, at least, of the creations of the youth movement, such as the Frankfurt *Musikheim* and the Silesian *Boberhaus*. If Paris was well worth a mass, was not a public avowal of confidence in the new rulers, or an open letter to Dr. Goebbels, a cheap price to pay for these cherished creations? There were indeed such considerations, but they do not wholly account for what happened. Only people who were in general sympathy with the new authorities could have been willing to make such gestures or declarations; no one else could have been so optimistic as to believe that Hitler would put up with any manifestations of the spirit of the youth movement in his totalitarian State.

The situation of the younger members of the *Bünde* who joined the Hitler Youth as individuals or in groups was more complicated. Not only could they plead the extenuating circumstances of their age and lack of political experience; it did seem, at the time, that there might be considerable scope within the Hitler Youth for former members of the *Bünde*. For in that summer of 1933 everything was in flux; the Hitler Youth, previously only a small movement, had just been inundated by hundreds of thousands of boys and girls. Might it not be possible under these chaotic conditions to build some youth-movement 'islands,' and thereby not only preserve cohesion and communication between the *Bündische*, but even in a measure denazify the Hitler Youth, by infusing it with something of their own spirit and tradition?

Such intentions were in fact entertained by some ambitious spirits, and they even had a little temporary success. They managed to gain positions of command in the *Jungvolk*, the junior section of the Hitler Youth, and kept them for about a year. In the groups which were thus infiltrated, the style of the *Bünde*, their attire, their songs, excursions, and magazines were adapted or copied, under a thin veneer of the approved ideology. However, once the dust of the initial scuffle had settled, these deviations from the norm were soon detected. Disciplinary measures were taken to eradicate *bündische* influences,[2] and the would-be reformers were expelled or transferred

---

[1] So was *Abwehr Zwei*, an important section of Admiral Canaris' Military Intelligence, that was considered by party stalwarts somewhat deficient in political enthusiasm.

[2] See *Deutsches Jungvolk*, April–August 1934, *passim; Wille und Macht*, 16, 1935. (G. Moegling, 'Bündische Jugend ist heute Bolschewismus.')

to positions of no consequence. A few groups survived within the Hitler Youth for some time after this, but as the *Gleichschaltung* became more effectual it finally ironed-out these last remnants of independence. What had begun as a compromise ended in unconditional surrender; there could be no reforming of the Hitler Youth from within.

Others had few serious reservations about Hitler and his movement. Today they refuse to admit any responsibility and plead immaturity and ignorance: the principles of National Socialism appeared to them pretty much like the tenets of the youth movement; they were young, inexperienced—and anyway, who was then to know where it was all leading? It is a familiar argument and can be extended without undue effort to the great majority of those who backed Hitler in 1933: only the Führer himself knew—the rest had abdicated all responsibility.

If much can be written off as political ignorance, in the last analysis the fatal weakness was moral relativism and indifference; the plain fact is that too many people in Germany were unable or unwilling to differentiate between right and wrong. The reactions of the youth movement in this respect were not very different from those of everyone around them in the Third Reich. The *Gleichschaltung* was complete, with the exception of a few *émigrés* and others who remained in Germany but preferred not to be identified with the regime. People who had been radical pacifists after the First World War now suddenly became eager to have a second go against England. The author of a learned treatise on the lyric poets of the youth movement now wrote anti-Jewish propaganda for an antisemitic propaganda centre. Another, who had been a prominent advocate for the Democratic party among the *Bünde* until January 1933, came out almost overnight with a book on Herbert Norkus, the Hitler youth 'martyr.' Yet another, who had preferred to leave the country, continued to submit his books for the approval of National Socialist literary juries. Even a 'Kulturbolschewist' whose books had been banned by the regime felt impelled to contribute to the war effort by producing anti-American literature. The list is long, and not very edifying.

But why single out those who were so incautious as to put themselves on record with books and plays, essays and poems, between 1933 and 1945? They were no better or worse than most. The youth movement had its anti-Fascist fighters and even martyrs, whom we shall remember presently. It also had its convinced, passionate Nazi Party members. But the majority of the former youth movement members, like the German people in general, muddled on somewhere midway between the devil and the deep waters: they supported

Hitler as long as the going was good. Within those limits there was a vast variety of attitudes; and within these again, doubtless as many nuances as individuals.

II

Unwilling that 'auld acquaintance' should be forgot, many former *Bündische* decided to keep together in groups, large or small, after the youth movement had been liquidated. Some did so within the framework of National Socialist organizations or upon such neutral meeting-grounds as sports clubs, mixed choirs, or literary societies. They even continued their excursions at home and abroad, arranged lectures, and went together to theatres and concerts. They carefully refrained from any public demonstrations; but sooner or later most of them were bound to fall foul of the Gestapo, or of the Hitler Youth's own private police which had been established to prevent separatist activities. Meetings and correspondence took place between such groups of friends, which existed in many cities, and the Gestapo soon had to have a special sub-section spying upon the behaviour of former members of the youth movement. Although the *Bünde* were dissolved in June 1933, the ban had to be repeated in February 1936, in May 1937, and again as late as July 1939, when the *Freischar*, the 'D.J.1.11' and a dozen other renitent groups were singled out by name. In July 1935, Gestapo branches throughout Germany were advised to prepare lists 'of all persons formerly active in the *bündische* youth.'[1] The Gestapo seem also to have been somewhat worried by what was called 'the infiltration of the Hitler youth by former members of the *Bünde*'; others were said to have established independent clubs, ostensibly devoted to recreations or the arts, in which they could carry on their subversive activities under a cloak of political neutrality.[2] And right up to the outbreak of the Second World War, illegal excursions were still fairly common.[3] Small groups could be spotted all over the roads of Europe, from Lapland to Sicily, despite the lack of foreign money, the strict frontier controls, and other obstacles.

The Communist and Socialist youth organizations were the earliest to be banned; nevertheless, a few of their local groups continued to carry on various anti-Fascist activities. In pursuit of the Popular Front policy of the Comintern, a Communist youth association

[1] Bavarian Political Police, circular letter of 5 July, 1935, No. 46057/35 in the B.D.C.
[2] Bavarian Political Police, Bnr. 23571/35, dated 4 June, 1935, in the B.D.C.
[3] Circular letter of the Gestapo, Munich, 24 May 1939, advising all branches that, with the beginning of the hiking season, the *bündische* youth 'which constitutes a danger to the State youth,' must be expected to renew its activities.

collaborated with Catholic scouts in West Germany and edited some magazines of the Catholic opposition—*Saint Georg* in the Ruhr, and *Rolandbriefe* in the Rhineland. Of the youth organizations grudgingly permitted a semi-legal existence, the Catholic groups were the only ones in which something of the spirit of the youth movement survived; they were kept under close surveillance and their activities restricted by special administrative measures. Certain Protestant groups also continued to be active, and took part in Boy Scout camps outside Germany.

But the 'Hitler Youth Law,' which was promulgated on 1 December, 1936, put an end to the semi-legal status of confessional groups. Every boy and girl now had to belong to the State youth organization. One noteworthy consequence was that, whereas National Socialism had in previous years attacked the *Bünde* for their élitist practices, the Hitler Youth now found itself forced to assume a still more invidiously élitist structure. Its rank-and-file members, enrolled by legal obligation, were sharply differentiated from the 'hard core' of earlier adherents, the so-called *Stamm* Hitler Youth, who provided leaders for the mass organization.

III

The *Bünde* had ceased to exist; but the Hitler Youth was imperfectly satisfied by its triumph. Elimination of its rivals by force of law was not enough; they must also be discredited ideologically, condemned before the bar of history so that their evil spirit could be exorcised for ever. Baldur von Schirach began his work on the youth movement with the words: 'What was previously called the German youth movement is dead.'[1] That was indisputable in 1934, but what was to be its place in history? Had it been a help or a hindrance to the resurrection of Germany under Adolf Hitler? His answer was that some of the ideas of the youth movement and a part of its way of life had influenced the Hitler Youth and been taken over by them[2] —for instance, the idea that youth should be led by youth only, the rejection of the concepts of bourgeois society, the exaltation of comradeship, of defence of the homeland and the *Volkstum*. But beyond this their ideas were nebulous, their aims confused, and the best thing about the Hohe Meissner was not the speeches but the boys and girls listening to them. In the view of von Schirach and other National

[1] *Die Hitler Jugend, Idee und Gestalt* (Leipzig, 1934), p. 13. Among members of the *Bünde*, Schirach was the most hated of the Party leaders; they had no such feelings about the 'decent' Hess, or Göring, or even Hitler. Yet in fact Schirach was both more honest and less clever than his colleagues—*vide* his subsequent career, and his behaviour at the war criminals trial at Nuremberg.

[2] *Ibid.*; also von Schirach, *Revolution der Erziehung* (Munich, 1938), p. 37 ff.

Socialist publicists, the youth movement had done good work up to the First World War, but had become a mainly destructive influence after 1918; the *Bünde* had all the weaknesses of the earlier *Wandervogel* without its merits. Most of their members had failed to recognize that a saviour had arisen in the person of Adolf Hitler; they had been weak and undecided; even those who accepted the basic truths of National Socialism had refused to draw the practical conclusions.[1] Some of those aristocratic individualists had even professed sympathy with the 'spiritual aims' of National Socialism, and then said they did not think Hitler was the right man![2]

There is little historical justification for these opinions; for, in fact, the *Wandervogel* took much less interest in politics than the *Bünde* did. The *Wandervogel* had a good press in the Third Reich because, in contrast to the *Bünde*, it had never tried to contract out of the Hitler movement: in the *Wandervogel*'s days there was no National Socialist party to join or not to join, so it could now be commended without incurring blame.

Another writer, apparently with some specialized knowledge of the subject, deplores the period between 1919 and 1924 as the 'saddest years,' those of 'the youth movement's dance of death,' while yet another affirms that its spiritual bankruptcy was not absolute and final until after 1929. All agree in condemning the very last phase of the *Jungenschaft* as one of 'cultural Bolshevism' or 'high treason,' and denounce the illegal groups that survived the liquidation as 'carriers of the Bolshevist bacillus' and therefore the worst enemies of the Hitler youth.[3]

These views prevailed within the Hitler Youth, but outside it there was some dissent, mainly from former *Bund* members who, although converted to National Socialism, cherished memories of their own past and were not disposed to take its total defamation lying down. Thus Hans Friedrich Blunck, chief of the German writers' organization and himself a quondam *Wandervogel*, declared that 'The German revolution began in the youth movement, and was carried on by National Socialism to victory.' This was in an essay with the revealing title *From the Wandervogel to the S.A.* 'The march of the young men of the S.A. is unthinkable without the spirit and the ideas of the so-called *bündische* movement.'[4] Another former leader of the *Bünde* declared that it was not only the dreams of the National Socialist comrades that had been realized in the events of 1933. . . . The roaring symphony of Germany's resurrection had yet another

---

[1] *Die Hitler Jugend* . . . , p. 34.
[2] F. W. Hymnen in *Wille und Macht*, 15 June, 1935.
[3] G. Mögling in *Wille und Macht*, 15 August, 1935.
[4] *Deutsche Jugend*, ed. Will Vesper (Berlin, n.d., ca. 1934), p. 2.

overture, of which the Hohe Meissner was one part and the *Bünde* another. It had culminated in the advent of the Führer, and it was the whole of the younger generation who were marching together to the strains of the Horst Wessel song in the torchlight parade of 30 January, 1933.[1]

Controversy persisted. German authors in the Third Reich, writing about the youth movement, show wide divergencies. Some thought that, for all its weaknesses, it had prepared the way for the new Germany—that, e.g., Karl Fischer had worked for an all-German Reich of youth, that the *Bünde* had been pioneers of the para-military *völkische* youth, that the *Wandervogel* in Austria and in the Sudeten region had done important spadework in the cause of racialism.[2] More numerous were the hostile critics of the youth movement who emphatically rejected the attempts of its apologists to make it respectable in the Third Reich. An early champion of National Socialism had denounced it as 'communist and pacifist,' and now Bäumler, the chief authority on education and philosophy, asserted that, far from having been a prelude to the National Socialist revolution, the manifestly individualistic youth movement marked the end of an age that was dying—it was the last emancipation movement of the epoch of liberalism.[3] Another learned doctor, in a dissertation published during the Second World War, denounced the cynicism of the *Bünde* and their anti-*völkisch* attitude, and denied that they had done valuable spadework for the Third Reich: the whole movement 'had done more harm than good,'[4] and this eventually became the generally accepted opinion in Germany under the Hitler regime.

IV

If Sodom could have been saved by the presence of ten just men, the youth movement deserves the forgiveness of posterity several times over. For if the majority capitulated, or went over to the camp of

[1] Arnold Littman, *ibid.*, p. 187. It has since been argued that the Vesper symposium (to which some twenty former leaders and friends of the *Bündische* youth contributed) was really an undercover attempt to keep their tradition in being, that the book was meant to 'save the youth movement' (Walther Jantzen, *Jugendbewegung und Dichtung*, Göttingen, 1960). But while some of the contributors to this book profess National Socialist sympathies less loudly than others, and while it did provoke Hitler Youth criticism, it was no more than an unsuccessful effort to improve the reputation of the youth movement in the eyes of the new authorities.
[2] Louise Fick, *Die deutsche Jugendbewegung* (Jena, 1939), *passim*; G. Pohl, *Bündische Erziehung* (Weimar, 1933), *passim*.
[3] Quoted in *Wille und Macht*, 15 February, 1936.
[4] Max Nitzsche, *Bund und Staat, Wesen und Formen der bündischen Ideologie* (Würzburg, 1942), p. 65.

the victors, enthusiastically or otherwise, there were others who never gave in but soon made grim acquaintance with the Gestapo. Some went to prison or to concentration camps, and a few were executed. The records of resistance to a totalitarian regime present complex problems to the historian. Not everyone who was arrested for interrogation by the Gestapo was a convinced enemy of the regime. In some cases resentment against the Party or the State arose from causes of little significance—the dissolution of their own group, or some vexatious disciplinary measure. But it happened more than once that a man who began by challenging a minor injustice on the part of the new authorities came gradually to realize that this was not due to their error, their ignorance or irritation, but part of a deliberate and consistent policy of tyranny and cruelty.

A good many of the offenders against the regime were boys and girls, former members of the *Bünde* who kept together in the small, illegal groups mentioned above, and were eventually caught. Some got off lightly; for instance, there was the case against Werner Karl Heise and his three associates in November 1936.[1] These members of the Hitler Youth, who had formerly belonged to the *Bünde*, were convicted of having gone on excursions in defiance of the ban, of reading to one another Klabund's novel about Peter the Great (*sic!*), and of singing their old songs about Admiral Kolchak the White army leader, and Ataman Platoff the Cossack hero of the Napoleonic wars. These were 'hostile activities' in the Third Reich; but even the Gestapo was not then in favour of the supreme penalty for such delinquents. The leader of the group was sentenced to a month's imprisonment and the others let off with a warning. There were dozens of similar trials; but as time went on the *bündische* opposition in so far as it continued to exist, grew more political, and the punishments more severe. In 1938, a sentence of three or five years penal servitude was no longer thought particularly harsh, and when the war had once begun the punishments became draconian. All the principal defendants were executed in the famous case of the 'White Rose' group in Munich, who had courageously protested against Hitler's war by distributing home-made leaflets.

These were rank-and-file resisters whose action was spontaneous; they had no leader, no unifying centre to guide or co-ordinate their efforts. None of them had been prominent in the *Bünde*; few had been more than fifteen or sixteen when Hitler came to power. Their anonymous outcry had the whole weight of the totalitarian State against it, with all its coercive and punitive machinery; theirs was a hopeless gesture, almost ridiculous but for its sincerity and bravery.

[1] 1. Sond. K. Ms. 854/36, copy in B.D.C.

These were indeed 'the last of the very last,' as one of their songs said; they fought a forlorn battle in Germany's darkest hour.

Among the older generation of the youth movement there were some active opponents of the regime. A few went into exile; one of these was Tusk, whose story we have already told. Another was Walter Hammer, who in the twenties had been the editor of a widely read youth movement journal (*Junge Menschen*) devoted to pacifism and the reformation of life, and one of the most courageous voices raised against the rising menace of National Socialism. He now went to Denmark and engaged in the distribution of illegal German literature. When Denmark was invaded and occupied, he was immediately arrested and spent the remaining war years in Brandenburg State penitentiary. Several former leaders of the *Junabu* (a right-wing group)[1] were brought to trial in Essen in 1937, and there were also proceedings against leaders of the Catholic youth associations. Chaplain Rossaint, head of the Catholic *Sturmschar* in West Germany, was sentenced to eleven years penal servitude, but survived the Third Reich. Karl Udo Widerhoff, a lawyer by profession and one of the chief defendants in the *Junabu* trial, died in mysterious circumstances in prison, before sentence had been passed. Another group of former right-wingers went to Holland, where they printed *Kameradschaft*, an anti-Hitlerite monthly appealing to the younger generation in the Third Reich, of which some copies were smuggled into Germany; it was a well-meant effort but a feeble one, for the quality of this, as of so many other *émigré* publications, was deplorably poor. An editor of *Kameradschaft*, Theo Hespers, was arrested when the Germans invaded Belgium, and executed in Berlin in September 1943, but his colleague Hans Ebeling succeeded in escaping to London.[2]

One of the leading members of the youth movement who died in a concentration camp was Robert Oelbermann; he was an old *Wandervogel* who had been a lieutenant in the war of 1914–18, and later on became head of the *Nerother Bund*. Hermann Maass, director of the executive of German youth organizations up to 1933, was executed after the abortive plot to kill Hitler in July 1944, as was Adolf Reichwein, another former *Wandervogel* and prominent Social Democrat. A fairly large number of the members of 'Kreisauer Kreis,' the main conservative resistance group during the war, had

[1] The public prosecutor praised the staunchly nationalist, even heroic, record of the defendants; pleading that they had been unable to understand that the time for Free Corps and *Landsknechte* was past and that there could now be no other *Führer* than Adolf Hitler. See *Kameradschaft* 1, November 1937.

[2] Another such periodical, which appeared for a while during 1938, was *Fanal*—edited in Holland, apparently by a small group of former members of the *Jungenschaft*.

taken part in the *Freischar* labour camps in 1928–29. Adalbert Probst, head of the Catholic *Jugendkraft*, was shot dead by the Gestapo in July 1934, 'while trying to escape,' and some of the former leaders of the Catholic *Quickborn*, such as Professor Alois Grimm and Wachsmann were also among the victims.[1]

The former leaders of the Social Democratic and Communist youth organizations were arrested and spent years in concentration camps, if they were lucky enough to survive at all.[2] Max Westphal, the leader of the Socialist youth, died like some others, after being tortured in a concentration camp. The illegal work of resistance claimed its victims. Katja Niederkirchner, a leader of the Young Communist League who had been parachuted into Germany, was captured in 1943, and Hilda Monte (Hilde Meisel) was also caught and executed, shortly before the end of the war; she was a member of the 'I.S.K.' (*Internationaler Sozialistischer Kampfbund*) and had been a courier between resistance groups in Germany and the West. The smaller Socialist factions were particularly active, and for a time perhaps more successful than either the Communists or the Social Democrats, probably because their members were younger and unknown to the Gestapo. The 'I.S.K.' was one of these, which traced its origin to the group founded by Professor Leonard Nelson; another was Karl Paetel's small *Sozialistische Nation*; and yet another the 'New Beginning' (*Neu Beginnen*) Circle. Both of the latter had centres in Paris until 1939.

But the real heroes of the German underground resistance were those of eighteen and nineteen years who faced the firing squad for having listened to foreign radio stations or for painting subversive slogans. One of these, a socialist or a communist, wrote on the day of his execution that he was about to die as a fighter for the liberation of Germany and the working class: 'Be of good cheer, as I am. I kiss and embrace my little mamma.' Another, also nineteen years of age, a former member of a Catholic youth group, who had been sentenced to death for trying to build a short-wave radio transmitter, wrote in a letter to a comrade: 'Dear Johnny. I have just heard that your sentence has been commuted. Congratulations. My application has been rejected. Which means that this is the end. Don't take it too tragically—you have succeeded, which is a lot. I have just received the holy sacrament and I am quite calm. If you want to do

[1] See Arno Klönne, *Gegen den Strom* (Göttingen, 1958), *passim*; Günter Weisenborn, *Der lautlose Aufstand*, *passim*; and Heinrich Roth, *Katholische Jugend in der NS Zeit* (Düsseldorf, 1959), *passim*.

[2] Some of the leading young Communists had formerly been members of the *Bünde*. One had been a Hitler Youth leader in Berlin between 1928 and 1931; cf. the biographies of Wilhelm Thews, Rudi Arndt, Wolfgang Thiess and others, in Stefan Hermlin, *Die erste Reihe* (East) Berlin, 1951.

something, say a few prayers for me. Good-bye!' His name was Walter Klingenbeck—and there were others like him.

The Muse of History has little use for losers. She prefers to celebrate victors, however transitory, and to record phenomenal actions, however monstrous. So much the worse for Germany, with its Hitler, Lidice, and Auschwitz. But there were witnesses to the survival of a more humane Germany, albeit submerged and none too numerous; these surely have a better claim upon our remembrance; and a good few of them came from the youth movement.

V

The mobilization of 1939 disrupted what remained of the illegal groups. For some of the old *Wandervogel*, this was the second world war in their lifetime; nor can it have been a great surprise to many members of the now-vanished *Bünde*, who in their war games ten years before had prepared themselves for the great battles to come. On the home front, the regimentation of the Hitler Youth provoked spontaneous opposition—from gangs of boys of fourteen and fifteen years of age. These, who gave themselves names such as *Edelweiss* or *Pack*, attacked Hitler Youth militants, mostly under cover of night. They were in any case too young to have had any direct contact with the old youth movement, and should perhaps be regarded as precursors of the 'teddy-boys' of the forties, rebelling against military drill and other forms of compulsion; in a totalitarian State even the teddy-boy problem takes on a political colour.

However, the great bulk of German youth reacted to the war as one would have expected; they were jubilant during the time of the great victories of the *Wehrmacht*, but became uneasy and despondent when the tide turned, and in the long nights of the bombs.[1] By 1944, many thought it was senseless to prolong the war, though they obeyed orders as mechanically as ever, while others still nursed hopes that something might yet turn up to ameliorate the outcome. Among the many appeals that came from prisoner-of-war camps during the final months, there was one calling upon the *bündische* youth to resist Hitler and save Germany from utter ruin,[2] but it had no more effect than other such appeals. German military resistance came to its end 'with a whimper'; the widely heralded 'Werewolves,' which were to have been made up of fanatical Hitler Youth battalions,

---

[1] *Jugend unter dem Schicksal* (Hamburg, 1950), is a very revealing collection of documents concerning the state of mind of young Germans during the last phase of the Second World War.

[2] Among those who signed it were Jürgen Riel, formerly of the *Freischar*, and Karl Oelbermann of the *Nerother*.

never materialized. Not only Hitler, but many foreign observers expected something of the sort—a heroic last stand, inspired by the myth of Hagen and the sinister last battle of the Nibelungs. Did not the battle-song of the Hitler Youth say that they would go marching on after everything was in ruins?[1]

By 1945 Germany was indeed in ruins; but nobody wanted to go on marching, not even the fifteen-year-olds who had just been conscripted for anti-aircraft service. One old *Nerother*, then a pilot in the Luftwaffe, stole an aeroplane somewhere in Czechoslovakia in May 1945 and flew home, dodging both the German and the Allied aircraft, and crash-landed near the Burg of his old *Bund*, where some of his friends had already assembled. For the others, the journey home was less dramatic and more protracted, lasting anything up to ten years.

The dreams of glorious war had been more than amply fulfilled for six years. Those who had set their hearts upon military status had attained it; the propagandists of the *Tat* and their friends, who had declared that a general holocaust was necessary to clear the way for the realization of the Germany of their dreams, certainly got more than they had bargained for. And what of those who had accepted the teaching of Moeller van den Bruck—that it was Germany's mission to disturb the peace of the world—or the opinion of Edgar Jung, that genuine war was an instrument of order?[2] That 'instrument of order' had rent their land in two, after reducing it to such a shambles as German history had not known for three hundred years.

---

[1] '*Wir werden weiter marschieren
        wenn alles in Scherben fällt,
   Und heute gehört uns Deutschland,
        und morgen die ganze Welt.*'

The poet, Hans Baumann, reappeared after the war, and has been praised in East Germany for his 'clean, humanist attitude, instinct with sincere friendship towards all peoples' (See *Neue Deutsche Literatur*, 1, 1960, p. 156).

[2] Neither of these men was a member of Hitler's party. Edgar Jung, secretary to von Papen and a former member of the youth movement, was killed in 1934 'while trying to escape.'

Twenty-one

THE POST-WAR PERIOD

I

'WHO talks of victory? To endure is all.'
Rilke's famous line had a peculiar ring of truth in a country that had suffered total defeat. The struggle for survival was the sole preoccupation of those who had escaped more or less unscathed from the war. The hunt for food and shelter, the search for dispersed relatives, the pursuit of work for a livelihood, left little time or energy for less urgent activities. The atmosphere of dejection and despair was almost unrelieved: never again, it seemed, would Germany be prosperous or independent.

On a gloomy day in 1946 a handful of former members of the youth movement gathered in Hesse to exchange wistful memories of the good old days and to ask one another what had become of whom; for in the general state of dislocation, each knew the fate of only a few others. They decided to invite as many old comrades as they could reach to a convention at the Altenburg convent in Hesse, at Whitsun 1947. A surprisingly large number of former leaders and members of the *Wandervogel* and the *Bünde* turned up: all previous differences and distinctions between the various groups had now become meaningless; they sat together as in the old days, telling one another with considerable candour how they had lived through the Third Reich. It was rather like the meetings of the *Freideutsche* after the First World War, but graver and more chastened in mood: there were no Communists or National Socialists among them; these were all sadder and wiser men than the *Wandervogel* lieutenants of 1919.

No one proposed to re-create the youth movement: that would be a task for the younger generation—if they wanted to. They were occupied mainly with reflections on the past—their own and that of their homeland. Had the German developments up to and after 1933 been inevitable? And if not, what responsibility did the youth movement bear for the disastrous course of events? Some said that complete frankness was necessary even if it meant opening old wounds.[1] For the actual emergence of the Third Reich, comparatively few in the youth movement could be said to bear any direct individual responsibility. But had they not all a collective responsibility for having propagated those ideals of Reich and *Gemeinschaft*, leadership and *Gefolgschaft* which National Socialism had taken over and perverted? There might be no question of moral guilt, but what of intellectual responsibility?[2] Worse still, those old ideals were now debased and discredited, perhaps forever, through their abuse by the Third Reich.

Others were inclined to pronounce a more lenient verdict: We must not be over-conscientious, they said; the youth movement was not guilty, it had merely failed through political naïvety. Its members had no idea of the realities of political power, and had really believed in the sincerity of the National Socialist propaganda; the motives that led them to join or to support Hitler in 1933 could not be fairly estimated from the standpoint of 1947.[3]

The debate again revealed the sterling qualities of the youth movement as well as its maudlin and muddled thinking. Everybody at Altenburg was deeply shocked by the crimes committed in and by the Third Reich, but not many were prepared to take any blame to themselves. Some, whether from pride or innate conservatism, refused to abjure the *völkische* ideals they had cherished all their lives, simply because these had now become unfashionable; others, still clinging to the old romantic beliefs, persisted in their rejection of 'intellectualism' and 'mass society.' Who, they asked, could say for certain that there had not been valid reasons, in 1933, for believing that National Socialism would end the class struggle and create a real *Volksgemeinschaft* (people's community), that it would provide a new political élite and, in the end, produce a true synthesis of freedom and order, of nationalism and socialism? This kind of self-justification came perilously near to rehabilitating a number of National Socialist ideals on the plea that they had failed only because of the nihilistic outlook and corrupt morals of the leaders.

Nevertheless, there were sincere attempts in these first meetings of the *Freideutsche* Circles (as they called themselves) to arrive at a true judgement upon their past, though the results were disappointing. Of these now middle-aged members of the former *Bünde*, many had been far too deeply and personally involved in the events they were discussing to evaluate them objectively. It was left to members of the

[1] *Freideutscher Rundbrief*, 3, March 1948, p. 8.
[2] *Ibid.*, September 1947, p. 9.   [3] *Ibid.*, p. 10.

younger generation, less directly concerned in the events of 1933 and their consequences, to draw some really valid conclusions from them.

The question of guilt gradually receded into the background; it had dominated their talk only in the dark and desperate days of 1946 and 1947, when people were brought closer together, as they usually are in a time of common emergency, and when the old community feeling fed upon the past and encouraged frank discussion. As life grew more normal and economic reconstruction got under way—that is, in the years between the currency reform of 1948 and the 'economic miracle' some years later—the new *Freideutsche* became more active externally but lost much of their immediate post-war impetus. The project for a German Fabian Society was shelved; the life ebbed out of the discussions on the future of Germany as a neutral bridge between East and West. The members were now fully occupied with their professional work, which as a rule left little time and energy for other activities. The *Freideutsche* Circles still met from time to time, but gradually gave up their more ambitious schemes; their regional and national meetings concentrated more and more upon educational topics and problems of social work—a natural development in view of the high proportion of educators in their ranks.

The *Freideutsche* was by no means the only group of youth that reassembled after the war. In 1946, Wyneken and Knud Ahlborn (a leading figure in the youth movement between 1908 and 1923) had tried, with friends in Göttingen and Hamburg, to set up an association of a more openly political character, but their appeal met with little success. A dozen or more similar groups with nation-wide ambitions subsequently emerged, and countless associations of regional scope. The more important of these decided, in 1957, to join forces in a central organization, the *Oeynhauser Ring*. Some of these old comrades' reunions devote themselves to such worthy tasks as regional planning, the preservation of ancient monuments, the establishment and maintenance of youth hostels, youth movement archives, etc.[1] All are avowedly non-political, but a good many of the leading members of some circles are *völkisch* in outlook, and this leaves its imprint on the cultural activities of their groups. Some of them had simply learnt nothing and forgotten nothing; others, fellow-travellers of the Third Reich, had suffered during the process of de-Nazification and were full of resentment against the post-war

---

[1] The central youth-movement archives are at Burg Ludwigstein near Witzenhausen, at the very border between West and East Germany. This fortress, formerly a ruin, was rebuilt by the soldiers of the *Wandervogel* who returned from the First World War, in memory of their fallen comrades. It is now one of the principal centres for meetings of youth-movement groups in Western Germany.

political order. They included a fairly high proportion of teachers and professors, former members of the National Socialist party, who were debarred from their profession for a number of years after 1945. Some of these men found part-time employment in former youth-movement circles, or used them as a platform for the expression of their opinions; they established, or renewed, contact with *völkische* writers such as Hans Grimm, Will Vesper, Ludwig Finckh and E. G. Kolbenheyer. Their influence was restricted, however, to certain associations (the *Freideutsche* were more or less free of it) and to the more elderly (fifty and over), and by 1960 they could claim only an inconspicuous place in German public life; some of these associations were doing useful work and the activities of others were slightly dubious, but none carried any social, cultural, or political weight. The happy memories of a rather distant past are the main reason for their continued survival.

II

But if the old were dreaming of the past, the young had visions of the future—if mainly of their own future. The first *Bund* to emerge—the *Jungenschaft*—did so only a few months after the war, in Stuttgart (Tusk's home town) and in Cologne. The *Deutscher Pfadfinderbund* (the scouts) was revived in Berlin in 1946 and then spread to West Germany. The *Freischar* made a strong come-back in the south-west and for a while seemed likely to become the leading organization of the autonomous youth movement; a promise which it did not, however, fulfil, owing to quarrels among its leaders. Some of these early leaders antagonized as many as they attracted by their extreme nationalistic views, and the discovery that they were not averse to collaboration with the East German communists did nothing to raise their prestige.

Other well-known old names reappeared—the *Nerother*, for instance, the *Fahrende Gesellen* and the *Wandervogel, Deutscher Bund*; and there were also newcomers like the *Sturmvaganten*, the *Zugvogel* and—biggest of all—the *Bund Deutscher Pfadfinder*. The Socialist youth group (*Falken*), as well as the Catholic (*Neudeutschland, Quickborn*) and the Protestant, had all been revived again by 1950. Literally hundreds of these autonomous *Bünde* sprang up; party, confessional, or neutral groups all complete with distinct uniforms, banners and internal news bulletins. And as the economic situation improved in Western Germany they found themselves in a much better material position than their predecessors; they could now get substantial public support for the asking.

It is a question whether these groups that have come into being since 1945, and still flourish, are to be regarded as the true descendants of the historic youth movement, or merely as its successors. The very word 'movement' conveys an idea of motion, and not even the best friends of the post-war *Bünde* would claim that they have been in any sense dynamic, or that they have developed new forms of youth activity. They were founded, with very few exceptions, by members of the old youth movement, most of whom were no more than thirteen to fifteen years old when Hitler took over, and even these dropped out after a time, to be succeeded by younger men, all of whose formative years had been spent under the Hitler regime.

This new generation has a very different outlook. It has been called 'jejune' by its detractors and 'sober' by its friends; discerning sociologists are impressed by its scepticism. Its preoccupation with private affairs, the pursuit of personal interests and individual careers, is perhaps the dominant characteristic. Less emotional, far less romantic and less idealistic than their predecessors, the members of the new movement are not rebels against the world of their elders: they have no irrepressible longings for a world of autonomous youth. This generation thinks more about its own professional education and prospects than about the destiny of the German people. Whereas the old youth movement grew largely in protest against the contemporary middle-class way of life, the new generation seems to have adopted bourgeois values without effort. And this is true of considerable sections of the working-class youth too. The earlier generation gladly took to the woods to show its dislike of the ugliness and squalor of the industrialized cities: the post-war generation has come to terms with urban conditions, and would be easily bored by 'Kibbo Kift' activities. The *Wandervogel* vigorously rejected the cheap cinema and dance music of its day, but by 1960 young people were finding modern jazz and jive more attractive than folk songs and dances. Moreover, the barriers between classes, castes, sexes and generations which existed at the beginning of the century have largely faded away, with a corresponding reduction of the tensions to which the classic youth movement was a conscious response.

Is this a development that ought to be welcomed? Anywhere else, the disappearance of enthusiasm and idealism might be a matter of justified concern, but in a country under treatment after a surfeit of romanticism, there may well be a greater need for other qualities, and a more sober, rational attitude may be welcomed. It is not, however, in all respects a healthy climate of thought: today as in Wilhelmian times, Western Germany's steady economic progress is accompanied by cultural indifference, aridity and, generally speaking, a lack of fresh air. It has been no more successful than the Weimar

Republic in creating a mystique of its own that appeals to the hearts as well as the heads of the rising generation. There can be little doubt, for instance, that the attitude of many of the younger German intellectuals towards their own country reflects a dangerous moral vacuum. A sound, healthy patriotism has indeed been one of the rarest things in German history, where patriotism has usually been all-or-nothing—either ultra-nationalist or nihilistic, without roots or loyalties. Within the last fifty years young Germans have been ready to fight for an autocratic regime and for a totalitarian one, but not for democracy. And although its attitude towards Bonn is free of the contempt that the youth movement professed for the First Republic, the readiness of the younger generation to defend their state against enemies, either within or without, does not seem at present to rest upon firm foundations.

All these defects are mirrored in the recent development of the German youth organizations. As far as numbers are concerned, the autonomous *Bünde* are not much weaker than their counterparts were in Weimar Germany, and are certainly stronger than the *Wandervogel* before 1914. But they are even more divided internally: most of them have only a regional basis, and very few have a nation-wide membership. They still make frequent excursions, often to other European countries, and they observe the tradition of the *Bünde* down to the smallest detail, but they have added nothing to it—whereas the fifteen-year period between 1918 and the dissolution of the *Bünde* saw the initiation of new forms of activity and new ideas, and produced new leaders at frequent intervals. It was a period of ferment and intense effort and of many crazy ventures, above all it was a time of great vitality.

The fifteen years since 1945, on the other hand, seem to have been barren of invention or originality. The old songs are still sung, the old books read and the old stories told; everyone has already been to Lapland, Greece and even North Africa; there are summer and winter camps, night attacks on other groups and attempts to steal their banners. The youth-movement magazines and calendars are published exactly according to the pattern evolved by Tusk in 1930. To assist German ethnic minorities, they now go to South Tyrol, instead of to Eastern Europe, as they used to do before 1933.

Thus the *Bünde* still exist, going through the traditional motions, though the traditional motive-power is a spent force. Such social protests as have been manifest in Adenauer's Germany assume very different forms—the riots of the *Halbstarke* (teddy-boys), and the demonstrations by the Socialist students against rearmament and the entire political climate in which they live; but in these there is nothing specifically youthful; and the *Halbstarke* riots, although undoubtedly spontaneous, do not—fortunately—amount to a movement, nor have they produced anything better than shattered glass and broken chairs.

The youth groups sponsored by churches and political parties have more moderate ambitions and have fared, as usual, somewhat better than the rest. Their religious or political work gives them a steadier basis. But they are no longer *bündisch* (as so many used to be in the nineteen-twenties) and, except for a few remnants of youth movement customs, their activities now resemble those of similar organizations outside Germany. The closely knit community is giving place to the ordinary youth club, making fewer demands upon the individual. This development is often (but mistakenly) called the 'Americanization' of youth; what it really represents is *modernization*—the evolving of ways of living more suitable, for better or worse, to modern industrial society.

III

The partition of Germany, and the establishment of a 'People's Democracy' in the eastern portion of the country, has had portentous consequences for the younger generation in what is now officially the 'German Democratic Republic.' The state youth organization, or *Freie Deutsche Jugend* (F.D.J.) has several million members: since the dissolution of the confessional youth groups in the early fifties, it has also a virtual monopoly of youth organization and indoctrination. As membership of the F.D.J. is not really voluntary, a detailed account of its tenets, structure, and educational method would be outside the scope of the present study; nor would it be of great political or social interest. The F.D.J. (like the Soviet *Komsomol* upon which it is closely modelled) exists to provide a reservoir of trained personnel for the Communist Party, and to assist that party in its current tasks.

Such close conformity was not always demanded of Communist youth organizations: in the early days of the Soviet *Komsomol* a certain measure of autonomy was permitted. Lenin's wife Krupskaya thought that youth organizations run by adults were bound to remain relatively small, and that only independent groups run by the young people themselves would be likely to attract a numerous following. In those early days there was much talk of spontaneity and even of *avant-gardism*, but the claims to autonomy lapsed with the emergence of the totalitarian regime in the late twenties, and the *Komsomol* became the official State youth organization, with about as much independence as the Soviet trade unions.

Similarly, the F.D.J. began by being—ostensibly at any rate—a politically neutral organization, although from the outset all the key positions in it were held by Communist Party members. It did not become officially Communist until April 1957. Its principal educational responsibility is for the political indoctrination of its members, but it owes a great deal (as the Hitler Youth did) to the traditions of the old youth movement—in its camps, excursions and war games; its songs, banners, camp-fires, sports competitions; and in its outward trappings in general. By a minor irony of history, this legacy from the *Wandervogel* and the *Bünde* reached the F.D.J. indirectly, via the *Komsomol*, which had taken it over from the German Socialist youth of 1910, who in their turn had copied it from the *Wandervogel*.

In contrast to the Hitler Youth, the F.D.J. does not appeal to emotions and instincts alone but also provides—for the higher age groups at all events—a 'scientific philosophy' (dialectical and historical materialism). This produces citizens far more 'conscious' and more ideologically sophisticated than National Socialism ever did; certainly the effect of the F.D.J. on the younger generation is incomparably more lasting than that of the Hitler Youth has been. Even when they lose faith or defect from communism, former members of the F.D.J. usually retain their belief in a Socialist order.[1]

For all that, we should not exaggerate the hold of the F.D.J. on the youth of East Germany. The younger 'pioneers' enthusiastically identify themselves with the ideals of Communism and the hatred of its enemies, but such identification with the ideals of their elders is common enough in the same age groups all over the world. At seventeen or eighteen years of age, on the other hand, the young men and women become much more reserved in their attitude: having left school and come in contact with realities, they discover to their consternation that there is a great gulf between the high ideals of socialism, democracy and humanism, and the society around them in which these ideals are ostensibly being realized. At this stage their Marxist-Leninist education often turns out to be a mixed blessing from their government's point of view; the young men and women apply the rational and dialectical thinking they have been taught to their own surroundings, and the results are often not what they were intended to be.

In the first years after the last war, the F.D.J. had branches in West Germany too, where it counted about 10,000 members by 1948.

[1] These conclusions are drawn from observations and conversations during visits to Berlin between 1953 and 1960. Useful sources are: the *Handbuch des Pionier Leiters*, (East) Berlin, 1952; Gerd Friedrich, *Die Freie deutsche Jugend*, Cologne, 1953, H. P. Herz, *Freie deutsche Jugend*, Munich, 1956; the official daily newspaper *Junge Welt*, and the fortnightly *Junge Generation*.

THE POST-WAR PERIOD

The F.D.J. was subsequently banned, together with other Communist party subsidiaries, and although some small groups undoubtedly carry on an illegal existence, their influence on the younger generation in the *Bundesrepublik* is quite insignificant. The activities of the F.D.J. in West Germany have been limited to occasional sallies from Berlin, and what may be called a strategy of indirect approach. To despatch a large group of members over the zonal borders to take part in meetings held in the West was a type of foray much in favour with the F.D.J. for a time, but it has been more or less dropped in recent years for lack of tangible results.[1] The East German Government has been more successful with its summer holiday camps, to which thousands of West German children were invited, free of charge or for a nominal sum. Many West German parents availed themselves of this offer.

The F.D.J. has endeavoured to infiltrate, and if possible to win over, both left- and right-wing youth organizations in West Germany, and also some of the revived *Bünde*. Considering the widespread lack of political education among West German youth, this was not an unpromising venture, but the results have been below expectations. At one time, the Communists had a strong foothold in the 'Falcons,' a Social-Democratic youth group, but it appears that most of their supporters have now been ejected.

The Socialist Students' association presents a more promising sphere for Communist infiltration, because of the fairly high percentage of conscious or unconscious fellow-travellers. Here the F.D.J. could count upon a certain amount of common ideological ground—however superficially held—in addition to the students' hostility to Adenauer's coalition Government. With the right-wing nationalist groups they have, at first sight, nothing in common. How often and how vociferously have they not protested against remnants and revivals of Hitlerism in West Germany? Yet on closer inspection, the F.D.J.'s anti-Fascism is curiously arbitrary and selective. All enemies and critics of the F.D.J. are branded 'Fascists' regardless of their real political records, but Communists have no scruples about collaborating in certain circumstances with individuals and groups whose past is, in this respect, not even doubtful. One such group was the *Kampfbund deutscher Jugend*, another was the *Autonome Jungenschaft*, and yet another the short-lived *Nationale Jugend*, and it is impossible to say for certain, about some extreme right-wing youth organizations, whether they are *bona fide* nationalist or crypto-communist. None of these factions

---

[1] Even Bertold Brecht was laid under contribution to this campaign, for which he wrote his *Herrnburger Bericht* (1951), a long poem unlikely to add much lustre to his reputation.

has attained much importance, but that is certainly not for want of trying on the part of the F.D.J.

The F.D.J. has shown less initiative in regard to the autonomous *Bünde*, perhaps only because of their great disunity and their relative unimportance. The early appeals of the F.D.J. to German youth were also signed by some representatives of the *bündische* youth, but it was never clear who these signatories were, or whom they represented. Some sections of the *Jungenschaft*, Tusk's old *Bund*, co-operated with the F.D.J. in various assemblies and other enterprises, but all that the Communists achieved was a strengthening of anti-government and neutralist views in some of these circles;[1] and it is doubtful how much of this was really the work of the F.D.J. It is much more likely that such views reflected a genuine anti-Fascism, and dissatisfaction with the cultural and social consequences of the 'economic miracle' which was strongly felt among the younger intellectuals in West Germany.

IV

Not even total defeat could wholly eradicate right-wing extremism in Germany. The Second World War, in which Hitler had led his adopted country to the brink of extinction, produced a *Fronterlebnis* just as the first had done; more than a few young lieutenants of the *Waffen* S.S. and similar units still thought that their years in the tanks and the trenches had been the most wonderful time of their lives. Those were the days! Days of excitement and comradeship, of heroism and high achievement. What a miserable contrast was presented by life under post-war conditions, the rat-race for daily bread, the absence of any spirit of community, the invidious de-Nazification and other national indignities! Hitler may have made some blunders, but the German soldier had been shown to be the best in the world, fighting against hopeless odds.

It was from such men, and some others who had held prominent posts on the 'home front' and lost them under the de-Nazification, that leaders emerged for new nationalist *Bünde*. Both the numerical strength and the political importance of these *Bünde* have been exaggerated.[2] The political victory of National Socialism in Germany

[1] The magazine *Pläne*, published in Hamburg, is one of the organs of this group.

[2] There are very good reasons for maintaining a vigilant attitude towards all manifestations of neo-Fascism in Germany, but this should not lead us to over-rate these organizations. Their membership in 1960 was not 50,000 to 60,000, as sometimes stated, but closer to 10,000. As there was also a certain amount of overlapping, the same girls or boys belonging to more than one organization, the actual membership may well have been smaller.

and its subsequent military successes were possible owing to a unique political constellation; in the atomic age a recurrence of such favourable conditions is inconceivable. The right-wing extremists have been an irritant, for they could do some damage to the prestige of the *Bundesrepublik*, but politically they are reduced to impotence. The fact that there is no longer even an outside chance of Germany's regaining great-power status makes the old war-horses feel frustrated, damps their fighting spirit; it also makes their ideas irrelevant. Like the veterans' associations that sprang up after the First World War, these right-wing radicals also are traditionalists in feeling, they lack the dynamic and the purpose for a potential mass movement.

The nationalist-*völkisch* elements are moreover in a state of hopeless internal division. Broadly speaking, there are[1] three different strands of opinion among them. Some, such as the *Deutschwandervogel*, the *Wikingjugend*, the *National Jugend* and the *Deutsche Jungsturm*, have engaged in activities much like those of the Hitler Youth. *Mein Kampf* is read and discussed at the meetings of certain groups, and units often go by names such as 'Schlageter' (a nationalist hero shot by the French in the Ruhr in 1923); 'Heinz Guderian,' 'Gerd von Rundstedt' or 'Walter Model' (the names of German generals in the last war). One of these *Bünde* proudly announced in 1955 that for the first time they were now using pistols in their war games. Almost all these groups are led by adults, many of them militant National Socialists. They are not usually thought of as part of the youth movement, because of their openly political character.[2]

The para-military organizations are probably somewhat stronger, and include the youth groups of the right-wing veterans' associations: the *Stahlhelm* youth, the *Kyffhäuser* youth, the youth corps *Scharnhorst*, the *Bismark* youth, the *Jungdeutschlandbund* and others. Their political conceptions follow the German right-wing tradition, in which *völkische* notions and aspirations to a greater Germany figure prominently. They have very little influence in the larger cities, but have gained some sort of foothold in several of the smaller towns of Lower Saxony, and in other traditional strongholds of National Socialism.

The only groups of this colour that may fairly be regarded as parts of the German youth movement today—in so far as that movement still exists—are to be found among some of those united in the

[1] The choice of the correct tense in which to write of these groups is a matter of some perplexity. Some have already disintegrated or been dissolved; others have changed their names. So rapid is the turnover in leaders, names and organizations on the extreme right that it is virtually impossible to keep track of them, the more so as most of these groups are quite small.

[2] Their central organization is the K.N.J. (*Kameradschaftsring Nationaler Jugendverbände*), to which a strong Austrian contingent, the ANJO, also belongs.

THE POST-WAR PERIOD

Ring deutscher Fahrtenbünde, such as the *Fahrende Gesellen* or the 'Young Eagles.' They are *völkisch* in their outlook and their cultural convictions, without being allied to any political movement: they regard *bündisch* education as more important than political activity. It is difficult to generalize about them, for there are great differences between individuals, leaders and groups; some are fairly openly anti-Western, anti-Jewish, and, usually, anti-government; others are more or less neutral. Many consider themselves to be the heirs of the Tusk tradition (minus Tusk's politics) and, in contrast to the para-military and neo-National Socialist organizations, they are élitist in principle. To this camp also belong the remnants of the *Wandervogel* in Austria.

The 'Young Eagles' has the historic distinction of being the first national *Bund* to re-emerge after the war: it came into being in Lower Saxony in 1947, and was soon dissolved by order of the British occupation authorities. When it reappeared on the scene four years later it had shed some of its political radicalism and relied more upon the *bündische* elements in its activities. Indeed, the 'Young Eagles' of 1951 had little in common with that of 1947 but the name, a fact which illustrates the difficulty of tracing the history of even a single group.

No fewer than seventy and perhaps as many as one hundred nationalist youth groups have existed in Germany in the post-war period, many with only a handful of members constantly merging, splitting and changing their names. An attempt to describe their development in detail would therefore not be very rewarding. The conclusion that emerges from a general survey of their vicissitudes is, however, somewhat reassuring, if negative. Considering how deeply the *völkisch* and militarist traditions are embedded in German thought, and remembering how conditions in West Germany (among the 9,000,000 refugees from the East, for instance) might well have favoured an upsurge of right-wing radicalism, the youth organizations of the extreme right have made little headway. They are indeed a relic of the past—an ugly fossil, viewed with grave suspicion by many, but of interest only as a museum piece.

CONCLUSION

TODAY, sixty-five years after the formation of the first *Wandervogel* group, the German youth movement has receded into the distant past, together with its early silhouettes, lute-playing and folk-dancing, with its interminable *Freideutsche* controversies and its lunatic fringe of groups dedicated to eccentric, if sometimes engaging, futilities. Fading recollections of its brief, golden age still haunt the minds of many people in Germany, mixed with memories of much else that abruptly vanished in the cataclysm of 1933.

It should now be far enough away for us to see it as a whole, to be able to sum it up. What has happened in Europe since the movement was trampled out has dwarfed its internal conflicts to insignificance and made its disputes with external critics irrelevant. The passions are spent, and many have forgotten what the quarrels were all about. Yet for all that, one feels a certain reluctance to draw conclusions and pass judgement on the youth movement, for its history was curiously unfinished. Other spontaneous movements can be said clearly to have either succeeded or failed in their vocation or mission; but that criterion cannot be applied to the *Wandervogel* or the *Bünde* without some injustice. Nor is this only, though it is partly, because the movement was an end in itself. It was 'always prepared' (as the scouts' motto has it), though its hour never came; and yet it has affected German public life in various ways, in education and other spheres. One is almost tempted to think—as some have suggested—that it existed in a sphere outside history, where strivings develop and mature, but was more like a love affair, a religious experience or some natural phenomenon that appears out of the blue and then passes away. But that is to treat the youth movement as if it were a 'pure

CONCLUSION

fool' in German romantic literature; and is anyhow far from the whole truth about it.

I

The youth movement has not been too lucky with its native annalists or with its foreign observers. Some have been interested only in its relations with National Socialism. One concluded that it was constituted mainly from the sons and daughters of the big industrialists, while another has explained it as an attempt by the petty bourgeoisie to divert the attention of the masses from the class struggle. One English writer deplored it for permitting an 'unbridled companionship of the sexes,' while another observer, a former member at that, described the movement mainly in terms of sexual inversion. A recent chronicler concentrated on the romantic element (Novalis's blue flower), and yet another sees the essential purpose of the movement in such highly practical achievements as the Silesian labour camps and the Frankfurt *Musikheim*. If there is a grain of truth (often a very small one) in these and many other conflicting opinions, no one of them nor even all together come near the heart of the matter. Some of the writers have been tendentious or prejudiced and others ill-informed: but the greatest impediment to any satisfactory description of the youth movement has always been its own formless and elusive character. Those who knew most about it from within were not accomplished writers, for it was not a literary movement: what they have left us in writing is only a part of the story, and not the most important part; the reality was almost always richer, of deeper human interest than its reflection in literature. The groups built themselves around charismatic leaders, who relied on personal example and force of character rather than ideas, principles or theories. It was they who *made* the youth movement, which was not produced by any of the philosophers and writers of the time whose ideas and doctrines the youth groups debated, adopted and discarded.

The experience of personal integration into a charasmatic group was the emotional basis of its membership, the very heart of its being. This non-rational process may be *re-thought* (as Hermann Mau wrote) but cannot be *re-lived*.[1] Thus the small group was not only the basic unit of a *Bund*, but the fount of its energy and enthusiasm. The group could exist without the *Bund*, but a *Bund* would be nothing

[1] 'Die deutsche Jugendbewegung, Rückblick und Ausblick' in the *Zeitschrift für Religions- und Geistesgeschichte*, 2, 1948. This is the best attempt so far to explain what some of the roots of the movement were, although the present writer cannot accept all Dr Mau's conclusions. Dr Mau, one of the most promising of the younger generation of German historians, was most unfortunately killed in an accident before he could carry out his intention of writing a study of the youth movement.

CONCLUSION

without its groups. You could not belong, as an individual, to a *Bund* as you can to a political party, for instance. You belonged to it only through your group. A history of youth movement politics could be written in terms of the *Bünde*, but an account of youth movement life would have to be based on studies of their constituent groups. Since no two groups were quite alike, and a history of groups is a manifest impossibility, the description of the quality of life in the youth movement will remain the task of the novelist and the social psychologist. What they have produced so far has not, it is true, done much to enlighten us in this respect, for reasons which are evident in the case of the social psychologists. A romantic phenomenon cannot easily be reduced to analyses of social motivation expressed in charts and statistics without losing its essence in the process. But it is strange that the whole generation of German writers who lived through the golden age of the youth movement should not have produced a single work that does justice to the subject.

It is not only the multiplicity of the groups that makes it wellnigh impossible to generalize about the youth movement. It had itself no 'general line'; it included National Socialists and Communists, militarists and pacifists, Jews and pious Catholics, purely academic groups,[1] and some *Bünde* that were openly and avowedly anti-intellectualist. On the doctrinal plane it could do nothing to unite them, for it had no leading political or cultural idea. Each group had its own little niche in a building that grew by accretion, not design: for since each constituent unit was absolutely autonomous, who was to say whether a group did or did not belong? Being thus incapable of uniformity—despite a growing love of uniforms—no efforts to unite them all into one super-*Bund* could possibly succeed. Some of these efforts were highly commendable in their motives; others were governed by merely personal ambitions, or by fear of a common danger from without, as in 1933.

All attempts to prolong the *Jugendbewegung* into later life were unsuccessful. Eternal youth is elemental to the romantic imagination—there can be no romantic hero of middle age or over. And not only did these boys grow up, their cohesion was rooted in the numinous experience of an adolescent life they had shared, but which was overlaid by other experiences after graduation from school—or from university at the latest. The other interests, impressions, friendships and loyalties that supervened as the individual matured and

---

[1] The list of members and associates of the Academic *Freischar* of Marburg, for instance, founded as a group on the periphery of the youth movement in 1912, reads like a page out of German cultural history—including the names of Martin Heidegger, Rudolf Bultmann, Paul Natorp, Nicolai Hartmann, *et alii*.

CONCLUSION

steered his own course through the adult world, seldom indeed eradicated the sense of a common experience. There was that peculiar scene at the first reunion of the *Freideutsche* after the Second World War, when former National Socialists sat side by side with veterans of the Spanish International Brigade discussing their widely different experiences since 1933 in the same spirit that had prevailed on the Hohe Meissner. But not even the happiest memories of a successful summer camp could bridge the gulf between the former inmate of a concentration camp and a comrade of his youth who had served in the S.S.

And, to take less extreme cases, could persons whose minds had matured in very different professions and circumstances be expected to find much in common because they had had the same adolescent experience? It is true enough that the youth movement had inculcated certain universal values and interests, some definite character ideals and a love of nature; but this was at a certain age and in chosen surroundings. Arising as it did in the cities, more especially the *big* cities of Germany and Austria, and conditioned by their culture, the youth movement was also psychologically and socially restricted—to middle-class youth still at secondary school. Most attempts to transplant it have failed.

II

'Intangible,' 'formless' and 'elusive'—the epithets we have had to fall back upon in our descriptions—are more usually applicable to romantic novels or poems than to a social movement. Should one then refrain from any question of success or failure? Perhaps so—had the *Wandervogel* and the *Bünde* regarded themselves only in the light of romantic heroes leaving the parental home to find their fortunes in the world, like an Eichendorff hero in an attack of *Wanderlust*. But though they were romantics, these young people were not individualists; they had a social conscience and wanted to change German society, or at any rate youth life.[1] The yearning of the romantic hero was to dream and brood, recumbent and alone in landscapes of unspoilt natural beauty, whereas the *Wandervogel* and the *Bünde* had much less interest in the experience of nature *per se*; hardly anybody ever went on a trip alone. The main thing was the *collective* experience, to which nature was the means; it was not an end in itself. For that reason, and because of their collective aspirations, the German youth movements cannot be treated as

[1] In French and English romanticism one finds similar aspirations to reform society, with an eye to the future rather than the past, but this has been rare in German romanticism.

CONCLUSION

societies of amiable dreamers chiefly interested in self-surrender to their ever-changing moods. They are entitled to be taken more seriously, for they did try spontaneously, if often awkwardly, to alter the human condition at a time when philosophers and sociologists were writing about the 'alienation of man,' the 'atomization of society,' the lessening of contact between human beings; when the anonymity and impersonality of life in modern societies, a loss of vitality in individuals and a growing social torpor, were already themes of contemporary social criticism.

The *Wandervogel* did not read Marx or Kierkegaard, or even Tönnies and the vitalist philosophers; but they certainly felt some deep disquiet about the society in which they found themselves—the society of Wilhelmian Germany at the dawn of this century. They were depressed by its conventions, its artificiality and materialism; they felt an absence of human warmth and sincerity; and it was in response to these conditions that their groups were formed, and developed into social centres where they could find the qualities of life to which they aspired.

Other groups, of course, were pursuing the same quest in very different ways—circles of artists, soldiers, sportsmen, etc.; the youth movement had no monopoly in this respect. In other countries where the social roots were firmer, and the barriers between parents and children, teachers and pupils less rigid, such a movement would have been less likely to arise. Indeed there have been some, viewing the *Wandervogel* and the *Bünde* in this light, who have said, in effect: Blessed is the land that has no need of them.

During the last sixty years German schools have altered their character, many customs and conventions have disappeared and the family itself has been affected by the winds of change. Some of the sources of the *Wandervogel* revolt no longer exist; the youth movement has become eminently respectable but also less relevant. In Western Germany today there is a strong reaction against collective living—and not only because of all the regimentation under the Third Reich. 'Community' is no longer a supreme value, and intensive group life has become unfashionable among the same age-groups that were so powerfully allured by it thirty or fifty years ago. People have learned to live with alienation; the younger generation of 1960 has not the same horror of the anonymity and squalor of the big cities that was felt by many of their parents. For one thing, many cities, and city life in general, have considerably improved. Alcoholism, prostitution and other evils still exist, but they are regarded as problems for social workers, to whose solution a youth movement has little to offer. Week-end trips have become part and parcel of urban life; and parents encourage their children to join youth movements, which the children are often reluctant to do. There are so many other attractions and distractions, and ways of meeting one's own friends. The pendulum has swung right over since 1900.

The old youth movement shook off the fetters of a rigid society, but could not break out of its own isolation. The forms of life it developed were possible only for middle-class youth within certain age limits; it could never have become a mass movement of adults. The very experience that held the members together was one that could not be extended to other classes or ages. And any common political action was precluded from the beginning by the lack of a central moral idea, to say nothing of a common ideology. But to say what it did not do is easy: it is not at all easy to point out its intangible but real achievements. The youth movement contributed much to the gradual transformation of German education and, to a lesser extent, to the change in German *mores*—for instance, to the prevalence of a more natural and unaffected social tone, both among the intelligentsia and in certain sections of the middle class. It invented and developed patterns of youth life—of groups, of leadership, of rambling and communal singing—that have survived widely in adapted forms. And it inculcated an attitude to life and a behaviour pattern that give its past members a certain distinction among other people. These achievements may be of less importance than some of them believe, but they are real.

The youth movement takes its place in German history as a lengthy footnote or appendix whenever neo-Romanticism, reform movements or (in some cases) the roots of National Socialism are under discussion. Attempts to trace a common denominator are perhaps unavoidable, but their value is dubious, as the present study has perhaps demonstrated. The youth movement was of course romantic in inspiration; it also contributed to the general climate of anti-rationalism, *Kulturpessimismus* and yearning for a total reform of life that set in about 1900; and its motives were not unlike those of the romantic revolt against the legacy of the Enlightenment and the neglect of all non-rational realities. But though it started under the same auspices as these and other movements of protest, its development was *sui generis*. Originating in the nineties, it was certainly neither *fin-de-siècle* nor decadent. Its own aims were the very antithesis of the individualism preached by neo-Romantic literature, which, like that of the high Romantic period, was emotionally egocentric, introspective and often refined to the point of femininity. The youth movement tended to apotheosize the group, not the individual; its manners were blunt and it was impervious to artistic or psychological subtleties. It was the expression of a fresh awakening to life. What has lately been said about the *Blaue Reiter*, the

CONCLUSION

contemporary group of expressionist painters, could well be said of the youth movement: that it confronted 'the anaemic intellectualism of a civilization self-consciously preening itself, while threatened with suffocation in the materialism of a utilitarian belief in progress, with the belief in a new world which, to them (to quote Nietzsche), still seemed abundant in beauty, strangeness, doubt, horror and divinity.'[1]

Many of the basic notions of the *völkische* camp out of which National Socialism grew were shared by the youth movement, but it moved in a different direction. It did not appeal to the mass instincts, nor did it develop an ideology of its own, because it saw the prospect of a better Germany not in terms of political action but of the education of a new élite from the ranks of the younger generation. It chose what is called in an untranslatable German phrase *den Weg nach Innen* ('the Inward Way'), whereas National Socialism was interested mainly in immediate political power.[2] It is therefore incorrect to classify the youth movement along with the Pan-German League or any other such body among the 'precursors of National Socialism.' It is equally beside the mark to speak of it, as Alfred Bäumler, the leading professional philosopher of National Socialism did, as a last offshoot of Liberalism. The youth movement had precious little in common with Liberalism beyond the fact that Hitler abominated both. Both in thought and action it moved on different levels from those of any other contemporary movement.

The early *Wandervogel* came into being spontaneously and was modest in its aims (we may discount latter day efforts to ascribe to Karl Fischer and his companions various meanings and intentions which they probably never had). But by 1910 it had grown into something more ambitious, and if it had failed to impress official Germany, it was having a profound influence on the younger generation, including some intellectual circles that had not at first been involved. In this period the youth movement included both a fairly strong *völkisch*, antisemite wing and a left-wing group, which found its way, later on, to Social Democracy and to Communism. The *Wandervogel* was patriotic, but for the most part not aggressively so; in 1914 hardly anyone had doubts about his duty to the Kaiser, the Reich and the German people in a just war of defence. But they took a dim view of the raucous jingoism of the beer-hall parties and

[1] H. K. Roethal's *Introduction* to the *Der Blaue Reiter* Catalogue, London, Tate Gallery, 1960, p. 5.

[2] Dr Heinz Dähnhardt, himself a leading member of the *Bünde* in the twenties, has recently pointed out some of the fundamental differences between the youth movement and National Socialism in an unpublished lecture (May, 1959): '*Die deutsche Romantik und der Nationalsozialismus. Ein Beitrag zur Phaenomenologie der Jugendbewegung.*'

CONCLUSION

sought to cultivate a new, inward love for fatherland and the folk. Theirs was not the patriotism of the philistines, but neither was it radically different in its motives or its consequences; a philosopher might have called it patriotism at a higher level of consciousness.

The *Wandervogel* phase finished with the war of 1914–18, though many of the *Bünde* managed to survive in one way or another. A great many of its members fell in the war and most of its survivors had grown beyond youth movement age. All attempts to maintain some form of organization among the older members failed; they had matured, and the kinds of shared experience which had been the bond of union between them had gradually lost importance in their present circumstances.

The *Bünde*, which emerged from the remnants of the *Wandervogel* and the scouts, quickly became the main force in the second phase of the youth movement: and if the vagrant scholar might be said to have been the *Wandervogel's* ideal, that of the *Bünde* was the soldier. Their militarist nostalgia is probably traceable to the fact that Germany was allowed only a small army under the terms of the Versailles Treaty. But the *Bünde* were by no means only para-military organizations; they were an order, more disciplined and more ambitious than the *Wandervogel*; on the whole more conscious of social and political realities, but lacking in some of the more amiable qualities of their predecessors; more tense, more self-consciously masculine; but also too easily taken in by notions emanating from their lunatic fringe. Altogether, they took themselves and their activities far too seriously. Their influence during this phase extended to all German youth and indeed further, to political, religious and sports youth groups, although, as we have seen, the spirit of the youth movement was not communicable and it was usually little more than general principles and forms of organization that were taken over elsewhere—such things as the leadership of youth by youth or the use of camps in the education of the young.

The third phase of the autonomous *Bünde*, which set in shortly before their general obliteration in 1933, was marked above all by the eccentricities of the *Jungenschaft*, which transformed the movement in some respects, and gave it a fresh impetus in others, but was on the whole merely symptomatic of the growing radicalization and the groping for desperate solutions in contemporary Germany. National Socialism speedily abolished the *Bünde*, but while many members joined the National Socialist party or one of its subsidiaries, some remnants of *Bünde* carried on an illegal existence in the Third Reich. By no means all were carried away in the stampede of 1933; a few resisted from the beginning.

After the war which ensued, many of the old *Bünde* revived and a

CONCLUSION

few new ones appeared; but this was a rehash rather than a revival. They lacked the *élan vital* of their predecessors: while the earlier movement had been, at times, the vanguard of German youth, the new one was no more than a marginal phenomenon, hardly relevant to the life that the younger generation had to face in the nineteen-fifties. The old movement, with all its faults, had never been sterile; it had produced an abundant crop of ideas almost every year, about the world in general and its own groups and *Bünde* in particular, adopting new and discarding old aims and activities. But the post-war movement developed nothing new in fifteen years: it merely took over and preserved the old traditions, much as an association of war veterans preserves its battle-flags and other relics.

The formative age of the movement spans two separate decades, from 1905 to 1914 and from 1923 to 1933. This was too short a time for an educational movement to produce an enduring effect upon German society, even if the *Bünde* had been clearer than they were in their views and aims. The movement showed signs of great promise, perhaps of universal significance; yet it was rendered largely ineffectual, probably less by its own weaknesses, inconsistencies and built-in limitations, than by the period of German history in which it had to bear its part.

Both the achievements of the youth movement and its shortcomings and failures ought to be judged on the background of that period. It produced a type of character; its young men and women developed qualities of sincerity, decency, open-mindedness and idealism, they tended to become free from petty egoism and careerism, opposed to artificial conventions, snobbery and affectation. The main defects of the youth movement were confused thinking, inadequate social courage and responsibility, and a profoundly illiberal outlook. It tended, like the Romantics before them, to venerate the Middle Ages in contrast to the modern world, and to exalt the peasant way of life above that of industrial society, to an extent which disqualified it for dealing with present realities. In general its members had too much of the German orientation towards a mythic past.[1] Like the Romantics before them, they disliked some of the consequences of the Enlightenment, an attitude that has not much to commend it in a country where the Enlightenment did not meet with conspicuous success anyway. The same anti-rationalism caused them to be easily swayed in different directions by philosophical charlatans and political demagogues preaching all kinds of eccentric doctrines.

In all this their immature minds reflected the contemporary German *malaise:* a nationalism running berserk (the typical concomitant

[1] Not that an 'orientation towards the future' would necessarily have been an unmixed blessing—*vide* Italian Futurism.

CONCLUSION

of an arrested national consciousness), the consequences of the war of liberation against Napoleon having been fought under reactionary auspices, the defeat of the rising of 1848, and the ensuing triumph of political autocracy and irrationalism which finally led Germany to disaster.

Democracy, freedom and humanism are much more than rational and utilitarian ideas; they presuppose a state of mind disposed to toleration. But toleration has never been a notable characteristic of the Germans as a nation; nor have they ever shown much feeling of responsibility *for* the State—all manifestations of the Prussian spirit notwithstanding. Far too few of them ever regarded the Weimar Republic as *their* State; there was a general readiness to abdicate all responsibility to the imaginary omniscience of a Führer. German bravery in battle is a virtue with a great tradition, which the youth movement did its part to maintain. Yet in less extreme situations, the individual German has generally reacted with more servility than *Zivilcourage*, and the youth movement—on the whole —not very differently.

National character is not at all necessarily static; doubtless it develops with a nation's experience. But a movement such as this whose history we have traced is no less a product of the national character than an effort to change it. Nor could the devotees of the *Wandervogel* and the *Bünde* have dispelled the curse that seems to have lain on German history ever since the defeat of the democratic revolution of 1848. Only a political or social movement that set itself in deliberate and radical opposition to the established order could have effectively dissociated itself from the main stream of developments—though it might not, even then, have prevented disaster.

But the *Wandervogel* and the *Bünde* could not aim so high. The fact that their movement lived and flourished at all was an achievement and a challenge. In twentieth century Germany such an effort was fated to be, at best, a splendid failure.

Appendix

THE FOREIGN POLICY OF THE *BÜNDE*

IN the days when the youth movement began, contacts between groups of the younger generation in the different European countries were rare, almost non-existent. The *Wandervogel's* occasional tours abroad, hiking in Sweden, England and other parts of the Continent, were something of an innovation, but these visits were of no greater political significance than those of any other groups of tourists. With the general expansion of 'tourism' after the First World War, however, the German youth groups' expeditions multiplied, forming various kinds of international ties, and something like a 'foreign policy' of the *Bünde* gradually emerged.

What the *Bünde* conceived to be their vocation in this field of action was then called *Volkstumsarbeit*; that is, work among the German minorities in lands beyond the borders of the Reich.[1] This was regarded as a national duty. Some of the German minorities were under considerable pressure, and visits by youth groups were designed to give them hope and encouragement, to strengthen their resolution not to abandon their native language and to maintain their ties with the fatherland. These visits lasted for periods of several weeks and sometimes involved fairly large groups. The boys and girls visited the German settlers in their homes, invited their sons and daughters to communal singing or amateur theatricals, and sometimes worked with them in the fields. The East German groups of the *Freischar* were pioneers in this activity: their excursions to German minorities in the Balkans set the pattern for many subsequent visits. The *Freischar* also invited young Germans from abroad to take part in holiday courses at its Silesian centre, the *Boberhaus*.

[1] Some of the *Bünde*, such as the *Nerother* and the 'd.j.1.11.', seldom joined in these activities, which they regarded as of a political character and therefore outside the scope of an autonomous youth movement.

THE FOREIGN POLICY OF THE BÜNDE

The whole question of this work among the ethnic minorities was bedevilled by the facts that, firstly, the activities of some of the *Bünde* were of a less innocent character than those of the *Freischar*, and, secondly, to draw the line between *bona fide* cultural work and subversive political activity is a highly delicate operation. Moreover, these activities were centralized in the Association for Germandom abroad (the V.D.A.) which was under right-wing influence from the beginning, and in 1933 passed into National Socialist hands.

Relations with youth organizations in other lands also grew in importance during the twenties. A long-enduring conflict arose between the World Scouts Organization and the German Scouts, because the world organization was unwilling to recognize more than one German *Bund*, and there were others who resented that decision. But over and above such official ties, there were developing contacts with youth in other countries and much interest in them. America was too far away and the Soviet Union's youth were insulated, but there were exchanges with France and Britain and some other European countries.

OTTO ABETZ

Otto Abetz, the arts teacher from Mannheim who became German ambassador to France, has been given a place in history as a very clever emissary of the Third Reich who did his best to subvert France and who afterwards held high office there, like many another Gauleiter. The truth about him is a good deal more complex: Abetz was in fact far from clever; he genuinely liked France and wanted to bring about a Franco-German *rapprochement*. But he did not realize until late in the day that his goodwill and the connections he had formed with outstanding French personalities of the younger generation were being exploited by his superiors who had nothing but enmity and contempt for the French. When there could no longer be any possible doubt about it, he did not dare to resign his post.

Abetz was born in a little village near Mannheim in 1903; as a youngster he joined one of the Nationalist *Wandervogel* groups, but soon came under the influence of the left wing of the *Freideutsche* youth.[1] In 1927, when he was a teacher at the Karlsruhe academy of art, he was elected president of the local executive of youth movements. Abetz believed that the youth groups in that border country had a special obligation to work for friendly relations with French youth; it was he who organized the first large-scale meeting with them on the Sohlberg in the Black Forest in 1930. The meeting was a success; a body later known as the *Sohlbergkreis* was formed,

[1] Otto Abetz, *Das Offene Problem* (Cologne, 1951), p. 19. See also Karl Epting, *Generation der Mitte* (Bonn, n.d., ca. 1953).

APPENDIX

further meetings followed and attracted attention in circles far removed from the youth movement. Here at last was a promising beginning, a real effort to transcend the old, disastrous enmity between the two nations.[1] What Romain Rolland had said in *Jean Christophe*—that Germany and France were the two wings of the Occident, and that neither could be injured without distorting the flight of the other—prefigured the hopes that inspired the early meetings of the *Sohlbergkreis*. Prominent intellectuals and youth leaders of both nations took part in subsequent meetings of the circle in Rethel, Mainz and Paris. But the situation in Germany was rapidly deteriorating; already, at the Mainz encounter in 1932, a Hitler Youth representative had fulminated against 'French rationalism.' When Hitler came to power Abetz was deposed from his Karlsruhe chairmanship even before the dissolution of the *Bünde*. At first he was definitely *persona non grata* with the authorities (had he not closely collaborated with 'Jews and Marxists'?), and he did not become a Party member until 1937. But somebody in Berlin had recalled his close personal contacts with French public figures, and he was encouraged to resume his activities.

A very different spirit prevailed at a conference that took place in Berlin in the summer of 1934. The French delegation was led by Drieu de la Rochelle, a gifted writer who became an open exponent of fascist ideas.[2] There was nothing of the Romain Rolland tradition about this debate, but much wild talk of a common struggle against rotten liberalism, parliamentary democracy and similar abominations. About the same time Abetz was called to Berlin to take over the French department of the Hitler Youth (and as late as 1950 he declared that 'the Hitler Youth did great work in the cause of German-French understanding'). From this appointment Abetz drifted into the Ministry of Foreign Affairs and was ultimately made German ambassador in France. He was brought to trial in Paris after the war; the French dealt leniently with him, for they knew he was probably the best German representative they could have hoped for in the circumstances, and that he had often interceded at Berlin to

---

[1] Abetz' counterpart on the French side was the editor of the French weekly *Notre Temps*, Jean Luchaire, who was executed in Paris in 1946 as a collaborationist. But in 1930 he was nearer to Briand than to fascism, and in his circle there were many who became prominent in the *Résistance*.

[2] Drieu, like Brasillach and other French pro-fascists, greatly admired the German youth. But Drieu was, at this time, perhaps closer to the National Bolshevists than to Hitler. He wrote in 1934 that his new movement was to rally 'les braves perdus' from both the extreme right and the extreme left, in the struggle against reaction, capitalist manoeuvres and liberalism. ('Contre la droite et la gauche.' *La lutte des Jeunes*, March 11, 1934, quoted in *Le Romantisme Fasciste*, Paris, 1959, p. 49.)

prevent or alleviate some severity on the part of the occupying power. After a few years he was released and returned to Germany. Otto Abetz and Suzanne his French wife were killed in a motor accident in Bavaria in 1958, on their way back from a meeting with his old comrades of the *Freideutsche* Circle, where he had been speaking upon his old subject, 'France and Germany'. . . .

It is the familiar story—of a young man, a former *Wandervogel,* full of praiseworthy intentions and with tremendous energy, fully convinced that he has a mission to work for a better world, but completely lacking in political instinct or principles, who becomes caught in the cogs of the machinery of the Third Reich. Perhaps not through idealism alone; it is not every day that an arts teacher is offered the rank of Ambassador in Paris. But essentially, this is the story of many another product of the youth movement under the Third Reich; too many of them thought they could both sign a pact with the devil and outsmart him. For the most part, it did not work.

RELATIONS WITH BRITAIN

In 1922 Rolf Gardiner, a young Englishman in his first year at Cambridge, visited Germany with a group of folk dancers and singers, and, like many of his contemporaries, was impressed and delighted by what he found there.[1] He formed close and lasting friendships with such distinguished leaders of the youth movement as Ernst Buske and Georg Götsch, and his name stood high in the esteem of youth movement circles long after the severance of relations between the two countries. When Adolf Reichwein, one of the martyrs of the German opposition (executed after 20 July 1944) sent an emissary to neutral Sweden during the Second World War, Gardiner's was the first name on the list of contacts he was to make.

The twenties were a time of social and cultural crisis and dissatisfaction in England as well as Germany. Rolf Gardiner has recorded his sense of this crisis when a student at Cambridge:

> 'A new Dark Age was descending on Europe and the world. The English were defying the inevitable with specious security. The humanism still cherished at our Universities was a withered shred of the great harvest of the Renaissance. When I stammered out my inchoate theories of the need to renew the roots of our culture, to revive religion of the soul through the soil, J. B. Priestley, taking out his pipe, flattened me by saying: "Yoong mun, all ye want is jest a few reforms" . . . To most of

[1] This feeling of admiration for young Germany lasted right up to 1933. Goronwy Rees writes in *A Bundle of Sensations* (London, 1960), p. 33, 'It is hard now, nearly thirty years later, to explain even to myself the kind of attraction which Germany exerted on men of my generation in Oxford.'

APPENDIX

my contemporaries what I was trying to say was bizarre balderdash . . . Cambridge was intellectually as uncongenial to me as it could be. The dons were steeped in scientific humanism, and the Bloomsbury elect were the intellectual heroes of the hour.'[1]

While some of the men and women of that generation sought a way out—temporarily—through Communism, Rolf Gardiner found in German youth the idealism he so sadly missed in England.

'The new Germans are young, brave, ardent, enthusiastic, alive. The modern British are mature, cautious, over-critical, over-prudent, tired. We are so terribly refined and so overweeningly self-conscious that we can no longer commit ourselves . . .'[2]

Gardiner, caught up in the movement for the revival of English folk song and dance, tried to impart to it the wider aims and regenerative ideals which inspired the German youth movement. But, as D. H. Lawrence warned Gardiner, in a sympathetic letter, it was 'very difficult to do anything with the English; they have so little *togetherness*, or power of togetherness . . .' And he added a few prophetic words about the future of German youth: 'Even the German *Bünde*, I am afraid, will drift into nationalistic, and ultimately fighting bodies; a new and necessary form of militarism.'[3]

Gardiner was not altogether unaware of the shortcomings and dangers in the mental and emotional make-up of the younger generation in Germany, and that its obsessive emphasis upon nationalism was really the symptom of a lack of self-assurance. Nevertheless, he believed in Germany as 'the sole country where there is a positive challenge to the mechanism and commercialism which we associate with America, but which we in England take lying down.' He was the moving spirit behind a number of exchanges between German and English youth in the twenties and thirties, notably the reciprocal visits of folk dancers and singers, and summer camps for agricultural work.

A symposium on Anglo-German relations, published in 1927, had among its British contributors Professor G. P. Gooch, the veteran historian, and Kingsley Martin, the editor of the *New Statesman*, then a young lecturer. The Germans included Professor Eugen Rosenstock, a conservative German philosopher of Jewish origin, and W. von Hentig, a diplomat. A British diplomat (whose identity

---

[1] *Wessex; Letters from Springhead.* 'D. H. Lawrence and the Youth Movements of the twenties.' p. 39. Privately printed and circulated by the author. Christmas 1959.

[2] *Britain and Germany. A frank discussion instigated by members of the younger generation.* Edited by Rolf Gardiner and Heinz Rocholl (London, 1928), p. 130.

[3] *Wessex* (*loc. cit.*), pp. 46–47.

was not revealed at the time—Sir William Montague Pollock) made the following observation about the English inability to understand the kind of nationalism (or the youth idealism) widely current in Germany: 'Nor are we impressed,' he wrote, 'by the conscious aspect of romanticism. To be intensely self-conscious seems to us to mean that we are not sure of ourselves—a kind of inferiority complex . . . A youth movement in England would have the flavour of being for the doubtfully young, and a patriotic movement for the doubtfully patriotic. British patriotism is such an old, inborn thing that it has almost passed out of the consciousness of the British people.'[1]

Exchanges continued during the early thirties, mainly with members of the *Junabu* and the *Freischar*, but politically they remained without significance. All that Rolf Gardiner saw and so deeply appreciated in German youth did exist, but it was by no means the whole of the picture. He relates, in his privately published recollections, that during his frequent visits to Germany before 1933 he hardly ever met a National Socialist. And despite the many repulsive features of the Third Reich that he witnessed after that date, he continued to believe in that 'other Germany' which was quite unknown to most of his compatriots. He—and not a few of his contemporaries—still clung to the belief that, with a sufficient measure of good will, the outstanding problems between the two countries could be solved. Nothing short of the eventual mobilization could quite convince them that a totalitarian dictatorship openly committed to conquest cannot be appeased, and is totally unresponsive to good will.

[1] *Britain and Germany*, pp. 91–92.

BIBLIOGRAPHY

It would be impractical and unnecessary to burden the present book with a list of all the primary and secondary works used in its preparation since an excellent bibliography is now available. *Die Deutsche Jugendbewegung*, a second-hand booksellers' printed catalogue, published by M. Edelmann in Nuremberg in 1960, lists 3,583 books, booklets, dissertations (printed and unprinted), songbooks, and a number of important articles published in periodicals. It took five years to prepare this catalogue and it is unlikely to be superseded.

A very full list of books and booklets on and by the German right-wing and the *völkische* camp (apart from National Socialism), can be found in Armin Mohler: *Die konservative Revolution in Deutschland 1918–1932*, Stuttgart, 1950 pp. 212–273. Most important works on German education and allied fields are listed in Wilhelm Roessler: *Jugend im Erziehungsfeld*, Düsseldorf, 1957, pp. 511–531. The most complete collection of youth movement books and periodicals is at Burg Ludwigstein, which also includes much unpublished material on the *Wandervogel* and the *Bünde*. Some information on the activities of the right-wing *Bünde* is to be found at the former *Reichsarchiv* (now in Potsdam) and at the former *Preussische Geheime Staatsarchiv* (now in Merseburg), while the Berlin Document Center (under American administration) has some interesting files about the dissolution of the *Bünde* and their illegal activities after 1933.

BOOKS

Only the more important secondary works are listed:

HEINRICH AHRENS: *Die deutsche Wandervogelbewegung von den Anfängen bis zum Weltkrieg*. Hamburg, 1939.

HOWARD BECKER: *German Youth: Bond or Free*. London, 1946.

HANS BLÜHER: *Wandervogel. Geschichte einer Jugendbewegung*. Berlin, 1912.

BIBLIOGRAPHY

FRITZ BORINSKI and WERNER MILCH: *Jugendbewegung*. London, 1945.
ELIZABETH BUSSE-WILSON: *Stufen der Jugendbewegung*. Jena, 1925.
LEOPOLD CORDIER: *Evangelische Jugendverbände*. Schwerin, 1926.
SIEGRIED COPALLE and HEINRICH AHRENS: *Chronik der freien deutschen Jugendbewegung*. Vol. I. Bad Godesberg, 1954.
WILHELM EHMER (ed.): *Hofgeismar*. Jena, 1921.
GÜNTER EHRENTHAL: *Die deutschen Jugendbünde*. Berlin, 1929.
VICTOR ENGELHARDT: *Die deutsche Jugendbewegung als kulturhistorisches Phaenomen*. Berlin, 1923.
LUISE FICK: *Die deutsche Jugendbewegung*. Jena, 1939.
Freideutsche Jugend. Jena, 1913.
Freideutscher Jugendtag. Hamburg, 1913.
GERD FRIEDRICH: *Die Freie Deutsche Jugend*. Köln, 1953.
ELSA FROBENIUS: *Mit uns zieht die neue Zeit*. Berlin, 1927.
MANFRED FUCHS: *Probleme des Wirtschaftsstils von Lebensgemeinschaften*. Göttingen, 1957
WALTHER GERBER: *Zur Entstehungsgeschichte der deutschen Wandervogelbewegung*. Bielefeld, 1957
WALDEMAR GURIAN: *Die deutsche Jugendbewegung* Habelschwerdt, 1924.
WERNER HELWIG: *Die blaue Blume des Wandervogels*. Gütersloh, 1960.
THEODOR HERRLE: *Die deutsche Jugendbewegung in ihren wirtschaftlichen und gesellschaftlichen Zusammenhängen*. Gotha, 1924.
H.P. HERZ: *Freie Deutsche Jugend*. München, 1957.
ARNO KLÖNNE: *Gegen den Strom*. Hanover, 1958.
ARNO KLÖNNE: *Hitlerjugend*. Hanover, 1960.
KARL KORN: *Die Arbeiterjugendbewegung*. Berlin, 1922.
Krieg, Revolution und freideutsche Zukunft. Jena, 1919.
CHARLOTTE LÜTKENS: *Die deutsche Jugendbewegung*. Frankfurt, 1925.
A. MESSER: *Die freideutsche Jugendbewegung*. Langensalza, 1923.
W. MÜNZENBERG: *Die dritte Front*, Berlin, 1930.
MAX NITZSCHE: *Bund und Staat*. Würzburg, 1942.
KARL O. PAETEL: *Jugendbewegung und Politik*. Bad Godesberg, 1961.
W. POHL: *Bündische Erziehung*. Jena, 1933.
ERNST POSSE: *Die politischen Kampfbünde Deutschlands*. Berlin, 1931.
MANFRED PRIEPKE: *Die evangelische Jugend im Widerstand gegen das dritte Reich von 1933-1936*. Frankfurt, 1960.
ADAM RITZHAUPT: *Die Neue Schar in Thüringen*. Jena, 1921.
H. ROTH: *Katholische Jugend in der N.S. Zeit*. Düsseldorf, 1959.
HELMUT SCHELSKY: *Die skeptische Generation*. Düsseldorf, 1957.
HERBERT SCHIERER: *Das Zeitschriftenwesen der Jugendbewegung*. Berlin, 1939.
BALDUR VON SCHIRACH: *Die Hitlerjugend*. Leipzig, 1934.
Schloss Prun. Regensburg, 1919.
KARL SEIDELMANN: *Bund und Gruppe als Lebensformen deutscher Jugend*. München, 1955.
HERTHA SIEMERING: *Die deutschen Jugendverbände*. Berlin, 1931.
OTTO ERNST SCHÜDDEKOPF: *Linke Leute von Rechts*. Stuttgart, 1960.
WILL VESPER (ed.): *Deutsche Jugend*. Berlin, 1934.

PERIODICALS

1. Youth movement periodicals

The serial publications of the *Wandervogel* and the *Bünde* often changed their names, and many appeared at irregular intervals. Out of the many hundred such periodicals the following have been of particular relevance in connection with the present study. Since the existing collections are in most cases far from complete, it has not been possible in many cases to establish the exact duration of publication.

Altwandervogel (1906–ca. 1920)
Der Anfang (1913–14)
Der Neue Anfang (1919–20)
Der Aufbruch (1915–16)
Der Bund (1919–21)
Der Neue Bund (1921)
Deutschwandervogel (1922–ca. 1930)
Eisbrecher (1932–1935)
Erkenntnis und Tat (1951–   )
Der Falke (ca. 1920– ca. 1933)
Freideutsche Jugend (1914–23)
Deutsche Freischar (1928–33)
Geusen
Der Herold (ca. 1928–33, and again after the Second World War)
Jugendland (1931–33)
Das Junge Deutschland (ca. 1926–33)
Junge Menschen (ca. 1920–27)
Jungdeutsche Stimmen (1919–21)
Jungnationale Stimmen (1926–31)
Jungwandervogel (1910–33)
Kameradschaft (1937–40)
Die Kommenden (1926–32)
Das Lagerfeuer (1931–2 and ca. 1952–58)
Nachrichtenblatt (Wandervogel Steglitz)
Das Nachrichtenblatt (Burg Ludwigstein) (ca. 1949–   )
Neuwerk
Der Pfad zum Reich
Pläne (ca. 1932 and again ca. 1958–   )
Politischer Rundbrief (1918–20)
Quickborn
Rundschreiben (Freideutscher Konvent) (1947–   )
Stimmen der Jugend
Vivos Voco (ca. 1920)
Der Wandervogel
Wandervogel (Illustrierte Monatsschrift)

BIBLIOGRAPHY

Wandervogel (Monatsschrift für Deutsches Jugendwandern) (1906–ca. 1925)
Wandervogel Führerzeitung (1912–19)
Wandervogel-Warte (ca. 1913–33)
Der Weisse Ritter (1920–27)
Wille und Werk (ca. 1926–33)
Der Zwiespruch (ca. 1919–30)

2. *Other Periodicals*

Deutsches Volkstum
Deutscher Volkswart
Free German Youth
Freie Schulgemeinde
Nationalsozialistische Monatshefte
Die Tat
Der Vorkämpfer
Der Vormarsch
Widerstand
Wille und Macht

INDEX

Abetz, Otto, 239–241
Adenauer, Konrad, 221, 224
'Agathon', 4
Ahlborn, Knud, 35, 37, 82n., 108n., 111, 115, 127, 218
Alverdes, Paul, 141n.
Ammon, Otto, 41
Angell, Sir Norman, 137n.
Anton, Georg, 193n.
Arndt, Rudi, 213n.
Arnim, Achim von, 6
Arnold, Eberhard, 119
Atatürk, Kemal, 182
Avenarius, Ferdinand, 34, 36

Baden-Powell, Lord Robert, 73
Banse, Ewald, 157
Barbizon, George, 59
Bartels, Adolf, 41
Barth, Karl, 70, 118
Barthel, Max, 112
Bauermeister, Friedrich, 101, 102
Baumann, Hans, 215n.
Bäumer, Gertrud, 34
Bäumler, Alfred, 210, 234
Bayer, Maximilian, 73
Becher, Johannes R., 112
Becker, Carl H., 146
Becker, Rolf, 180
Benjamin, Walter, 59n., 103
Bergsträsser, Arnold, 111, 148
Bernfeld, Siegfried, 59, 64, 65

Berns, Peter, 185, 200
Bewer, Max, 80
Bismarck, Otto von, 35, 155
Bittel, Karl, 100, 101n., 102, 103, 111–113, 115, 126
Blüher, Hans, 10, 21–23, 50–53, 64, 65, 74, 95, 97, 101n., 103n.
Blumenthal, Herbert, 59, 60
Blunck, Hans Friedrich, 74n., 209
Böckh, Joachim, 142n.
Bölcke, Oswald, 90
Bondy, Curt, 80n.
Bondy, Max, 80, 126
Borinski, Fritz, 148
Brecht, Bert, 224n.
Brentano, Clemens von, 6
Breuer, Hans, 7, 13, 23, 56, 97
Bronnen, Arnold, 112
Brooke, Rupert, 87
Brückner, Helmuth, 194n.
Buber, Martin, 48n., 115, 116
Buchhold, Maria, 120
Bückmann, Karl, 158
Bultmann, Rudolf, 230n.
Burte, Hermann (H. Strübe), 43–45
Buske, Ernst, 99n., 128, 142, 144–154, 171, 172, 241

Calvary, Moses, 80
Carlyle, Thomas, 33
Carnap, Rudolf, 112
Caruso, Enrico, 77

INDEX

Chamberlain, Houston Stewart, 9, 41, 74n., 106, 109, 157
Chuang Tse, 48n., 121
Cichon, W., 104
Clauss, Ludwig Ferdinand, 157
Copalle, Siegfried, 20–23, 41, 50, 74
Cordier, Leopold, 196
Cromwell, Oliver, 195

Dähnhardt, Heinz, 159, 234n.
Darré, Walter, 158
Dehmel, Hans, 113, 142, 145
Dehmel, Richard, 97
Diederichs, Eugen, 33
Dingräve, Leopold (E. W. Eschmann), 148
Dinter, Arthur, 106
Dostoevsky, Fedor, 121, 126, 181

Ebeling, Hans, 159, 185, 186, 212
Eckhart, Meister, 116
Ehlen, Nicolaus, 71
Eichendorff, Josef von, 6, 17n., 231
Ellis, Havelock, 137n.
Engels, Friedrich, 101, 118
Erikson, Erik H., 197n.
Eschmann, Ernst W., 151
Eulenburg, Philipp zu, 52

Fabricius, Wilhelm ('Hartmut'), 161
Fichte, Johann Gottlieb, 33, 101
Fidus (H. R. K. J. Höppener), 18
Finckh, Ludwig, 157, 219
Fischer, Frank, 24, 97
Fischer, Karl, 7, 16–22, 27, 41, 50, 51, 56, 75, 122, 210, 234
Fischer, Walter, 24, 79, 101, 107, 112
Flex, Walter, 46, 47, 107
Flitner, Wilhelm, 156
Foerster, Friedrich Wilhelm, 82, 96, 101
Fontane, Theodor, 50
Förster, Paul, 41, 75, 108
France, Anatole, 137n.
Frank, Ludwig, 67, 97
Freud, Sigmund, 51, 61n., 64, 65

Freyer, Hans, 148, 150
Friedländer, Benedict, 51
Fries, Jacob Friedrich, 33
Friese, Hermann, 21
Fritsch, Theodor, 42, 75, 76, 77, 107, 109
Fulda, Friedrich Wilhelm, 76–78, 81, 91, 105, 112

Galiev, Sultan, 182
Gardiner, Rolf, 241–243
Geheeb, Paul, 53
George, Stefan, 48, 54n., 77, 97, 102, 116, 135, 136, 138
Gerber, H., 122
Gerlach, Dankwart, 81, 83, 99n., 105
Gerlach, Kurt, 94n.
Glatzel, Frank, 105, 107, 114, 115, 122
Gneisenau, August Neithardt von, 36
Gobineau, Josef Arthur Count, 41
Goebbels, Josef, 109, 194, 195, 199, 205
Goebel, Ferdinand, 127
Goethe, Johann Wolfgang von, 36, 47, 75
Gogarten Friedrich, 70
Gollong, Heinz, 180, 186
Goltz, Kolmar von der, 72
Gooch, George Peabody, 242
Göring, Hermann, 200, 208n.
Götsch, Georg, 142, 145, 146, 150, 152, 156, 241
Gräf, Otger, 81, 91, 93, 97, 105–108, 122
Gregory, K. F. A. von, 194n.
Grimm, Alois, 213
Grimm, Hans, 219
Grimmelshausen, Hans Jakob Christ von, 5
Gruber, Kurt, 191, 192, 193, 195
Guardini, Romano, 71
Guderian, Heinz, 226
Gurian, Waldemar, 71
Gurlitt, Ludwig, 20, 34

INDEX

Haake, Heinrich, 194n.
Habbel, Friedrich Ludwig, 133, 142n.
Hahn, Eduard, 135n.
Halm, August, 156
Hammer, Walther, 212
Hänisch, Konrad, 123
Harden, Maximilian, 51
Hargrave, John, 136, 137
Hartmann, Nicolai, 230n.
Hasenclever, Walter, 48n.
Hasselblatt, M., 111
Hauer, Jakob Wilhelm, 106, 148, 205
Hauptmann, Gerhard, 34
Haverbeck, Werner, 194n.
Hegel, Georg Wilhelm Friedrich, 36n.
Heidegger, Martin, 230n.
Heimann, Eduard, 59, 111, 112, 118
Heine, Heinrich, 75
Heise, Werner Karl, 211
Heisenberg, Werner, 141n.
Hensel, W. (Julius Janiczek), 156
Hentig, Werner von, 242
Herzfelde, Wieland, 59n., 103
Hespers, Theo, 212
Hess, Rudolf, 194, 204, 208n.
Hesse, Hermann, 48, 116
Hielscher, Friedrich, 106, 110, 186
Himmler, Heinrich, 158
Hindenburg, Paul von, 151, 200, 201
Hirsch, Helmuth, 176
Hitler, Adolf, 8, 55, 78n., 108, 109, 110, 119, 140, 144, 153, 157, 159, 163, 167, 174, 177, 178, 180, 182, 183, 184, 185, 186, 187, 191, 192, 194, 196–215, 220, 225
Hodann, Max, 60, 61, 65n., 96
Hofer, Andreas, 198
Hoffmann-Völkersamb, Hermann, 15, 16, 22
Hofmannsthal, Hugo von, 48
Hölderlin, Friedrich, 5, 139
Holfelder, H., 192
Holzapfel, Rudolf, 116

Höss, Rudolf, 31n.
Hugenberg, Alfred, 185

Illgen, Johannes, 89
Illgen, Walter, 97
Immelmann, Max, 90

Jahn, Friedrich Ludwig, 8, 41, 72
Jansen, Wilhelm (Willie), 21–23, 51
Jantzen, Walther, 13
Jensen, Werner, 109
Jöde, Fritz, 156
Joel, Ernst, 100–103
Jordan, Wilhelm, 80
Jung, Edgar, 215
Jünger, Ernst, 90, 110, 170, 183, 186

Kelber, Willi, 124, 128
Kenstler, Georg, 158
Kerschensteiner, Georg, 34
Keyserling, Hermann Count, 121
Kierkegaard, Sören, 101, 232
Kittel Helmuth, 135n., 141, 142n., 145, 146, 199
Klabund, 211
Klages, Ludwig, 34
Klatt, Fritz, 60
Kleist, Heinrich von, 198
Klingenbeck, Walter, 214
Köbel, Eberhard (Tusk), 167–178, 212, 219, 227
Kolbenheyer, Erwin Guido, 219
Kolchak, Alexander, 171, 211
König, Eberhard, 112
König, René, 165n.
Konopacki-Konopath, 92n.
Korsch, Karl, 117
Kossina, Gustav, 157
Kotzde, Wilhelm (Kottenrodt), 108, 157, 158
Kötschau, Georg, 91
Krebs, Albert, 109, 194n.
Kropotkin, Pyotr, 112
Krupskaya, Nadezhda, 222
Kurella, Alfred, 60, 61, 102, 103, 104, 112, 113, 115, 125
Kurella, Heinrich, 104

INDEX

Küsel, 200
Kutschera, Fritz, 92n., 97

Lagarde, Paul de, 9, 33, 41, 109
Landauer, Gustav, 100, 101, 112, 121
Langbehn, Julius, 9, 41
Lange, Friedrich, 75, 107
Lass, Werner, 181n., 185, 186, 192n.
Lawrence, David Herbert, 137, 242
Lemke, Bruno, 34, 37
Lenin, Vladimir Ilich, 112, 121, 173, 180, 182, 222
Lenk, 191
Lenz, Friedrich, 186
Leonhard, Rudolf, 103
Liebknecht, Karl, 112
Lienhard, Friedrich, 41
Lietz, Hermann, 53
Lion, Alexander, 73
Lissner, Hans, 23
Luchaire, Jean, 240n.
Ludendorff, Mathilde, 106
Luntowski, Adalbert, 92n., 94, 105n.
Luserke, Martin, 35, 53
Luther, Martin, 197
Lützow, Adolf von, 198
Luxemburg, Rosa, 112

Maass, Hermann, 212
Maeterlinck, Maurice, 137n.
Mahraun, Arthur, 164
Mann, Klaus, 156n.
Martin, Kingsley, 242
Marx, Karl, 100, 101, 118, 173, 232
Maschke, Erich, 142n.
Mau, Hermann, 229, 232
Mehnert, Rudolf, 128
Meisel (Monte), Hilde, 213
Meyen, Albrecht, 112
Meyen, Wolf, 12, 17n., 56
Model, Walther, 226
Moeller van den Bruck, 118, 141, 180–182, 184, 215
Moltke, Helmuth von, 198
Morocutti, Camillo, 92n.
Mosley, Sir Oswald, 138

Moutchka (Mautschka), Hans, 92n. 97
Muck-Lamberty, Friedrich, 115–117
Müller, Gustav, 106
Müller, Karl Christian (Teut), 161, 173
Münchhausen, Börries von, 157
Münzenberg, Willi, 125
Mussolini, Benito, 185

Napoleon, 6, 8, 32, 36, 72, 237
Natorp, Paul, 34, 37, 230n.
Naumann, Friedrich, 34
Nelson, Leonard, 46, 96, 160, 213
Neuendorff, Edmund, 23, 72, 79, 87, 91, 107, 128
Niederkirchner, Katja, 213
Niekisch, Ernst, 31, 160, 182–186
Nietzsche, Friedrich, 8, 9, 95, 234
Nohl, Hermann, 156
Norkus, Herbert, 206
Novalis (Friedrich von Hardenberg), 5, 229

Oelbermann, Karl, 162, 214n.
Oelbermann, Robert, 90, 162, 212
Ollenhauer, Erich, 69, 156n.

Paasche, Hans, 34, 35, 45, 46, 101
Paetel, Karl O., 110, 185–187, 213
Pannekoek, Anton, 68
Pannwitz, Rudolf, 116
Papen, Franz von, 215n.
Parvus (Helphand), Alexander, 68
Pastenaci, Kurt, 164
Petrich, Eckart, 115
Piper, Rudolf, 90
Plato, 197
Platoff, Ataman, 211
Pleyer, Kleo, 185, 186
Pohl, Guntram Erich, 105n.
Pollock, Sir William Montague, 243
Popert, Hermann, 44, 45, 58, 80
Priestley, John Boynton, 241
Probst, Adalbert, 213
Pross, Harry, 140
Proudhon, Pierre, 197
Pudelko, Alfred, 92n., 108n.

INDEX

Rathenau, Walther, 33n.
Rauch, Karl, 142n.
Redl, Colonel, 77
Reich, Wilhelm, 65n.
Reichenbach, Bernhard, 101n.
Reichenbach, Hans, 101n.
Reichwein, Adolf, 173n., 212, 241
Reiner, Paul, 124
Remarque, Erich Maria, 72
Richthofen, Manfred von, 90
Riel, Jürgen, 214n.
Rieniets, Carl, 115, 124
Rilke, Rainer Maria, 48, 153, 216
Ritter, Karl Bernhard, 71
Rochelle, Drieu de la, 240
Rolland, Romain, 137n., 240
Römer, Beppo, 164, 185
Roquette, Otto, 17n.
Rosenberg, Alfred, 106, 109, 161, 180, 182, 194
Rosenstock-Huessy, Eugen, 148, 242
Rossaint, Chaplain, 212
Rossbach, Gerhard, 109, 181n., 191, 192
Rousseau, Jean Jacques, 165
Rundstedt, Gerd von, 226
Rust, Franz, 74
Rüstow, Alexander, 118

Sachs, Hans, 18
Salomon, Bruno von, 185, 186
Salomon, Ernst von, 186
Sand, Karl, 8
Schapke, Richard, 186
Schauwecker, Franz, 186
Scheler, Max, 109, 116
Scheringer, Wilhelm, 185, 186
Schiller, Friedrich, 75
Schirach, Baldur von, 161n., 175, 191–195, 199, 200, 201, 206n., 208
Schlageter, Albert, 226
Schleicher, Kurt von, 152, 184, 198
Schmid, Carlo, 59n.
Schmid, Fred (Sebastian Faber), 161, 172, 173n.
Schmückle, Heinrich, 104

Schneehagen, Christian, 97
Scholl, Inge, 176
Schubert, Franz, 6
Schüller, Hermann, 124
Schultz-Hencke, Harald, 61n, 111, 126
Schultze-Boysen, Harro, 173n.
Schumacher, Kurt, 156n.
Schumann, Robert, 6
Schwab, Alexander, 124
Schwaner, Wilm, 33n.
Seidel, Ina, 87
Sidow, Max, 89
Sievers, Rudolf, 97
Simmel, Georg, 109
Socrates, 95
Sohnrey, Heinrich, 17, 41
Sombart, Werner, 109
Spann, Othmar, 141, 150, 157
Spengler, Oswald, 116, 118, 121, 141, 151
Spitteler, Carl, 48, 116
Spranger, Eduard, 24, 156
Stählin, Wilhelm, 71, 107, 113, 122
Stalin, Yosef Visarionovich, 171
Stammler, Georg, 109
Stapel, Wilhelm, 109, 122
Stauff, Philipp, 76
Stauffenberg, Klaus von, 136
Steiner, Rudolf, 116
Stöcker, Adolf, 74
Strasser, Otto, 106, 185, 186, 194
Streicher, Julius, 77, 191n.
Suso, Henry, 116
Süsskind, Heinrich, 126

Tagore, Rabindranat, 116
Tanzmann, Bruno, 109
Terboven, Josef, 194n.
Thews, Wilhelm, 213n.
Thiede, Bruno, 20, 23
Thiess, Wolfgang, 213n.
Tieck, Ludwig, 6
Tillich, Paul, 70, 118
Tolstoy, Leo Nikolayevich, 100
Tönnies, Ferdinand, 232
Tormin, Helmuth, 112
Trakl, Georg, 48

INDEX

Traub, Gottfried, 35, 112
Trotha, Admiral von, 199–201

Uhse, Bodo, 185, 186
Ursin, Karl, 122

Vesper, Will, 210n., 219
Voelkel, Martin, 133, 134, 136, 138, 139, 140, 142n., 161, 169
Voggenreiter, Ludwig, 133, 142n., 199
Vorwerk, Friedrich, 103, 114

Wachler, Ernst, 80
Wagner, Richard, 43
Weber, Alfred, 34, 37
Weber, Friedrich, 78, 164
Weber, Max, 116
Weber, Richard, 20, 23
Weddigen, Otto, 90
Weininger, Otto, 95

Werfel, Franz, 48n.
Wessel, Horst, 210
Westphal, Max, 213
Whitman, Walt, 101
Wickram, Jörg, 5
Widerhoff, Karl Udo, 212
Wilhelm II, 5, 50
Wittfogel, Karl August, 103, 112, 118
Wix, Hans, 97
Wolf, Friedrich, 46n.
Wulle, Reinhold, 108
Wyneken, Gustav, 13, 33, 35, 36, 37, 38, 43, 50, 53–55, 58, 59, 61, 64, 76, 82, 96, 97, 100, 107, 116, 123, 156, 169, 218

York von Wartenburg, Johann David, 198

Zehrer, Hans, 184n.
Zietz, Luise, 68